INFORMATION
Representation
and Retrieval
in the Digital Age

Second Edition

Heting Chu

ASIST Monograph Series

Published for the
American Society for Information Science and Technology by

 Information Today, Inc.
Medford, New Jersey

First printing, 2010

Information Representation and Retrieval in the Digital Age, Second Edition

Library of Congress Cataloging-in-Publication Data

Chu, Heting, 1957-
    Information representation and retrieval in the digital age / Heting Chu. -- 2nd ed.
        p. cm. -- (ASIS&T monograph series)
    Includes bibliographical references and index.
    ISBN 978-1-57387-393-2
        1. Information organization. 2. Information retrieval. 3. Information storage and retrieval systems. I. Title.
Z666.5.C48 2010
025--dc22

                                                                    2009042497

President and CEO: Thomas H. Hogan, Sr.
Editor-in-Chief and Publisher: John B. Bryans
Managing Editor: Amy M. Reeve
ASIST Monograph Series Editor: Samantha Hastings
VP Graphics and Production: M. Heide Dengler
Book Designer: Kara Mia Jalkowski
Cover Designer: Dana J. Stevenson
Copy Editor: Bonnie Freeman
Proofreader: Penelope Mathiesen
Indexer: Beth Palmer

www.infotoday.com

Contents

Figures and Tables

Preface to the Second Edition

Around eight years have passed since I completed the manuscript for the first edition of this book in July 2001. The time span itself spells out the need for a new edition in the rapidly developing field of information representation and retrieval (IRR). In addition, at least two-dozen reviews were written for the previous edition of the book. Those reviews contain many valuable suggestions and comments, which I not only appreciate highly but also would like to incorporate into this book. These two factors combined subsequently became the catalyst for writing the second edition.

While the entire book is updated and revised, the following list details the major changes I made to individual chapters in the present edition:

- Chapter 1: New section §1.1.2.5 Karen Spärck Jones (1935–2007)

- Chapter 2: New sections §2.1.4 Social Tagging and §2.3.1.4 RSS

- Chapter 3: New section §3.1.3.3 Digital Object Identifiers

- Chapter 4: New sections §4.4.1 Taxonomies, §4.4.2 Folksonomies, and §4.4.3 Ontologies

- Chapter 5: Added Search/Retrieve Web Service (SRW) and Search/Retrieve via URL (SRU) into §5.1.2.4 Multiple Database Searching

- Chapter 8: Added next generation of OPACs into §8.3 OPACs: Computerized Library Catalogs as Information Retrieval Systems; Major updates of §8.4.2.4 Ranking Techniques; New section §8.5.2 Web 2.0 and Information Retrieval Systems

- Chapter 9: Major updates of §9.1 Multilingual Information, §9.2.2 Sound Retrieval, and §9.2.3 Moving Image Retrieval

- Chapter 10: New section §10.2.2 Other User-Centered Models of Information Retrieval; Added organic user interface (OUI) into §10.3.1.4 Other Models of User-System Interaction

- Chapter 11: Deleted §11.2.2 Evaluation Criteria for CD-ROM Systems; New sections §11.2.4 Evaluation Criteria for Multimedia Retrieval Systems and §11.2.5 Usability as

Evaluation Criteria; Major updates of §11.3.2.1.4 Retrieval Tasks

- Chapter 12: Expansion and major revision, including deletion of §12.2.2 The Natural Language Model; new sections §12.2.2 Automatic Summarization, §12.2.3 Question Answering, §12.2.4 Natural Language Searching, and §12.3 The Semantic Web

In addition, I would like to clarify the focus and orientation of this book based on the feedback I received about the previous edition. First, IRR in this book is examined and discussed from the perspective of library and information science rather than from the viewpoint of computer science. Thus, systems design and implementation specifics such as algorithms are not included in this book. Second, information representation is presented as one necessary component in the process of IR and not treated as a domain parallel to information retrieval. Therefore, coverage of information representation in this book is much less than that of IR. Third, certain topics (e.g., information-seeking behavior), are only described briefly in this book for two reasons: 1) This book is not intended to treat them extensively, and 2) excellent coverage of them can be found in other publications that are typically listed as references at the end of related chapters.

Finally, I wish to thank Long Island University for granting me sabbatical leave, without which I would not have been able to write a second edition of this book. The efforts of my graduate assistant, Fenfei Ouyang, in gathering materials for me are also gratefully acknowledged. Furthermore, I truly appreciate the advice and guidance of Samantha Hastings, ASIST Monograph Series Editor, Amy Reeve, Managing Editor of Books, and John B. Bryans, Editor-in-Chief and Publisher, Information Today, Inc., during the course of preparing the current edition. It is a pleasure to work with them all as always.

Heting Chu
Long Island, New York

Preface to the First Edition

Another book on information retrieval (IR)? Yes, because there are new topics and developments that need to be discussed in this field as we enter the digital age. In addition, two chapters of this book are devoted exclusively to information representation, a step that must be taken before information becomes retrievable.

We begin with an overview of information representation and retrieval (IRR) in Chapter 1, which reviews key concepts, key people, key events, and major developmental stages of the field. Chapters 2 and 3 examine basic approaches to information representation and other related topics. Given the significance of language in information representation and retrieval, Chapter 4 discusses natural language and controlled vocabulary, the two types of languages used in the field, along with their relationship and characteristics. Chapters 5, 6, and 7 focus on various aspects of retrieval: retrieval techniques, retrieval approaches, and retrieval models. Major types of information retrieval systems are then considered in Chapter 8 with special coverage of internet retrieval systems, the rising star in the family of IR systems. Chapter 9 explores the retrieval of multilingual information, multimedia information, and hyper-structured information. The user dimension, a fundamental aspect in information representation and retrieval, is covered in Chapter 10. Chapter 11 surveys the complex and multifaceted evaluation issue in the field, including evaluation measures, evaluation methodology, and major evaluation projects. The last chapter of the book, Chapter 12, analyzes the role and potential of artificial intelligence (AI) in information representation and retrieval.

I have attempted to present a systematic, thorough, yet nontechnical view of the field by using plain language, wherever possible, to explain complex topics. The emphasis of the book is placed upon the principles and fundamentals of information representation and retrieval rather than on descriptions of specific procedures, systems, or corresponding practices in the field. Once the reader understands these IRR principles and fundamentals, he or she should be able to apply them in different situations and environments. Attention is also paid specifically to topics and developments regarding information representation and retrieval in the digital age.

While *Information Representation and Retrieval* has an orientation toward the user, IRR system designers should find it helpful for understanding the field from the perspective of users. My intent is a book that will be useful to anyone who is interested in learning about the field, particularly those who are new to it. I strongly recommend that beginners read the book in the order in which it is organized, as later chapters are built upon the earlier ones.

Looking back, I might not have written this book at this point in my career if my colleague, Richard Smiraglia, had not initiated the contact for me with the publisher. My gratitude also goes to my students, who have shared my interest and enthusiasm in the field. I appreciate as well the sabbatical leave granted by Long Island University, without which I would not have had the luxury of time for undertaking this project. In addition, I would like to thank Michael Koenig, dean of Palmer School with which I am affiliated, and John Bryans, editor-in-chief of the book publishing division of Information Today, Inc., for making the publication of my manuscript a reality.

This book to a large extent was an integral part of my family life during the time of writing as my husband and daughter were also deeply involved with my work. For example, the book became a regular topic at our dinner table, and my family often had to spend weekend and evening hours without me at home. My daughter, Fangfei, is perhaps exposed more to *information retrieval* than any other kids her age. She continually urged me to work on my book even though, in her heart, she would have preferred I spend the time with her. The love, understanding, and support from my family have continuously been a source of energy and inspiration.

Heting Chu
Long Island, New York

CHAPTER 1

Information Representation and Retrieval: An Overview

Information representation and retrieval (IRR), also known as abstracting and indexing, information searching, and information processing and management, dates back to the second half of the 19th century, when schemes for organizing and accessing knowledge (e.g., the Dewey Decimal Classification of 1876) were created (Wynar, 1980). However, research on IRR did not become a key field in information science until the breakout of World War II. Since then, great minds from various disciplines have been attracted to this emerging field, while information technologies with different degrees of sophistication and maturity are applied to facilitate research and development in IRR.

The history and development of IRR are illustrated here with a focus on the main features of each period and the outstanding pioneers of the field. The key concepts involved in this book are then explained, followed by a discussion of the major components in IRR. This chapter concludes with an exploration of the essential problem of the field, namely, how to obtain the right information for the right user at the right time.

1.1 History and Development of Information Representation and Retrieval

The history of IRR is not long. A retrospective look at the field identifies increased demand, rapid growth, the demystification phase, and the networked era as the four major stages IRR has experienced in its development.

1.1.1 Major Stages

1.1.1.1 Increased Demand (1940s–early 1950s)

World War II denoted the official formation of the field of IRR. Because of the war, a massive number of technical reports and documents were produced to record the research and development activities surrounding weaponry production. Never before had people confronted such an enormous task of IRR, without considering other aspects of information processing and management such as selection, dissemination, and preservation. As Bush (1945) wrote:

There is a growing mountain of research. But there is increased evidence that we are being bogged down today as specialization extends. The investigator is staggered by the findings and conclusions of thousands of other workers—conclusions which he cannot find time to grasp, much less to remember, as they appear. (p. 101)

Indeed, the need for representing and organizing the vast amount of information became quite obvious and pressing. In the fields of chemistry and biology, for example:

The biomedical press, for example, has been estimated to publish 2 million papers each year (McCandless, Skweir, & Gordon, 1964, p. 147). These papers can be read at the rate of two per hour—assuming that the reader is attentive, can read approximately 70 languages, and has the documents at hand. If journal reading is limited to 1 hour per day and 365 days per year, then it will take more than 27.4 centuries to read the output of 1 year of the world's biomedical press. (Borko & Bernier, 1975, p. 6)

Although the exact amount of technical information produced during the 1940s and 1950s may not be accurately determined, its magnitude can be estimated according to the previously described biomedical field. People could no longer rely exclusively on their own skills, memories, or individual file cabinets for organizing and retrieving information efficiently whenever there was a need. Rather, collective efforts in the area of IRR were called for, resulting in systems specifically designed for that purpose even though they were manual ones such as the coordinated indexes introduced in 1951 (Gull, 1956).

1.1.1.2 Rapid Growth (1950s–1980s)

The decades in this period represent the golden years in the development of IRR. Computers were formally introduced to the field between 1957 and 1959, when Hans Peter Luhn used one to handle not only keyword matching and sorting tasks but also the intellectual work related to the content analysis of written texts (Salton, 1987).

The emergence of online systems such as DIALOG in the 1960s and 1970s signified the shift from manual to computerized information retrieval (IR). Hahn (1996) described the pioneer online systems developed during that time:

[They] had some remarkable advanced features such as online thesauri, ranked output, automatic inclusion of synonyms in the search formulation, Boolean logic, right and left-hand truncation,

cited-reference searching, and natural language free-text searching. Some systems had automatic data collection programs to
monitor use and satisfaction. (p. 34)

Along with the growth and maturity of the online systems, automated and
automatic techniques for IRR were being created and experimented with,
supported by advancements in computing technology. People from different
fields, especially computer science, devoted their efforts to research and
development in this area. However, additional problems were waiting to be
researched, just as Salton (1987) summarized in one of his writings:

Even though great progress has been made in the past 30 years
in text processing and information retrieval, especially in the
areas of text editing and document production, index term
assignment, and dynamic collection search and query formulation, few substantive advances are apparent in the true text
understanding areas. (p. 379)

1.1.1.3 Demystification Phase (1980s–1990s)

Although the online systems previously described were built for users with
various kinds of information needs, those systems were not designed in such
a way that the users could search them directly, without any training or assistance from information professionals. In other words, only intermediaries
such as librarians and other information professionals were able to perform
the search task on behalf of the users. Moreover, it was very costly to use such
systems for locating information because a remarkable array of fees (e.g.,
telecommunication, connection, and database fees) would be charged for
every single search. The term *end users* then referred to those who had some
information need but would not conduct the actual online search themselves. The meaning of the term end user changed gradually when personal
computers began to be employed in IR and when CD-ROM and online public access catalog (OPAC) systems were implemented in the mid-1980s.

Online IR systems in the past were accessed via assorted means, such as
printer terminals and Cathode Ray Tube (CRT) terminals. Needless to say, the
interaction between the searcher and the system was not inviting or friendly.
When personal computers were introduced into IR, end users found that the
retrieval process seemed much less intimidating because some form of
friendly "conversation" or interaction could be carried out between the user
and the system.

The implementation of CD-ROM and OPAC systems made it possible for
end users to search for themselves by demystifying IR systems that had

existed previously in online form only and were geographically located in remote places, users no longer needed to be concerned with the online costs when they searched CD-ROM or OPAC systems. Since then, IR systems have increasingly become systems built for and used by end users.

1.1.1.4 The Networked Era (1990s–Present)

IR, up to this point, was a centralized activity, meaning that databases of IR systems were physically managed in one central location. If people intended to use several IR systems, they had to establish connections with respective IR systems individually. In comparison, distributed searching allows people to access database information using the network infrastructure. IR systems are no longer restricted to one single geographical area. The advent of the internet truly makes networked IR a reality by providing the infrastructure needed for this implementation.

In addition to the feature of distributed searching, the internet has redefined the field of IRR. Never before in the history of information representation have statistical keywords and similar methods been applied so extensively to such a huge amount of hyperstructure and multimedia information. Never before in the history of IR have so many users conducted online searches without the help of intermediaries. As a result, the quality of information representation in this environment seems so mixed that the term *organized chaos* has been coined specifically for describing the status quo. On the other hand, full-text retrieval has become the norm rather than the exception on the internet. Retrieval techniques that were previously tested only in lab experiments are readily available in internet retrieval systems such as AltaVista and Google. Overall, research results obtained from controlled environments are now widely applied to IRR on the internet.

The networked era is symbolized by the internet, which provides a novel platform as well as a showcase for IRR in the digital age.

1.1.2 Pioneers of the Field

The field of IRR has attracted so many talented and devoted people in the past 50 years that it is impracticable to list all of them here. Nevertheless, the following people deserve individual discussion in this book because their contributions to the field are so great. Another criterion for selecting the IR pioneers in this section is that all of them had concluded their academic careers by the time of this writing.

1.1.2.1 Mortimer Taube (1910–1965)

Mortimer Taube earned his doctorate in philosophy at the University of California at Berkeley. He worked as a librarian for circulation, cataloging, and acquisitions before he took a position at the Library of Congress to become the assistant chief of general reference and bibliography in 1945 (Shera, 1978). In 1952, Taube founded Documentation Inc., where he and his colleagues began to explore new methods for information indexing and retrieval under contract to the U.S. Armed Services Technical Information Agency (Smith, 1993).

The new approach to indexing and searching eventually became the well-known *coordinate indexing*. Taube, with Alberto F. Thompson, presented a report titled "The Coordinate Indexing of Scientific Fields" before the division of chemical literature of the American Chemical Society as part of its Symposium on Mechanical Aids to Chemical Documentation. The report was never officially published in a journal or book, but Gull (1987) included it later in one of his publications as an appendix.

The need for new indexing and retrieval methods at the time was twofold. First, a huge number of technical reports and other scientific literature, generated by research conducted for World War II, indicated the inadequacy of the existing indexing and retrieval systems, which were primarily manual. Second, the two established methods of representing information, the alphabetical and the hierarchical (e.g., subject headings and classification schemes), were unable to accommodate the new disciplines, new technologies, and new terminology that evolved from research and development related to World War II (Smith, 1993). It was in this particular circumstance that in 1952 Taube and Thompson proposed coordinate indexing (Gull, 1987).

Breaking away from traditional methods for indexing and searching, coordinate indexing is based on the implementation of uniterms and application of Boolean logic in IR. Uniterms are individual terms selected by indexers to represent different facets of a document. Uniterms can, in a sense, be regarded as today's keywords because both are derived from original documents, and no effort is made toward vocabulary control (e.g., checking synonyms and homographs). Typically, several uniterms are used to represent a single document, as with keyword indexing.

Boolean logic, a subdivision in philosophy, was put forward by George Boole in 1849 on the basis of his detailed analyses of the processes of human reasoning and fundamental laws that govern operations of the mind (Smith, 1993). To Boole, the processes of reasoning were either the addition of different concepts, or classes of objects, to form more complex concepts, or the separation of complex concepts into individual, simpler concepts (Boole, 1854). The former is summarized as the AND operator, and the latter includes the OR and NOT operators. Almost a century later, Taube brought these principles to the field of IRR in the form of coordinate indexing.

Taube's cumulative efforts in coordinate indexing laid the foundation for Boolean searching in the computerized environment. If disciplines can be broken down into single ideas represented by uniterms, computers can be used to organize and search for information put in that format. This insight eventually led to the development of various retrieval systems that performed all types of Boolean searching, a topic explored further in other parts of this book. Meanwhile, indexes that were developed using the coordination method became known as coordinate indexes. The process of searching these indexes by combining ideas to find needed information was called *concept coordination* (Smith, 1993).

The phrase *coordinate indexing* is, however, a misnomer (Gull, 1987). More accurately, it should be called *coordinate indexing and searching* or, in today's terminology, *coordinate representation and retrieval*, because it does not appear to be just an indexing method. Rather, it has been used for searching as well. In addition, the emphasis of the method was put on analysis over synthesis, which led some critics (e.g., Gull, 1987; Pao, 1989) to question whether coordinate indexing combined words or concepts/ideas. The problem of false coordination also caused concern because there was no mechanism in the method to prevent false drops. For example, if the desired search topic is *computer desk*, the retrieval results may contain documents related to *computer desk*, as well as *desk computer* and other phrases that happen to have the words *computer* and *desk* in them (e.g., *desktop computer*). As uniterms are assigned without reference to controlled vocabularies, all the disadvantages associated with indexing and retrieval using natural language (see Chapter 4) are present in coordinate indexing. Furthermore, if coordinate indexing is limited to single words only, it seems just a restriction imposed on the old alphabetical and hierarchical methods rather than a novel third method for indexing and retrieval (Gull, 1987).

Nevertheless, Taube's contribution to the field is remarkable in that he created coordinate indexing and introduced Boolean logic to indexing and retrieval. As summarized by Gull (1956), the uniterm system exhibited the following characteristics, in comparison with classification and subject catalogs:

- Lower cost
- Smaller size
- Faster analysis
- More access points per unit cataloged
- Faster searching
- Slower rate of growth
- Slower rate of obsolescence
- Greater specificity

- Universality

- Logical structure

- Neutrality

- Simplicity

- Suitable for cumulative publication

There is certainly little doubt that the real impetus to modern methods of IR was given by Mortimer Taube, founder of Documentation Inc. (Lancaster, 1968). As we move from the electronic age to the digital one, the influence and impact Taube had on indexing and retrieval remain apparent.

1.1.2.2 Hans Peter Luhn (1896–1964)

If Taube is regarded as the pioneer who laid the foundation for the application of computers in IR by incorporating Boolean logic in his uniterm system, Hans Peter Luhn is the individual who actually created computer-based applications for the field.

Born in Germany, Luhn was an engineer by education who became a famed IBM inventor with more than 80 patents. Luhn's initiation into information science in general and IR in particular came in the period 1947–1948, when James Perry and Malcolm Dyson approached him and asked whether an IBM machine could be designed to search chemical structures coded according to the Dyson notation system (Harvey, 1978). Luhn quickly became interested and joined with them to develop and test a pioneer electronic information searching system that, in 1948, Luhn called an electronic searching selector. This machine later came to be known as the Luhn scanner (Schultz, 1968). By 1953, he was spending an increasing amount of time in IR and published his first paper in the area, titled "A New Method of Recording and Searching Information" (Luhn, 1953). He also became the manager of IR research at IBM. Luhn explored and worked out many of the important computer-based IR applications that now seem commonplace in the field.

One such application is the KeyWord In Context (KWIC) system, which encompasses three elements fundamental to IRR. The first element is that keywords, rather than terms obtained from conventional classifications and subject headings, are used to represent and retrieve the plural facets of a document. Keywords, in a sense, can be considered a descendant of Taube's uniterms, although few people have attempted to make this association. This keyword approach has since been widely implemented in applications such as automatic indexing, automatic abstracting, and keyword searching. The second element of the KWIC method derives from the concordances our ancestors created as early as the 13th century (Wellisch, 1995). While all the sentences in a document make up a concordance, titles and similar artifacts (e.g., topic sentences) form the so-called context for KWIC products. For instance, titles are processed to generate KeyWord In Title (KWIT) indexes, one extension of the KWIC application. The third element of the KWIC approach is the permutation of keywords contained in titles and other equivalents. The permutation typically assumes two display formats: KWIC with a particular keyword aligned within the context, and KeyWord Out of Context (KWOC) with a particular keyword displayed and left aligned outside the context. KWOC, like KWIT, is a variation of the KWIC application. Luhn, who coined the KWIC terminology in 1958, successfully produced a KWIC index for *Chemical Titles*, bringing his idea to a practical result (Fischer, 1966). The KWIC approach is unarguably a significant milestone in IRR.

Automatic indexing and abstracting represent major contributions made by Luhn to the IR field. Using statistical methods, Luhn developed and promoted algorithms for producing indexes and abstracts automatically. For automatic indexing, the procedure is based mainly on the selection of significant words (i.e., keywords) that carry meanings from documents. Words that appear frequently (i.e., high-frequency words such as articles, conjunctions, and prepositions) or seldom in the document (i.e., low-frequency words or words people rarely use in communication) and *noninforming words* (i.e., general nouns such as *report* and *summary*, as well as terms constantly used in a particular collection, e.g., *information retrieval* in a document database for IR) can be eliminated by adopting a stop-word list or statistical word-frequency procedure (Luhn, 1958). This approach for producing KWIC indexes, KWIC variations (e.g., KWOC and KWIT), and other keyword indexes became the first and—to this day—the only fully automatic indexing method. For automatic abstracting, two measures are suggested for identifying significant words and subsequently significant sentences that can be the most representative of a given document. The keyword approach, as described earlier for automatic indexing, furnishes one of the two measures for constructing automatic abstracts. The other measurement relies on the relative position within a sentence of significant words. According to Luhn (1958), proximity of four or five nonsignificant words between significant words appears useful for selecting significant sentences from a document. A combination of keyword frequency and keyword proximity within a sentence seems a viable methodology for generating auto-abstracts.

Luhn's third notable contribution to the field was the development of selective dissemination of information (SDI) systems. SDI is an application for effective dissemination of new scientific information to target users based on their profiles. Luhn (1961) outlined its components and various steps for operating an SDI system, of which the creation and maintenance of user profiles is the most important and critical task. The profile of user interests includes a list of words, along with their current weights, each indicating the balance between additions and subtractions resulting from the profile maintenance procedure. The profile is then checked against document representations (e.g., abstracts and index terms) at a specified temporal interval (e.g., weekly or monthly). As conceived by Luhn, intelligent systems could be built for business, science, and other types of literature with the implementation of the SDI concept (Stevens, 1968).

Obviously, Luhn put quite a few ideas into practice for IRR with the aid of computers even though not all of them originated from him (Stevens, 1968; Wellisch, 1995). As all the aforementioned applications are computer-based, the efficiency of those IR-related operations has been drastically improved. However, these applications cannot attain the quality generally associated with indexes, abstracts, and retrieval tasks that are done manually.

Luhn's contributions to the field, especially to computerized IRR, earned him an important place in the history of information science, of which IR is a key component. Based on an analysis by Carlos Cuadra (1964), Luhn's name led all the rest on three out of four of the listings of major contributions as perceived by four experts in information science. Luhn also ranked fourth among the top 25 authors in terms of publication density, a score calculated by Cuadra using bibliographic data. In addition, Luhn was positioned in the top 10 in the four bibliographies of the most frequently cited authors in the field. All the findings confirm that Luhn stands out as a prominent researcher in information science, particularly in IR, regardless of the evaluation method (e.g., expert advice, textbook analysis, and citation analysis) used (Cuadra, 1964). It is Luhn who brought computers into our field, pioneered many IRR applications, and catalyzed empirical research in IRR.

1.1.2.3 Calvin N. Mooers (1919–1994)

Compared with Taube and Luhn, Calvin N. Mooers' contributions to IRR came much later. Mooers' areas of study were mathematics and physics, but he did devote a considerable amount of his time to information and computer science after attending the Massachusetts Institute of Technology in 1946 to capitalize on his computing experience (Corbitt, 1992).

In 1950 Mooers in fact coined the term *information retrieval*, which has since been seamlessly integrated into the vocabulary of information science. According to Mooers, IR means finding information whose location or very existence is a priori unknown (Garfield, 1997). Mooers (1960) was also credited with proposing Mooers' law for IR systems:

An information retrieval system will tend not to be used whenever it is more painful and troublesome for a customer to have information than for him not to have it. (p. ii)

Mooers' law has been paraphrased, and one version reads, "An information system will only be used when it is more trouble not to use it than it is to use it" (Koenig, 1987). Garfield (1997) further suggested a corollary to Mooers' law: "The more relevant information a retrieval system provides, the more it will be used." In sum, Mooers' law indicates quintessentially that systems that reflect users' needs and practices are more apt to be consulted readily (Henderson, 1996).

In addition to coining the term *information retrieval* and authoring Mooers' law, Mooers developed the zatocoding system for storing a large number of document descriptors on a single, specially notched card by superimposing random, eight-digit descriptor codes. The use of the zatocoding system would result in only a small but tolerable number of false drops in a bibliographic search (Garfield, 1997). Mooers was also responsible for creating two applications oriented toward computer science: the Text Reckoning and Compiling (TRAC) and VXM computer languages. TRAC was designed specifically for handling unstructured text in an interactive mode as opposed to the batch mode. VXM was used for multicomputer network systems (Corbitt, 1992; Henderson, 1996).

In recognition of his outstanding contributions to the field of information science, Mooers was honored with the American Society for Information Science Award of Merit in 1978. The award citation states that he "has affected all who are in the field of information and his early ideas are now incorporated into today's reality" (Henderson, 1996). Indeed, Mooers was one of the great pioneers in the growing field of IRR.

1.1.2.4 Gerard Salton (1927–1995)

Everyone in the IR community agrees that Gerard Salton was one of the preeminent figures in the field. He was the man "most responsible for the establishment, survival, and recognition of IR ..." by spending 30 years of the latter part of his life "carefully nurturing it and sustaining it when the professional climate was inhospitable, and defending it until it could support itself" (Crouch, et al., 1996). If the entire field of IR were regarded as a domed architecture, Salton would be the dome, and his colleagues and protégés would serve as pillars or other supporting parts of the structure.

Salton's main research tool was the System for the Manipulation And Retrieval of Texts (SMART), also humorously known as "Salton's magical automatic retriever of text." His ideas fundamentally changed full-text processing methods on computers and provided the field of IR with solid underpinnings (ACM SIGIR, 1995). "His research contributions span the gamut of information retrieval: the vector space model, term weighting, relevance feedback, clustering, extended Boolean retrieval, term discrimination value, dictionary construction, term dependency, text understanding and structuring, passage retrieval—and, of course, automatic text processing using SMART" (Crouch, et al., 1996). Each of these contributions can easily be a topic for extensive discussion and some are discussed in other parts of this book. Nevertheless, it is not an exaggeration to say that Salton brought computer science and contemporary techniques to IR.

IR systems that operated commercially in the 1960s were basically using Boolean logic and other pre-SMART retrieval technology. Today, dozens of well-known commercial systems use the ideas and technology developed in SMART. For example, Individual (a news clipping service) licensed the SMART technology directly. Others, such as the wide area information servers (WAIS) and DOWQUEST, a tool for the Dow Jones newswire, are directly derived technology. Many new systems have leveraged off the years of research, including WIN, a legal retrieval system run by the West Publishing Company, and INQUERY, another eminent research tool (ACM SIGIR, 1995). IR techniques, previously only tested in SMART, are now commonly implemented, even in the newest species of IR systems: internet retrieval systems.

All these systems show the influence and application of Salton's IR concepts and research in the electronic and digital environments. In addition, Salton was a prolific writer. He published five texts on IR and more than 150 research articles in the field throughout his career (ACM SIGIR, 1995). He also dedicated his outstanding services to the field. In return, Salton received numerous awards.

1.1.2.5 Karen Spärck Jones (1935–2007)

Karen Spärck Jones completed her undergraduate degree first in history and later in philosophy at the University of Cambridge, U.K. It was her education in philosophy that led her to the field of IR, particularly in what is now labeled natural language processing (NLP). In her PhD dissertation in 1964, titled "Synonyms and Semantic Classification," she employed the theory of clumps for term clustering (Wilks, 2007).

Spärck Jones, working in IR for more than four decades, made significant contributions to several areas and influenced many around her, both colleagues and students. Chronologically speaking, the experimental approach to IR was the first of such areas. During the final years of Spärck Jones' dissertation research, the epic Cranfield tests entered their second phase, and Spärck Jones began showing a strong interest not only in the experimental approach Cranfield took but also in the details of experimental methods and materials (Robertson & Tait, 2008). She consequently used the Cranfield collection in experiments to test term clustering for semantic classification, which she had begun exploring in her doctoral research.

Her experimental research in IR did not stop, however, when the Cranfield tests ended in 1967. Rather, she led a joint effort of U.K.-based researchers in the 1970s to develop a new "ideal" test collection so that experiments could be carried out beyond a single one like the Cranfield tests. Although this effort was not brought to fruition due to the insufficient financial support available in the U.K., she continued toiling tirelessly in this area nevertheless. Spärck Jones edited *Information Retrieval Experiment* (Spärck Jones, 1981), the only monograph devoted primarily to experimental methods in IR. She also wrote two of the papers in that book. On the other hand, when the Text REtrieval Conference (TREC) series commenced in 1992, Spärck Jones had attained the ideal test collection she and her colleagues had been unable to create almost two decades earlier. From the very beginning, she enthusiastically participated in the TREC series in various capacities (e.g., informal advisor to the organizers, program committee member, and research team participant). More important, Spärck Jones authored a series of papers summarizing and comparing different teams' performances in the TREC experiments. She also reflected on the lessons the IR community could learn from the multitude of disparate results by TREC participants (Spärck Jones, 1995, 2000). No one seemed more appropriate than Spärck Jones to undertake this tremendously significant task, given her lifelong interest in and commitment to the experimental approach to IR.

The paper Spärck Jones published in 1972 on inverse document frequency (idf) represented another area of her research: statistical methods in IR (Spärck Jones, 1972). She explained in that paper, still one of the most highly cited papers in the field, that a document is relevant not only because key terms are frequent in it but because those terms are infrequent in other nonrelevant documents. In conjunction with the term frequency (tf) algorithm developed by Salton's group at Cornell University, the tf.idf combination became the most common default weighting scheme for many years. The idf criterion further led to relevance weighting in the probabilistic model Robertson developed in collaboration with Spärck Jones (Robertson & Spärck Jones, 1976). In a sense, Spärck Jones' work on idf inspired a series of well-founded experimental investigations of term weighting. The statistical methods, exemplified by the idf and other measures of a similar nature, have proven to be inexpensive and competitive in IR, and the most recent testimony can be seen in the TREC series (Spärck Jones, 1995).

Extending her research on statistical methods in IR into a larger and different but closely related area, Spärck Jones started work in the 1980s on natural language processing, with a specific focus on automatic summarization, question answering, and natural language querying. She strongly believed that "words stand only for themselves" (Wilks, 2007) and found it strange to represent text using languages (e.g., subject headings) other than the natural language (Spärck Jones, 1994). Her research on NLP (e.g., Spärck Jones, 2005, 2007) eventually built her a reputation at least as significant in that area as in others, although NLP is different from them in comparison. Because of Spärck Jones' important contribution to natural language processing, a book titled *Charting a New Course: Natural Language Processing and Information Retrieval* (Tait, 2005) was published in her honor. This book is not the only publication that manifests her contribution and influence in NLP. In fact, in addition to many other publications she authored, she jointly edited a reader in NLP as early as 1986 (Grosz, Spärck Jones, & Webber, 1986).

Spärck Jones' research in later years involved spoken document retrieval. With colleagues, she authored two award-winning papers about their innovative work on this topic (Maybury, 2005). Robust unrestricted keyword-spotting algorithms and adapted, existing text-based information retrieval techniques were among the research Spärck Jones conducted on voice data such as speeches and broadcast news.

The IR field has benefited enormously from Spärck Jones' work in the idf weighting method, natural language processing, spoken document retrieval, and the experimental approach to IR (Willett & Robertson, 2007). Her influence on the IR community as a researcher, mentor, and advisor will continue to be felt for many years.

1.2 Elaboration on Key Concepts

The title of this book contains four distinct concepts: information, information representation, IR, and digital age. Each of the concepts, without exception, has synonyms and can be interpreted and understood differently in different contexts. The following discussion is intended to explain and clarify the meaning and connotation of the concepts in this book.

1.2.1 Information

Information, as a concept, has been considered and contrasted extensively with such terms as *data*, *knowledge*, and *wisdom* (e.g., Meadow, 1992). Hence, there seems little need for this book to repeat or continue those discussions or debates. On the other hand, the words *information*, *text*, and *document* are often used interchangeably in the field (e.g., *text retrieval* and *document representation*). According to Larsen (1999):

> In our field, documents are characterized by having a "price," they can be counted in "numbers," and are in that capacity the basic components of library statistics. Most of them "take up space," they can be "damaged in use," and they may "deteriorate" over time. (p. 1020)

In addition to Larsen's definition, documents may contain multimedia. If *text* refers to textual information only, *document* could include multimedia information (i.e., any combination of audio, video, image, and textual information). It appears that *information* encompasses both text and document, having the broadest connotation among the trio.

In recent years, research has been done on passage retrieval as opposed to document retrieval (Spärck Jones, 2000). *Passage retrieval* (also called information retrieval) denotes finding the very information or document passage (e.g., a paragraph or an arbitrary length of document segments) the end user needs. In contrast, *document retrieval* implies getting a full document for the end user, even if only one short passage is needed. If the word *information* is treated as a synonym of *passage*, as in *passage retrieval*, one exception must be made to the previous discussion regarding the implication of *information*.

1.2.2 Information Representation

No matter which format a piece of information may take, it needs to be represented before it can be retrieved. Information representation includes the extraction of some elements (e.g., keywords or phrases) from a document or the assignment of terms (e.g., descriptors or subject headings) to a document so that its essence can be characterized and presented. Typically, information representation can be done via any combination of the following means: abstracting, indexing, categorization, summarization, and extraction. *Information processing* and *information management*, though having different meanings, are often regarded as synonyms of *information representation*. While *information processing* refers to how information is handled for retrieval purposes, *information management* deals with the full range of activities associated with information, from information selection to information preservation.

In this book, the term *information representation* will be used to cover the various aspects and methods of creating surrogates or representations (e.g., indexes and abstracts) for IR purposes.

1.2.3 Information Retrieval

Information retrieval has been treated, by and large, as a subject field covering both the representation and retrieval sides of information (Spärck Jones & Willett, 1997). The retrieval dimension is further referred to as *information access, information seeking,* and *information searching.* These terms can be considered as synonyms for *retrieval.* However, each of them does have its different orientation with regard to implications. The term *information access* emphasizes the aspect of getting or obtaining information. In contrast, *information seeking* focuses on the user who is actively involved in the process. As for *information searching,* the center of attention appears to be on how to look for information.

In addition to the aforementioned terms, *data mining* and *resource discovery* have often been found in the information professional's vocabulary in recent years when IR is discussed. Both terms are normally used in the business and networked environment. At this time, it remains to be seen whether *data mining* and *resource discovery* will be incorporated into the permanent vocabulary of people from the field of IR.

Another layer of meaning in IR is *information storage,* which mainly deals with the recording and storage of information. However, such usage is gradually becoming a past practice because *information storage* is no longer a major concern, thanks to the advances made in information storage and access technology. Therefore, IR in this book encompasses information seeking, information searching, and information access but excludes information storage.

1.2.4 Digital Age

The word *digital,* as opposed to *analog,* is a relatively new concept. Both *digital* and *analog* are terms related to electronic technology, according to the following account provided by Tech Target (2001), a company also defining terminology in information technology:

> Digital describes electronic technology that generates, stores, and processes data in terms of two states: positive and non-positive. Positive is expressed or represented by the number 1 and non-positive by the number 0. Thus, data transmitted or stored with digital technology is expressed as a string of 0's and 1's. ... Prior to digital technology, electronic transmission was limited to analog technology, which conveys data as electronic signals of varying frequency or amplitude that are added to carrier waves of a given frequency. Broadcast and phone transmission has conventionally used analog technology.

With the advent of the computer, the internet, and other information technologies, we have apparently been entering into a digital age. Various activities, including research and development, related to IRR increasingly take place in the digital environment. This book is thus titled accordingly, signifying the state of the art for the field.

1.3 Major Components

IRR in its totality can be divided into several major constituents: database, search mechanism, language, and interface. People (including the user, the information professional, and the system developer), information, and systems are the three intertwining entities that function jointly in the process of IRR although they are not discussed specifically in this section.

1.3.1 The Database

Databases in IRR comprise information represented and organized in a certain manner. In the traditional sense, a database (e.g., an online database) is typically made of records that can be further decomposed into fields, the smallest and most natural units for sorting, searching, and retrieving information. In a database of journal publications, for instance, author and title are two fields. Traditional databases consist of two parts: *sequential files* and *inverted files*. The sequential file is the database source, containing information organized in the field-record-database structure. It is called a *sequential* file because the records in it are ordered according to the sequence they take when being entered into the database. The inverted file, also known as an index, provides access to the sequential file according to given search queries. It is called an *inverted* file because the order in which information is presented (access point first and locator second) is the reverse of that in sequential files (locator first and access point second).

In a nontraditional sense, a database (e.g., as in internet retrieval systems) may still have sequential and inverted files. But the composition of the sequential file for an internet retrieval system, for example, is different from its counterpart for traditional IR systems (e.g., online systems) in that the composition of the sequential file does not take the field-record-database structure. Rather, the sequential file is made of fieldless information presented in proselike format. In addition, information contained within is not a surrogate (e.g., abstract) but a part or the full content of an original internet document (e.g., a webpage). In traditional IR systems, however, information in sequential files is usually some type of representation in the form of bibliographical descriptions, abstracts, summaries, extracts, and the like.

The content and coverage of the database determine what can be retrieved later from the IR system.

1.3.2 The Search Mechanism

Information represented and organized systematically in a database can be searched and retrieved only when a corresponding search mechanism is provided. A search mechanism can acquire any degree of sophistication in search capabilities, which are defined ultimately by the search algorithms and procedures the IR system incorporates. All search procedures can be categorized as either basic or advanced. Basic search procedures are commonly found in the majority of operational IR systems, while advanced search procedures have been tested and experimented with mainly in laboratories or prototype systems. However, in recent years, advanced search algorithms have increasingly been integrated into internet retrieval systems.

Procedures such as keyword searching, Boolean searching, truncation, and proximity searching belong to the basic search algorithm cluster. As noted earlier, these procedures often form the search mechanism embedded in many IR systems. End users with little training or search experience should be able to perform simple searching tasks in retrieval environments of this kind. Advanced search procedures, such as weighted searching, are employed mostly in newer retrieval systems and are generally designed for people with professional training and search experience.

The capacity of a search mechanism determines what retrieval techniques will be available to users and how information stored in databases can be retrieved.

1.3.3 The Language

Information relies on language, spoken or written, when being processed, transferred, or communicated. In this context, language is one of the crucial components in IRR. Language in IRR can be identified as either natural language or controlled vocabulary. What people naturally use for representing information or forming a query is called *natural language*. If an artificial language, whose vocabulary, syntax, semantics, and pragmatics are limited, is applied in IRR, that language is termed *controlled vocabulary* (Wellisch, 1995). There are three common types of controlled vocabulary: classifications, subject heading lists, and thesauri, each with its own special usage in IRR.

Natural language, generally speaking, allows the highest degree of specificity and flexibility in representing and retrieving information. People do not need any training or practice in using natural language because it is what they use for oral and written communication every day. In contrast, it is costly to create and maintain a controlled vocabulary, and people have to learn how to use it by practice and training. Nevertheless, controlled vocabulary is able to reduce the intrinsic difficulties (e.g., complexity, subtleness, and ambiguity) in using natural language for representing and retrieving information (Lansdale & Ormerod, 1994). The debate in this field about natural language versus controlled vocabulary has been going on since the end of the 19th century (Rowley, 1994). However, language remains an essential part of IRR regardless of debate outcomes.

Language, to a certain degree, determines the flexibility and artificiality in information representation and retrieval. Chapter 4 of this book is devoted to the discussion of language in information representation and retrieval.

1.3.4 The Interface

Interface, according to Shaw (1991), is what the user sees, hears, and touches while interacting with a computer system. In IRR, interface refers to the interaction occurring between the user and related activities. Also, with this component of IRR, the user dimension appears obvious yet is intermingled with the other three components: database, search mechanism, and language.

Interface is regularly considered when judging whether an IRR system is user-friendly. As defined by Mooers' law, user-friendly systems will attract more people than user-hostile ones in terms of usage. The quality of an interface is decided by interaction mode (e.g., menu selection), display features (e.g., screen layout and font type), and other related factors. Adaptive and affective technologies are beginning to be applied in interface design and implementation as more attention is paid to the human dimension in IRR. Interface determines the ultimate success of a system for IRR, especially if the system operates in the digital environment.

In sum, database, search mechanism, language, and interface constitute the major components of IRR that interact with the human dimension at one stage or another during the IRR process.

1.4 The Essential Problem in Information Representation and Retrieval

The essential problem in IRR remains how to obtain the right information for the right user at the right time despite the existence of other variables (e.g., user characteristics or database coverage) in the IRR environment. Before exploring the essential problem any further, we should first consider the process of IRR.

1.4.1 The Process of Information Representation and Retrieval

In the IRR process, the user initiates the search and receives any results retrieved, while the information professional is responsible for designing, implementing, and maintaining the IRR systems. Figure 1.1 illustrates the IRR process.

Any information retrieved from the database must first be represented by the information professional according to the language chosen for IRR. Discrepancies are likely to occur during the course of information representation and can be serious problems if a controlled vocabulary is used for the following reasons: First, when information recorded in forms such as journal articles or technical reports is represented as abstracts, indexing terms, and the like, a genuine rendering of the original information does not seem achievable. One could argue that we represent, for example, a big circle with a smaller one. Even so, the size dimension has been distorted. Second, any controlled vocabulary is merely a subset of the natural language with which the original documents were created. It is therefore often hard to find, for example, an exact match between a term in a document and a descriptor from a thesaurus. For representation purposes, the indexer then has to

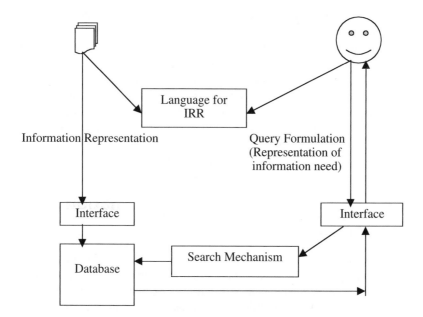

Figure 1.1   Process of Information Representation and Retrieval

choose from related terms, narrower terms, or broader terms listed in the thesaurus. Third, inconsistency in information representation (including concept analysis) appears inevitable, especially if more than one person or system handles the task. Cleverdon (1984) reported that even two experienced indexers, using the same controlled vocabulary, could assign only 30 percent of terms in common to the same document. Similarly, Humphrey (1992) found that inter-indexer consistency in MEDLINE by selecting terms from Medical Subject Headings (MeSH) was less than 49 percent.

On the other hand, users are required to transform their information needs, using the chosen IRR language, into queries that can then be executed in the database with the searching mechanism provided. Researchers have long been aware of the complexity involved in this task. For instance, Blair and Maron (1985) pointed out, "It is impossibly difficult for users to predict the exact words, word combinations, and phrases that are used by all (or most) relevant documents" (p. 295).

In addition, any use of controlled vocabularies and search features (e.g., Boolean operators) will add to the difficulty. Natural language searching, that is, searching with complete phrases or sentences as used in everyday communication without forming any structured queries (e.g., why is the sky blue?), is becoming available on the internet, but there is still a long way to go before researchers in natural language processing—a subdivision of artificial intelligence (AI)—make substantial breakthroughs in their endeavors.

In other words, whether a search will be successful or not depends solely on whether a match is found between the represented information in the system and a query submitted by the user. To be more specific, a search is successful if a match is made between a query and the information represented in the database chosen for the task. Otherwise, a search cannot turn up any useful results. Matching is, therefore, the fundamental mechanism in IRR. As shown in Figure 1.1, there are several points in the IRR process that can cause discrepancies in matching. The ultimate goal for quality IRR is, through the use of various methods and techniques, to minimize or even eliminate the discrepancies that can occur during the process. These methods and techniques are discussed at length in later chapters.

1.4.2 The Limits of Information Representation and Retrieval

While a great amount of research has been done on IRR, there are certain limits that appear insurmountable. When Swanson (1988) pondered the prospect for automatic indexing and retrieval, he borrowed the term *postulates of impotence* (PIs) from E. Taylor Whittaker and formulated nine PIs stating things that cannot be done in IRR. Although made in 1988 with reference to the automatic domain, several of the statements still seem quite relevant and are quoted here:

> PI 1: An information need cannot be fully expressed as a search request. ... The question cannot be precisely formed until the answer is found.

> PI 3: ... Relevance is not fixed, it is judged within a shifting framework.

> PI 4: It is never possible to verify whether all documents relevant to any request have been found. ...

> PI 9: In sum, the first eight postulates imply that consistently effective fully automatic indexing and retrieval is not possible. The conceptual problems of IR—the problems of meaning—are no less profound than thinking or any other forms of intelligent behavior. (p. 96)

The conceptual problems of IR, as Swanson put it, are critical to the understanding and development of the field. With a close examination of the IRR process, it is apparent that what IRR implies, as suggested earlier, is essentially term matching rather than concept searching in the digital environment. When the search term is, for example, *public transportation*, documents indexed under *buses* or *subway* are not likely to be retrieved unless cross-references are made in the controlled vocabulary. Will IRR one day move beyond term matching and closer to concept searching? The answer is being sought and explored vigorously via trial and error (Swanson, 1977).

References

ACM SIGIR. (1995). Gerard Salton: In memoriam. *IRList Digest*, 12(34). Retrieved January 19, 2009, from www.cs.virginia.edu/~clv2m/salton.txt

Blair, David C., and Maron, M. E. (1985). An evaluation of retrieval effectiveness for a full-text document-retrieval system. *Communications of the ACM*, 28(3), 289–299.

Boole, George. (1854). *An investigation into laws of thought, on which are founded the mathematical theories of logic and probabilities*. London: Walton and Maberley.

Borko, Harold, and Bernier, Charles L. (1975). *Abstracting concepts and methods*. New York: Academic Press.

Bush, Vannevar. (1945). As we may think. *Atlantic Monthly*, 176(1), 101–108.

Cleverdon, C. W. (1984). Optimizing convenient online access to bibliographic databases. *Information Services and Use*, 4, 37–47.

Corbitt, Kevin D. (1992). *Calvin N. Mooers papers, 1930–1978* (CBI 81). Minneapolis: Center for the History of Computing, Charles Babbage Institute, University of Minnesota. Retrieved October 3, 2009, from www.libsci.sc.edu/bob/isp/mooers.htm

Crouch, Carolyn, et al. (1996). In memoriam: Gerard Salton, March 8, 1927–August 28, 1995. *Journal of the American Society for Information Science*, 47(2), 108–115.

Cuadra, Carlos A. (1964). Identifying key contributions to information science. *American Documentation*, 15(4), 289–295.

Fischer, M. (1966). The KWIC index concept: A retrospective view. *American Documentation*, 17(2), 57–70.

Garfield, Eugene. (1997). A tribute to Calvin N. Mooers, a pioneer of information retrieval. *The Scientist*, 11(6), 9.

Grosz, Barbara J., Spärck Jones, Karen, and Webber, Bonnie Lynn (Eds.). (1986). *Readings in natural language processing*. Los Altos, CA: Morgan Kaufmann.

Gull, Cloyd Dake. (1956). Seven years of work on the organization of materials in the special library. *American Documentation*, 7(1–5), 320–329.

Gull, Cloyd Dake. (1987). Historical note: Information science and technology: From coordinate indexing to the global brain. *Journal of the American Society for Information Science*, 38(5), 338–366.

Hahn, Trudi Bellardo. (1996). Pioneers of the online age. *Information Processing and Management*, 32(1), 33–48.

Harvey, John F. (1978). Luhn, Hans Peter (1896–1964). In Bohdan S. Wynar (Ed.), *Dictionary of American library biography* (pp. 324–326). Littleton, CO: Libraries Unlimited.

Henderson, Madeline M. (1996). In Memoriam: Calvin N. Mooers, October 24, 1919–December 1, 1994. *Journal of the American Society for Information Science*, 47(9), 659–661.

Humphrey, Susanne M. (1992). Indexing biomedical documents: From the-saurai to knowledge-based retrieval systems. *Artificial Intelligence in Medicine*, 4, 343–371.

Koenig, Michael E. D. (1987). The convergence of Moore's/Mooers' Laws. *Information Processing & Management*, 23(6), 583–592.

Lancaster, F. Wilfrid. (1968). *Information retrieval systems: Characteristics, testing and evaluation.* New York: Wiley.

Lansdale, Mark W., and Ormerod, Thomas C. (1994). *Understanding inter-faces: A handbook of human-computer dialogue.* London: Academic Press.

Larsen, Poul Steen. (1999). Books and bytes: Preserving documents for pros-perity. *Journal of the American Society for Information Science*, 50(11), 1020–1027.

Luhn, H. P. (1953). A new method of recording and searching information. *American Documentation*, 4(1), 14–16.

Luhn, H. P. (1958). The automatic creation of literature abstracts. *IBM Journal of Research and Development*, 2(2), 159–165.

Luhn, H. P. (1961). Selective dissemination of new scientific information with the aid of electronic processing equipment. *American Documentation*, 12(2), 131–138.

Maybury, Mark T. (2005). Karen Spärck Jones. In John I. Tait (Ed.), (2005). *Charting a new course: Natural language processing and information retrieval* (pp. xi–xxiii). New York: Springer.

McCandless, R. F. J., Skweir, E. A., and Gordon, M. (1964). Secondary journals in chemical and biological fields. *Journal of Chemical Documentation*, 4(2), 147–153.

Meadow, Charles T. (1992). *Text information retrieval systems.* San Diego: Academic Press.

Mooers, Calvin N. (1960). Mooers' Law: Or, why some retrieval systems are used and others are not. *American Documentation*, 11(3), ii.

Pao, Miranda Lee. (1989). *Concepts of information retrieval.* Englewood, CO: Libraries Unlimited.

Robertson, Stephen, and Spärck Jones, Karen. (1976). Relevance weighting of search terms. *Journal of the American Society for Information Science & Technology*, 27(3), 129–146.

Robertson, Stephen, and Tait, John. (2008). In memoriam: Karen Spärck Jones. *Journal of the American Society for Information Science & Technology*, 59(5), 852–854.

Rowley, Jennifer. (1994). The controlled versus natural indexing languages debate revisited: A perspective on information retrieval practice and research. *Journal of Information Science*, 20(2), 108–119.

Salton, Gerard. (1987). Historical notes: The past thirty years in information retrieval. *Journal of the American Society for Information Science*, 38(5), 375–380.

Schultz, Claire K. (Ed.). (1968). *H. P. Luhn: Pioneer of information science: Selected works.* New York: Spartan Books.

Shaw, Debora. (1991). The human-computer interface for information retrieval. *Annual Review of Information Science and Technology*, 26, 155–195.

Shera, Jesse H. (1978). Taube, Mortimer (1910–1965). In Bohdan S. Wynar (Ed.), *Dictionary of American library biography* (pp. 512–513). Littleton, CO: Libraries Unlimited.

Smith, Elizabeth S. (1993). On the shoulders of giants: From Boole to Shannon to Taube: The origins and development of computerized information from the mid-19th century to the present. *Information Technology and Libraries*, 12(2), 217–226.

Spärck Jones, Karen. (1972). A statistical interpretation of term specificity and its application in retrieval. *Journal of Documentation*, 28(1), 11–21.

Spärck Jones, Karen (Ed.). (1981). *Information retrieval experiment.* London: Butterworths.

Spärck Jones, Karen. (1994). *Finding the information wood in the natural language tree* [Videotape]. Talk presented at the Grace Hopper Celebration of Women in Computing meeting. 41 min.

Spärck Jones, Karen. (1995). Reflection on TREC. *Information Processing & Management*, 31(3), 291–314.

Spärck Jones, Karen. (2000). Further reflections on TREC. *Information Processing & Management*, 36(1), 37–85.

Spärck Jones, Karen. (2005). Some points in a time. *Computational Linguistics*, 31(1), 1–14.

Spärck Jones, Karen. (2007). Automatic summarising: The state of the art. *Information Processing & Management*, 43(6), 1449–1481.

Spärck Jones, Karen, and Willett, Peter (Eds.). (1997). *Readings in information retrieval.* San Francisco: Morgan Kaufmann.

Stevens, Mary Elizabeth. (1968). H. P. Luhn, information scientist. In Claire K. Schultz (Ed.), *H. P. Luhn: Pioneer of information science: Selected works* (pp. 24–30). New York: Spartan Books.

Swanson, Don R. (1977). Information retrieval as a trial-and-error process. *Library Quarterly, 47*(2), 128–148.

Swanson, Don R. (1988). Historical note: Information retrieval and the future of an illusion. *Journal of the American Society for Information Science,* 49(2), 92–98.

Tait, John I. (Ed.). (2005). *Charting a new course: Natural language processing and information retrieval.* New York: Springer.

Tech Target. (2001). Digital. Retrieved December 3, 2008, from whatis.techtarget.com

Wellisch, Hans H. (1995). *Indexing from A to Z.* 2nd ed. New York: H.W. Wilson.

Wilks, Yorick. (2007). In memoriam: Karen Spärck Jones (1935–2007). *IEEE Intelligent Systems, 22*(3), 8–9.

Willett, Peter, and Robertson, Stephen. (2007). In memoriam: Karen Spärck Jones. *Journal of Documentation, 63*(5), 605–608.

Wynar, Bohdan S. (1980). *Introduction to cataloguing and classification.* 6th ed. Littleton, CO: Libraries Unlimited.

CHAPTER 2

Information Representation I: Basic Approaches

Information, recorded formally in different types of documents (e.g., proceedings papers and technical reports), needs to be represented before it can be retrieved. In no case can information retrieval be performed with the original documents themselves. Rather, the retrieval activity takes place with document surrogates in the form of indexes, abstracts, summaries, and the like. Representation in this book refers to the essence or the subject content of a document via a certain approach, although the end product can take a variety of forms. Ideally, the representation process should be conducted simply and efficiently; however, as Lesk (1997) noted:

> If we had a single knowledge representation scheme that let us put each idea in one place, and if the users knew this scheme and could place each of their queries in it, subject retrieval would be straightforward. ... In practice, it seems unlikely that any single knowledge representation scheme will serve all purposes. (pp. 99–100)

Furthermore, how the representation scheme could be applied consistently and precisely still poses challenges to information professionals even if the choice of schemes is not a concern and some methods (e.g., abstracting) do not require a scheme to get implemented. Information representation, in a nutshell, means challenge, complexity, and subtlety.

2.1 Indexing

Indexing has been a widely adopted method for information representation. It uses terms (i.e., words or phrases), either derived or assigned, to represent important facets of the original document. The number of index terms used to represent a document ranges from several terms in bibliographical databases to hundreds in full-text systems.

Conceptual analysis and translation of the document to be indexed constitute the intellectual portion of the indexing practice. To be more specific, conceptual analysis in indexing involves the identification of key concepts covered in the document, whereas the translation phase actually converts a chosen concept to index terms based on a preselected indexing language.

Indexing language will be discussed specifically, together with retrieval language, in Chapter 4.

2.1.1 Types of Indexing

Indexing type is normally dependent on how the terms are obtained. If the terms are extracted from the original text of a document, it is called derivative indexing. Correspondingly, if the terms are assigned to a document, it is labeled as assignment indexing. Derivative indexing can also be treated as a synonym for keyword indexing because index terms are selected directly from keywords in the text, and no controlled vocabulary is consulted. By comparison, a controlled vocabulary must be used in assignment indexing to ensure the use of appropriate terms.

Indexing terms assigned from a controlled vocabulary are customarily called descriptors even though the controlled vocabulary used might not be a thesaurus. If a concept to be indexed is new or happens to be a proper name (e.g., *Great Wall*) and no equivalent can be found in the controlled vocabulary, an identifier can be created in assignment indexing. In other words, identifiers are terms assigned by the indexer but not taken from a controlled vocabulary. As mentioned earlier, terms selected in the derivative indexing process are called keywords.

Indexing without a controlled vocabulary is sometimes referred to as free indexing (Fugmann, 1993). Free indexing is generally applied in derivative indexing. Similarly, assignment indexing is typically performed by using a controlled vocabulary. Whether a controlled vocabulary should be used in indexing has been an issue over the years, and the debate continues. Overall, as more information becomes available digitally, controlled vocabulary will be applied less in indexing because of quality and quantity factors.

2.1.2 Automated and Automatic Indexing

All the activities involved in indexing can be categorized into two types: intellectual and mechanical. The intellectual part of indexing was described in §2.1. The mechanical elements in indexing mainly include activities such as alphabetizing and formatting index entries. While the intellectual portion of indexing remains to be accomplished by human beings most of the time, given the current state of research in artificial intelligence, indexing operations of a mechanical nature can be completed satisfactorily by computers. If computers are used to handle both the mechanical and the intellectual parts of indexing, we have automatic indexing. If computers are used only for the mechanical operations of indexing and human indexers are responsible for the intellectual portion of indexing, we have automated indexing.

Automatic indexing, also known as machine indexing, appears to be a very attractive solution to the inconsistency problem and the high cost associated with manual indexing. However, the intrinsic weakness of automatic indexing is that the computer can deal with the intellectual part of indexing only as well as the human indexer and, in most cases, much worse than the information professional. The reason is obvious: The computer cannot, in truth, think and does not have the analytical power of a human being. In comparison, automated indexing can relieve human indexers of the tedious and repetitive indexing tasks so that they are able to concentrate more on the intellectual undertakings of indexing.

On the other hand, the value of automatic indexing should not be underestimated, especially when the amount of information to be indexed is gigantic. Automatic indexing usually relies on a variety of algorithms, among which the keyword frequency approach seems the most popular and has been implemented extensively. Other automatic indexing approaches are generally based on keyword proximity, location, probability, and linguistics. Controlled vocabularies are incorporated in some automatic indexing practices as well. But the success of such a method is negatively affected by the mechanical nature of computerized indexing.

2.1.3 Indexing in the Hyperstructure Environment

More and more information is becoming available in the hyperstructure environment, which is symbolized by the World Wide Web. For web-based information, index terms are most naturally presented as hyperlinks that embody both the index term and the locator mechanism. In other words, hyperlink names serve as index terms, whereas the hyperlink mechanism seamlessly leads the user to where the index terms are pointing. In comparison with other indexing environments, this setting is unique in the following respects.

First, index terms in the hyperstructure environment are embedded within the document itself rather than existing as separate entities outside the context. Second, index terms and locators are merged into one unit instead of being listed individually. Third, the subject hierarchy or the concept of subentries in traditional indexing is not exactly reflected in the hyperstructure environment. Fourth, only content-based links in the hyper- structure can be regarded as index terms, whereas organizational links, such as "Next page" and "Top of document," should not be (Chu, 1997). Fifth, authors assume the role of indexer when they prepare hyperstructure documents, and indexing is done simultaneously with, if not before, document creation. As a result, terms (e.g., *click here*) that are unlikely to be chosen by an indexer would often appear as link names in the hyperstructure environment. Sixth, less discrepancy will occur between the original document and the index terms in this process of information representation because the author decides, while writing the document, which terms should become links, whereas in traditional indexing, the author writes a document, and then an indexer tries to analyze it for representation purposes.

Given the unique features of indexing in the hyperstructure environment, hyperdocuments should be indexed with methods appropriate to them. For example, one should choose link names carefully when writing hyperdocuments (Chu, 1997).

2.1.4 Social Tagging

Social tagging, entirely different from tagging with an identification code (e.g., RFID—radio frequency identification), has been gaining in popularity since 2003 as a means for the end user to "index" information on the internet. Social tagging, in conjunction with other applications aiming for user participation (e.g., blogging and wikis), belongs to the Web 2.0 movement (O'Reilly, 2005). Early systems with tagging mechanisms include Flickr, a well-known photo sharing website, and del.icio.us, whose domain name was changed to Delicious.com in 2007. At such tagging sites, people can describe and comment on what they view and hear by tagging with words or phrases of their own choosing.

Tagging, to a large extent, is an activity similar to keyword indexing described earlier in this section, except that keyword indexing is performed by indexers, authors of scholarly publications, and information retrieval systems, while tagging is done by any internet user. Because of this major dissimilarity, tagging does not seem equivalent to keyword indexing, although taggers tend to choose nouns and noun phrases as tags most of the time (Kipp, 2007; Xu & Chu, 2008). In addition, problems that have plagued keyword indexing (e.g., synonyms, homographs, and word form variations) are all present in tagging, if not on a larger scale. Nevertheless, tagging as an emerging and alternative method for information representation has great potential in facilitating information retrieval because user-generated tags, among their other benefits (e.g., providing more access points), are more likely chosen by end users themselves as query terms for locating information.

As an emerging approach to information representation, tagging has also brought about innovations that enrich the field of information retrieval (Smith, 2008). Folksonomy is one example of such innovations. The word folksonomy was coined by Thomas Vander Wal in 2004, a portmanteau of *folks* and *taxonomy* (Vander Wal, 2007). In other words, a folksonomy is a taxonomy built with tags created by folks or end users. Further discussion of both taxonomies and folksonomies is presented in §4.4.

Folksonomies commonly take the form of a tag cloud, which is a visual aggregation of tags generated at a tagging site based on tagged frequencies. The tag cloud can help users choose appropriate terms in either the tagging or the retrieval process.

2.2 Categorization

Categorization denotes the successive and hierarchical representation of information by categories. Two types of categorization exist depending on whether a systematically developed scheme is used.

2.2.1 Types of Categorization

Traditionally, categorization is done according to an established classification scheme such as Dewey Decimal Classification (DDC) and Library of Congress Classification (LCC). Such categorization practices are thus universally called classification, which is generally applicable to publications collected by libraries and information services. Notations for classification include numbers, alphabets, or alpha-numerals.

With the advent of the internet, a lot of information has been posted to that new platform. Information on the internet overall shares the following attributes: ephemeral, mixed quality, and huge quantity. The classification method therefore seems too costly, inappropriate, or unjustified for representing information on the internet. Rather, taxonomy based on loosely structured categories appears the right framework for organizing information of that nature. Yahoo! is undoubtedly a pioneer in this practice, which has become one model for representing information on the internet, especially on the web. Categories in taxonomies for representing web-based information are listed directly as hyperlinks. No notations (e.g., numbers, alphabets, and alpha-numerals) are used to reflect the hierarchical or other relationships in the framework of taxonomy. Further coverage of taxonomy is provided in Chapter 4, along with a discussion of folksonomies and ontologies.

2.2.2 Principles of Categorization

When categorization is chosen as the information representation method, one category, or occasionally two for items covering interdisciplinary topics, will be assigned to a given document. In other words, a given document should be assigned to a specific category listed in an existing system for categorization. This practice requires that categories selected for the categorization system must be both of the following:

- Exhaustive
- Mutually exclusive

That is to say, all categories possibly needed for representing information should be included in the categorization system. At the same time, none of these categories should be mutually exclusive among themselves. If the first point is not satisfied, some information cannot be represented by categories available in the scheme. If the second point is not observed, then more than one category can be chosen to represent the same document. Other principles, such as flexibility and ease of use, though important, are not as fundamental as these two.

2.2.3 The Convergence of the Two Categorization Approaches

What differentiates one categorization approach from another lies mainly in the nature of the framework adopted for the purpose of information representation. Classification, having endured tests of various kinds, has established itself as a plausible method for representing information. Taxonomy, in contrast, has been regarded as a quick and rough approach to information representation. As more substantive and quality information becomes available on the internet, classification is beginning to be utilized to categorize network-based information (e.g., McKiernan, 2001). In the meantime, frameworks developed for taxonomy purposes are improved and enhanced by incorporating time-tested features that originated from classification schemes, such as hierarchical representation.

In addition, text categorization by automatic means (e.g., Boley, et al., 1998; Yang, 1999) has increasingly been explored with an orientation toward taxonomy rather than classification, as a growing amount of information is available digitally. While automatic classification once attracted a lot of attention from researchers, the brainpower needed for rigorous classification seems unattainable in purely machine-based algorithms.

2.3 Summarization

Summarization, unlike indexing or categorization, tries to represent a document with a paragraph or two—a précis or a condensed version of the original. The degree of condensation and the method used define the different summarization approaches.

2.3.1 Types of Summarization

2.3.1.1 Abstracts

An abstract is a concise and accurate representation of the contents of a document. Abstracting, the act of writing an abstract, has basically been carried out by human beings, although automatic efforts (e.g., Luhn, 1958) have been attempted in the past. Abstracts ideally should be written in a style similar to the original, but that criterion is hard to meet because of the inevitable loss of authenticity during the abstracting process.

Abstracts can be further divided into three kinds: informative abstracts, indicative abstracts, and critical abstracts. Informative abstracts contain substantial information from the original document, so they may serve as a substitute. Based on an informative abstract, people can decide whether they need to read the full document. Indicative abstracts, by comparison, simply describe the "aboutness" of the original document, excluding specific details such as methodology and findings, and therefore cannot be treated as a replacement for the original. People have to consult the original document to get a thorough understanding of it. Critical abstracts are so named because they not only represent the document's contents under consideration but also try to evaluate them. This form of abstract is not recommended because abstracts by definition should be free of any interpretation and judgment. Generally speaking, no critical abstracts should be written unless one is required to do so.

As mentioned earlier, researchers have explored ways of producing automatic abstracts. However, the end products at present look essentially more similar to auto-summaries or auto-extracts than auto-abstracts because they consist purely of key sentences extracted from the original document.

2.3.1.2 Summaries

A summary is a restatement of the main points of an original document, placed either at the beginning or at the end of a document. Although very close to an abstract, a summary usually assumes that the reader will have the opportunity to peruse the full document. Hence, certain elements essential to a complete understanding of the document, such as sections on background, purpose, and methodology, tend to be absent from a summary (Rowley, 1992).

Algorithms for automatically summarizing texts, especially those in digital format, have been developed in recent years (e.g., Spärck Jones, 2007; Spärck Jones & Endres-Niggemeyer, 1995). Automatic summarization in fact emerges as an active research area in artificial intelligence (AI). Some researchers may label their end products of representation as abstracts. However, it is well known that only AI research will be able to make automatic abstracting a reality, and such AI algorithms have not been successfully worked out. Further discussion of automatic summarization is provided in §12.2.2.

2.3.1.3 Extracts

An extract comprises one or more portions of a document selected to represent the whole. Extracts are unlikely to offer a good representation of the original document. Nevertheless, they may be valuable to the reader who is interested in the outcome of a particular study. In no case can extracts be regarded as substitutes for original documents.

Extracts, though their representativeness is inferior to that of both summaries and abstracts, can be constructed entirely by automatic methods. The majority of internet retrieval systems, including Google, employ auto-extracts for information representation purposes. An infamous feature of auto-extracts produced by internet retrieval systems is that the extract often ends with an ellipsis when it has reached the cutoff point set up by the system. The quality of auto-extracts, therefore, is a serious concern when they are used to represent documents.

2.3.1.4 RSS

RSS, which initially stood for Rich Site Summary, is another Web 2.0 application that can be used for information representation purposes. More specifically, RSS relies on file formats called feeds to aggregate newly updated information from multiple sources on the web. People who subscribe to certain feeds via a reader (i.e., an aggregator program) can receive at their own computers the up-to-date information those feeds provide. RSS can thus be considered a current awareness service in the web environment that offers to its subscribers a summary of information newly available from sources in which they are interested. In that sense, Rich Site Summary seems a fitting name for this application.

Realizing the value of RSS, developers at World Wide Web Consortium (W3C) created a new version of RSS when Netscape, the company that developed the first graphic web browser, could no longer support the RSS it first built. Because the newer version of RSS was based on the Resource Description Framework (RDF) standard that W3C set up as part of the semantic web architecture, the RSS abbreviation was changed to stand for RDF Site Summary to differentiate it from its predecessor, Rich Site Summary (Kelly, 2005). Really Simple Syndication is yet another meaning of RSS that was developed after the W3C version (Lerner, 2004).

Compared with other summarization methods described in this section, RSS is accomplished automatically on the web. On one hand, this automatic feature adequately meets the needs of the many end users who desire the latest information. On the other, the quality of summary information provided by RSS is undoubtedly inferior to that of other summarization methods, such as abstracts. Representativeness is one criterion commonly used in judging the quality of summarization.

2.3.2 The Issue of Representativeness

All four different forms of summarization—abstracts, summaries, extracts, and RSS—are legitimate means of information representation. As described previously, however, they differ from each other in terms of representativeness. To rank the four by that criterion, abstracts would be scored the highest, while RSS appears to have the least representativeness in this group. Summaries and extracts would be ranked somewhere between the other two. This comparison, although brief, sheds some light on how each summarization method can be best applied for different tasks of information representation.

2.4 Other Methods of Information Representation

If indexing, categorization, and summarization are considered the conventional methods of information representation, the techniques discussed in this section are unique and atypical.

2.4.1 Citations

Citations are references that authors make when they compose their writings. In general, a citation implies a relationship between a part or the whole of the cited document and a part or the whole of the citing document (Malin, 1968). Ever since Eugene Garfield, founder of the Institute for Scientific Information (ISI), which publishes citation indexes, introduced this novel approach to the field of information representation and retrieval, a great deal of discussion has been devoted to deciphering the implication of the citation relationship, or determining why a citation is made. Garfield tried in 1965 to summarize reasons for the citation practice in 15 points, which include, for example, paying homage to pioneers and giving credit for related work (Garfield, 1965).

Although the real motivation for citing others' works might be different from person to person, citations can be regarded as what the citing authors select to represent in their own publications. The representations in this context take the form of citations rather than the usual surrogates, such as abstracts and index terms. Citations are in fact bibliographical information about documents, which can be further decomposed into units such as titles and authors. In other words, citations provide a rich source for representing information. Moreover, there is no need to create and maintain a framework (e.g., a thesaurus or classification scheme) for representation purposes, whereas such a framework is a must in classification and controlled vocabulary indexing.

Citing authors are in fact indexing their own work with readily available resources, namely, references or citations. The elimination of intermediaries in citation indexing, however, has both positive and negative impacts on representation. The positive impact is that the author, as the indexer, knows his or her own work the best and needs to expend no effort to interpret the original document. The negative impact is that the true reason for citation is really unknown. Therefore, we can always question whether the right citations have been used to represent a document. Another concern about citation indexing as a method of information representation is the limited coverage of citation databases. Yet people customarily use them because creating one from scratch often seems impractical and too time-consuming.

Because citation indexing requires little human intelligence, the whole procedure can be automated easily. Indeed, the entire process of citation indexing can be completed without any human intervention, which appears unachievable with the other methods of information representation.

2.4.2 Strings

While citations can serve as surrogates for original documents, string indexing (Craven, 1986) is another approach to information representation. Strings can be a phrase, a group of phrases, or a statement, all specifically prepared for representing a document. *Use of World Wide Web for distributed learning in higher education* is an example of such strings.

There are many different types of string indexes, but they share two main characteristics: 1) manually create a string to summarize the theme of a document, and 2) mechanically generate index entries based on the given string for representation purposes. String indexing, therefore, is a distinctive case of automated indexing, briefly described in §2.1.2.

PREserved Context Index System (PRECIS) and NEsted PHrase Indexing System (NEPHIS) are two of the best-known systems developed for string indexing. In both systems, a string is first prepared by a human indexer. A PRECIS string is a mini-abstract loaded with relevant indexing terms, and a NEPHIS string is a summary statement for indexing a document. These strings are then coded to indicate which terms could become access points and determine the composition of index entries. The actual displaying algorithms adopted by each string indexing system may vary greatly. But all the mechanical tasks in string indexing can be effectively handled by automatic means.

The integration of the human selection of index strings with computer-assisted manipulation of index displays makes string indexing an appealing method for information representation. On one hand, it retains the quality associated with human indexing by having human beings prepare index strings. On the other, string indexing can preclude the dissatisfaction associated with the tedium, inefficiency, and inconsistencies of manual approaches. The digital age is, after all, rapidly emerging. Computers are expected to play an increasingly important role in information representation as well as information retrieval.

2.5 A Review of Basic Approaches to Information Representation

As shown in previous sections, there are various methods for information representation. Table 2.1 recapitulates the major representation approaches discussed so far, from the perspectives of representation type, entities represented, representation framework (whether a controlled vocabulary is used), and production method. Each of these approaches has strengths and weaknesses. When a particular method is selected for representing information, as Meadow (1992) states, it should do the following:

> (1) discriminate between different entities, (2) identify similar entities, (3) allow accurate description of entities, and (4) minimize ambiguity in interpretation. (pp. 41–43)

As anticipated, not a single method can completely fulfill the requirements Meadow specified. One method's weakness may be another's strength. For instance, indexing alone can reveal only certain facets of a document while abstracting is meant to represent a document in its entirety. Therefore,

Table 2.1   Basic Approaches to Information Representation

Approach Feature	Indexing		Categorization		Summarization			Other	
Representation Type	Derivative	Assignment	Classification	Taxonomy	Abstract	Summary	Extract	Citation	String
Entity Represented	Part		Whole		Whole		Part	Whole	
Representation Framework	No	Yes	Yes	No	No			No	Maybe
Production Method	Automatic	Manual & Automatic	Manual	Manual & Automatic	Manual	Manual & Automatic		Automatic	Automated

methodological pluralism (i.e., using more than one method) has been the choice when one needs to select from the diverse approaches to information representation. In practice, an assortment of representation methods (e.g., classification with abstracting or summarization with indexing) has been implemented. Emerging approaches such as RSS and tagging are increasingly used to meet the changing needs of information representation in the digital age.

References

Boley, Daniel, et al. (1998). A client-side web agent for document categorization. *Internet Research: Electronic Networking Applications and Policy*, 8(5), 387–399.

Chu, Heting. (1997). Hyperlinks: How well do they represent the intellectual content of digital collections? *Proceedings of the 60th Annual Meeting of the American Society of Information Science*, 34, 361–369.

Craven, Timothy C. (1986). *String indexing*. New York: Academic Press.

Fugmann, Robert. (1993). *Subject analysis and indexing: Theoretical foundation and practical advice*. Frankfurt/Main, Germany: Indeks Verlag.

Garfield, Eugene. (1965). Can citation indexing be automated? In Mary E. Stevens, et al. (Eds.), *Statistical methods for mechanized documentation* (pp. 189–192). Washington, DC: National Bureau of Standards.

Kelly, Brian. (2005). RSS: More than just news feeds. *New Review of Information Network*, 11(2), 219–227.

Kipp, Margaret E. I. (2007). @toread and cool: Tagging for time, task and emotion. *Proceedings of the 8th Information Architecture Summit*. Las Vegas, Nevada, March 22–27, 2007. Retrieved January 19, 2009, from eprints.rclis.org/10445/1/mkipp-iasummit2007.pdf

Lerner, Reuven M. (2004). At the forge: Syndication with RSS. *Linux Journal*, 2004(126), 8. Retrieved November 12, 2008, from www.linuxjournal.com/article/7702

Lesk, Michael. (1997). *Practical digital libraries: Books, bytes and bucks*. San Francisco: Morgan Kaufmann.

Luhn, H. P. (1958). The automatic creation of literature abstracts. *IBM Journal of Research and Development*, 2(2), 159–165.

Malin, Morton V. (1968). The Science Citation Index: A new concept in indexing. *Library Trends*, 16, 374–397.

McKiernan, Gerry. (2001). Beyond bookmarks: Schemes for organizing the web. Retrieved January 19, 2009, from www.public.iastate.edu/~CYBER STACKS/CTW.htm

Meadow, Charles T. (1992). *Text information retrieval systems*. San Diego: Academic Press.

O'Reilly, Tim. (2005). What is Web 2.0? Retrieved October 4, 2009, from oreilly.com/web2/archive/what-is-web-20.html

Rowley, Jennifer E. (1992). *Organizing knowledge: An introduction to information retrieval*. Brookfield, VT: Gower.

Smith, Gene. (2008). Tagging: Emerging trends. *Bulletin of the American Society for Information Science and Technology*, 34(6), 14–17.

Spärck Jones, Karen. (2007). Automatic summarising: The state of the art. *Information Processing & Management*, 43(6), 1449–1481.

Spärck Jones, Karen, and Endres-Niggemeyer, Brigitte (Eds.). (1995). Summarizing text [Special issue]. *Information Processing & Management*, 31(5).

Vander Wal, Thomas. (2007). Folksonomy. Retrieved November 20, 2008, from vanderwal.net/folksonomy.html

Xu, Chen, and Chu, Heting. (2008). Social tagging in China and the USA: A comparative study. *Proceedings of the Annual Meeting of the American Society for Information Science and Technology*. Columbus, Ohio, October 24–29, 2008 [CD-ROM].

Yang, Yiming. (1999). An evaluation of statistical approaches to text categorization. *Information Retrieval*, 1(1/2), 69–90.

CHAPTER 3

Information Representation II: Related Topics

Chapter 2 discussed basic approaches to information representation with an emphasis on traditional practices and their variations or extensions. In this chapter, other topics related to information representation are explored, including metadata, full text, and multimedia representation.

3.1 Metadata

Metadata is a term coined in the late 1990s for referring to those descriptions that are specifically created to represent digital information accessible on the internet. Metadata was initially applied only to electronic resources and networked information. The connotation of the term has been expanded to include all practices for information representation because metadata has become a very fashionable term and the internet is increasingly becoming a platform for accessing a wide variety of information.

3.1.1 What Is Metadata?

Metadata nowadays can be defined in two different ways: One is narrower in scope, implying descriptions provided for networked information and digital resources by following a standard or framework (e.g., Dublin Core) that is specifically created for this purpose. The other definition is broader in coverage, including cataloging and indexing data created for any kind of documents through the use of traditional methods for describing and organizing information. In this sense, for example, cataloging data produced with Dewey Decimal Classification (DDC) and Anglo-American Cataloging Rules/MAchine Readable Cataloging (AACR/MARC) is also regarded as metadata.

Metadata can be derived or assigned by authors, repository managers, and third-party creators (Dempsey & Heery, 1998). Some metadata information can also be embedded in the hyperstructure environment in the form of hypertext markup language (HTML) tags or hyperlinks. Although metadata provides frameworks for representing information, especially for networked resources, in addition to the existing ones (e.g., classifications and cataloging rules), Wool (1998) believes that metadata provision is essentially an extension of the traditional cataloging process. As briefly mentioned in §2.2.1, the traditional cataloging process is not feasible for organizing digital resources on the internet because of the unique features discussed in the following sections.

3.1.2 Characteristics of Digital Information on the Internet

Digital information, compared with printed resources, has its own characteristics. One must rely on certain hardware and software to view the content of digital information. In addition, digital information must be recorded in some kind of format that changes constantly as the hardware and software are upgraded. Sometimes, different versions of the same software program are compatible, but more often they are not. The compatibility issue becomes worse if one works with digital information generated with different software packages.

Furthermore, digital information on the internet is commonly recorded in the form of hyperstructure, which contrasts sharply with the flat structure of printed information. The advent of the internet makes it easy for people to communicate and share resources. But the absence of a quality control mechanism on the internet results in a flood of information whose quality has a large variance. Therefore, different methods should be adopted for describing and organizing digital information on the internet because existing standards (e.g., DDC and AACR/MARC), developed before digital information was produced in huge quantities, are designed primarily for representing printed information. Metadata has emerged just to cope with the problem of representing digital information that is uniquely formatted, constantly changing, uneven in quality, and enormous in quantity.

3.1.3 Examples of Metadata Standards

Although the concept of metadata is relatively new in the realm of information representation, a considerable number of metadata standards have been developed, and more are being conceived. Dublin Core (DC) and Resource Description Framework (RDF) are some examples of metadata standards.

3.1.3.1 Dublin Core

DC is a simple content description model for electronic resources (Weibel, 1997). DC is a joint effort among experts from the library world, the networking and digital library research communities, and a variety of content specialists in a series of focused, invitational workshops called the Dublin Core Workshop series. DC consists of 15 elements: title, creator, subject, description, publisher, contributor, date, type, format, identifier, source, language, relation, coverage, and rights. As Weibel (1997) explained:

The Dublin Core is not intended to replace richer description models such as AACR2/MARC cataloging, but rather to provide a core set of description elements that can be used by catalogers or non-catalogers for simple resource description. (p. 9)

In practice, DC is used mainly to provide simple descriptions for networked resources such as websites. It seems to be the best-known standard among all the metadata models. Moreover, DC is the prototype application that drove the development of RDF in the World Wide Web Consortium (W3C). Developers of the DC are closely involved in the W3C's RDF effort.

3.1.3.2 Resource Description Framework

RDF was developed under the auspices of the W3C, becoming a W3C recommendation in February 1999 and subsequently a key component in the semantic web envisioned by Berners-Lee and his coworkers (e.g., Berners-Lee, Hendler, & Lassila, 2001; Shadbolt, Hall, & Berners-Lee, 2006). A discussion of the semantic web from the perspective of information representation and retrieval (IRR) is presented in §12.3. According to Shafer (1998):

RDF is an infrastructure for encoding, modeling and exchanging metadata. At the heart of RDF is a simple three-part model: metadata is about a resource, the resource has one or more properties, and each property has a value. (p. 21)

RDF uses eXtensible Markup Language (XML) as the transfer syntax. RDF is evolving to support the many different metadata needs of vendors and information providers (Weibel, 1997). RDF does not stipulate semantics but rather provides the ability for each resource description community to define a semantic structure that reflects community requirements. In other words, unlike DC, RDF does not specify the particular elements the framework should have. Rather, it lets users choose and define the specifications within its framework, based on their needs. RDF is therefore a foundation for processing metadata. According to Lassila (1997), RDF can be used in a variety of application areas: for example, in resource discovery, to provide better search engine capabilities, and in cataloging, for describing the content and content relationships available at a particular website, webpage, or digital library. Further elaboration on RDF is provided in §12.3.1, where semantic web architecture is considered.

3.1.3.3 Digital Object Identifiers

Different from DC and RDF, the Digital Object Identifier (DOI) illustrates individual digital entities (e.g., journal articles, video clips, and music pieces) with its own specific scheme. The International DOI Foundation (2009), an organization established to develop and manage the DOI system, states at its homepage (www.doi.org):

> The Digital Object Identifier (DOI) System is for identifying content objects in the digital environment. DOI names are assigned to any entity for use on digital networks. They are used to provide current information, including where they (or information about them) can be found on the Internet. Information about a digital object may change over time, including where to find it, but its DOI name will not change.

The DOI system consists of three parts: identifiers, a directory, and a DOI system database. Each identifier contains a prefix and a suffix, separated by a forward slash (/). The *prefix*, also known as the *publisher ID*, is assigned by a DOI registration agency to the publisher; the *suffix*, also called the *item ID*, is assigned by the publisher (Wang, 2007). The makeup and assignment of a DOI are in essence similar to those for an ISBN (International Standard Book Number) and ISSN (International Standard Serial Number), the two systems that have been used since the 1970s for uniquely identifying books and serials. In addition, the DOI system uses a central directory to rectify problems regarding digital content ownership and location changes. The information about the object identified is stored in the DOI system database (Nair & Jeevan, 2004).

There are two features that make DOIs distinctive among all the methods for representing digital resources. First, a DOI can be applied to either a digital object in its entirety (e.g., an ejournal) or any portion of it (e.g., a section, a figure, or a table). This characteristic in DOI application literally allows information representation at any level of granularity, which is rarely done in the field but has positive implications for passage retrieval. Second, a DOI is stable and persistent, once registered and assigned, in linking its content and a directory that always contains the current location of that digital object, regardless if its predecessor changes or disappears from the internet.

The DOI system not only provides an alternative approach to information representation but also enables seamless access to digital objects so identified. An exemplary implementation of DOIs is CrossRef (www.crossref.org), a nonprofit organization of publishers and libraries aiming to connect users via DOIs to primary research content such as books, journal articles, and conference proceedings. Publishers affiliated with CrossRef assign DOIs to each item they publish, and users can in turn access those items through the DOI linkages.

The DOI system is, however, more a uniform, permanent linking mechanism than a metadata standard in that each DOI is associated with a series of metadata as well as a set of bibliographical and commercial information relating to its content (e.g., title, author, publication date, and price). When the DOI information is transferred to the publisher, it will look up the DOI in its bibliographic data and find the content via the linking information stored in the central directory. The user's digital content would then appear on the computer screen.

Other metadata standards have also been or are being developed for describing digital information on the internet. Zeng and Qin (2008) completed a comprehensive survey of current metadata standards and grouped them into eight categories (e.g., general purposes, cultural and visual resources, archives and preservations). The need for such metadata standards is growing, as are the concerns and questions.

3.1.4 Some Questions and Concerns About Metadata

As indicated earlier, metadata is created basically for describing and organizing digital resources. But in consideration of the nature of digital information or internet resources, what is having metadata worth? In the printed world, every publication in a library collection is cataloged. The same practice apparently does not seem applicable for digital information on the internet because of the aforementioned reasons. A similar question also surfaces: Who would create the metadata, given the huge quantity and mixed quality of networked resources?

The life expectancy of digital information to a large extent depends on the availability of the technology (e.g., hardware and software) used for information creation and access. As information technology develops rapidly, how can we ensure that digital resources, once described, can be located and retrieved throughout their lifetime?

In the printed world, the content of a publication remains the same until a new edition is released. But in the digital environment, the content of a document can be changed constantly. Then how do we deal with the dynamic contents of many of these resources when we try to provide metadata for them?

As discussed earlier, there are metadata standards for representing digital information on the internet. Meanwhile, we also have standards such as DDC and AACR/MARC that we have been using over the years for describing printed resources. Now, how should metadata be incorporated into other existing frameworks? Dempsey and Heery (1998) have pointed out that the library community is only beginning to address how to bring "book world" metadata and "network" metadata into the same context of use. One such attempt is OCLC's efforts in enhancing DDC with tools such as WordSmith, which extracts new and emerging concepts and terminology from unrestricted text and then links them to the DDC (Vizine-Goetz, 1997).

In addition to what has been summarized here, the interoperability issue remains at the core of the metadata movement (Rowley & Hartley, 2008). Interoperability refers to the ability of multiple systems or components with different platforms, interfaces, and data structures to exchange and share data with minimal loss of content and functionality (Zeng & Qin, 2008, p. 321). Zeng and Chan (2004) specifically addressed issues in establishing interoperability among knowledge organization systems that are often used for creating metadata. It is clearly not easy to achieve interoperability, although great efforts have been made in that direction. Furthermore, individual metadata standards have their own distinctive issues and concerns. Take DOIs as an example (Wang, 2007): What metadata standard should be used when assigning DOIs? Should different DOIs be assigned for each manifestation and for each version?

The questions and concerns enumerated here have by no means exhausted all the challenges we face in representing digital data on the internet with the metadata approach. Furthermore, there is no general plan to specifically deal with these questions and concerns. Selective description, scheduled updating, and planned archiving are some of the current practices used in providing metadata for digital resources. Metadata, no matter how the current and future practices may change, is ultimately intended to facilitate the representation of digital information so that it can be more effectively retrieved later.

3.2 Full Text

When computer space was precious and computing time was costly, only surrogates of full-text (e.g., bibliographical and indexing) information could be stored digitally for retrieval purposes. Today, even a regular desktop computer can be powerful in terms of storage space and computing capacity. In the digital age, full-text storage and retrieval are no longer rare commodities.

3.2.1 Representation of Full-Text Information

Representation of full-text information stored digitally is apparently a result of information technology advancement (Meadow, 1992). However, representation of full text is neither "every word a descriptor" (Fugmann, 1993) nor "no indexing necessary." Either invisible or embedded representation other than the full text itself is needed to make the information retrievable. Representation of full text shares most of the properties of derivative indexing by the adoption of a stop-word list plus stemming and similar techniques. This approach is nothing other than what Luhn called *keyword indexing*, which typically can be done automatically. Popular internet retrieval systems such as Google use the same method of keyword indexing to represent the full text they collect in their databases.

3.2.2 Difficulties in Representing Full Text

While representation of full text appears desirable to users, the outcome is often mixed and overwhelming because of the low precision problem. A pertinent example would be the results turned out by most internet retrieval systems. More often than not, a keyword search on the web will retrieve at least several thousand sites, among which only a few are probably relevant to the input query. Fugmann (1993) wrote:

> Full text storage imposes particularly high demands on storage space and on search time. The latter does not only comprise machine time consumption, but also, more important, the human's time and patience for weeding out the excessive amount of retrieval noise. (p. 99)

Full-text storage, as explained earlier, is no longer an issue in information representation and retrieval, thanks to the advancement of computing technology. However, the quality of representation for full-text information remains far from satisfactory, which reflects unmistakably in results produced by the majority of internet retrieval systems. Future breakthroughs in solving this fundamental problem largely depend on research in natural language processing (NLP). Some of the important tasks NLP researchers must undertake include 1) determination of the syntactic structure of a sentence (e.g., Time flies like an arrow), also known as parsing, and 2) determination of the meaning of a word (e.g., duty) in context or of multiple meanings of a word (Knight, 1999). Further discussion of natural language processing will be provided in Chapter 12, "Artificial Intelligence in Information Representation and Retrieval."

Typically, nontextual information such as diagrams or tables is inaccessible for retrieval in full-text information systems (Fugmann, 1993) if the representation is done automatically. But how about other types of multimedia information, such as sound and moving images that are available in the digital format? How is multimedia information represented in a retrieval system? This topic is examined in the next section.

3.3 Representation of Multimedia Information

More and more multimedia information is produced in the digital age, and the advent of the World Wide Web makes access to such information much easier than before. The booming of multimedia information, however, also presents unprecedented challenges to the field of information representation and retrieval.

3.3.1 Types of Multimedia Information

Multimedia is any combination of sound, image, and textual information, in which images include both still or moving images. The words *sound* and *audio* may be treated as synonyms; however, there is a tendency to replace the term audio with sound. Sometimes, the phrase *spoken document* is used for referring to textual information recorded orally (e.g., speeches and talks). As for image information, still images comprise pictures, photos, posters, and the like. Moving images may be with or without sound. Images without sound are animations or silent movies. Moving images with sound become video or movies. Text could appear in sound information as annotations and in images as captions and subtitles. Figure 3.1 illustrates the different types of multimedia information.

3.3.2 Two Major Representation Approaches

In the past, multimedia was usually represented by descriptions based on, for instance, creator's name, image size, captions or subtitles, and keywords. This approach was thus called description based and has long been employed by librarians and other information professionals to represent multimedia. However, the description-based representation of multimedia must always be done by people, yet the quality of end products fluctuates because, among other reasons, multimedia in some cases can hardly be explicitly and objectively described. For example, how can one describe explicitly an image that looks like a sunset or a piece of music that sounds soothing and peaceful? In addition, how can people have consistent and accurate representations of multimedia information through the use of this subjective approach?

The so-called content-based approach, that is, representing multimedia by their own properties, such as image color and sound pitch, has been developed to overcome the limitations of the description-based approach. Dictated by the key technologies (e.g., speech recognition, pattern recognition, and image understanding) used in the analysis of multimedia for representation purposes, the content-based approach is normally adopted by

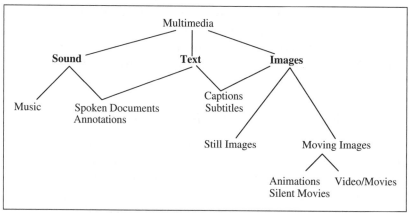

Figure 3.1 Taxonomy of Multimedia Information

researchers in computer science. This approach also symbolizes a paradigm shift in multimedia representation. If the description-based representation of multimedia is accomplished by describing the "ofness" (e.g., creator's name and publication year) and "aboutness" (e.g., keyword and subject) of the object, the content-based representation is attained by analyzing multimedia properties or attributes such as image color and sound pitch.

Multimedia attributes are multifaceted. Common attributes of still images include color, shape, and texture, which can be decomposed further by directionality, randomness, roughness, contrast, and the like. For sound information, properties such as pitch and speed are often considered for representation purposes. These primitive or low-level features can usually be abstracted automatically or semi-automatically, which eliminates the need for costly, yet not always rewarding, human involvement in the representation process. Attributes for video information can be scaled down to those for still images and sound after the segmentation procedure, described in §3.3.3.

Between these two distinctive approaches for multimedia representation, which one is used more often in research and practice? Chu (2001) conducted a citation analysis of the literature published in the field of image indexing and retrieval, and found that the content-based approach has been dominating the area, especially in recent years. The complexity associated with the adoption of the description-based approach and the advancement of the key technologies employed in the content-based approach explain in part the emergence and growth of the content-based method of multimedia representation. Chu's findings do not imply, however, that the content-based approach should be the only method chosen for representing multimedia. To the contrary, the description-based approach, if used properly and consistently, is able to achieve quality representation that would be hard to attain with the content-based approach. An integration of the two different approaches by combining the jewels of both seems to be an ideal road to take in representing multimedia.

3.3.3 Challenges in Representing Multimedia

Aside from the aforementioned problems associated with both representation approaches, moving image segmentation and speech parsing appear to be major stumbling blocks in representing multimedia. Moving image segmentation is a step necessary for decomposing moving images into, for instance, element units (e.g., camera operations and salient stills) and keyframes (i.e., frames that are representative of each shot) that would then serve as the basis for content analysis and representation (Zhang, et al., 1995). Other methods may use different algorithms and techniques for moving image segmentation. But the essence of the process remains the same: dividing moving images into smaller and meaningful entities so they can be represented adequately and accurately.

Speech segmentation refers to the process of segmenting full-length speeches into paragraphs, sentences, phrases, and words so that their subject contents can be examined and represented. The criteria for either moving image or speech segmentation are hard to formulate because of the very nature of moving images and sound information. That is, moving images are continuous in time and space. Yet, boundaries between consecutive camera shots cannot always be relied on for segmentation. Similarly, speech information does not contain punctuation, spaces between words, or other types of markers, as written information may, to guide segmentation. In addition, many constraints that pertain to speech information make the segmentation task more difficult. Some examples of speech constraints (Spärck Jones, et al., 1996) are nonspeech events (e.g., loud breath and tongue clicks), disfluencies (e.g., partially spoken words, pauses, and hesitations), and functional events or components (e.g., *and* or *in addition*). Because of these difficulties, more research is needed before we can have quality automatic methods for segmenting speech and moving images. Human involvement still seems necessary in representing multimedia, even using the content-based approach.

Generally speaking, less research has been done in multimedia representation than in text information. Of all the different kinds of multimedia, sound information appears the least studied in terms of representation. Meanwhile, the digital age has been witnessing an increasing amount of multimedia information. How to represent multimedia information therefore poses a serious challenge if we want to make multimedia information accessible when needed.

3.4 Further Elaboration on Information Representation

Information representation is essential in information retrieval for two reasons: First, information must be represented before it can be retrieved; second, representation quality directly affects retrieval performance. We generally base our representation on the ofness and aboutness of information, with the exception of the content-based approach for representing multimedia. Ofness includes attributes such as author, language, and publication year, whereas aboutness deals with the subject content of the information. In comparison, information representation based on ofness is straightforward and less challenging, whereas representations of aboutness are much harder to accomplish.

Retrieval performance suffers when information representation is not properly done. The importance of having quality information representation cannot be overemphasized. We should therefore aim for quality information representation so that we can find what we are looking for in the world of digital information.

References

Berners-Lee, Tim, Hendler, James, and Lassila, Ora. (2001). The semantic web. *Scientific American*, 284(5), 35–43.

Chu, Heting. (2001). Research in image indexing and retrieval as reflected in the literature. *Journal of the American Society for Information Science and Technology*, 52(12), 1011–1018.

Dempsey, Lorcan, and Heery, Rachel. (1998). Metadata: A current view of practice and issues. *Journal of Documentation*, 54(2), 145–172.

Fugmann, Robert. (1993). *Subject analysis and indexing: Theoretical foundation and practical advice.* Frankfurt/Main, Germany: Indeks Verlag.

International DOI Foundation. (2009). Welcome to the DOI system. Retrieved July 18, 2009, from www.doi.org

Knight, Kevin. (1999). Mining online text. *Communications of the ACM*, 42(11), 58–61.

Lassila, Ora. (1997). Introduction to RDF metadata: W3C note 1997–11–13. Retrieved January 19, 2009, from www.w3.org/TR/NOTE-rdf-simple-intro-971113.html

Meadow, Charles T. (1992). *Text information retrieval systems.* San Diego, CA: Academic Press.

Nair, Saji S., and Jeevan, V. K. J. (2004). A brief overview of metadata formats. *DESIDOC Bulletin of Information Technology,* 24(4), 3–11.

Rowley, Jennifer E., and Hartley, Richard J. (2008). *Organizing knowledge: An introduction to managing access to information.* Burlington, VT: Ashgate.

Shadbolt, Nigel, Hall, Wendy, and Berners-Lee, Tim. (2006). The semantic web revisited. *IEEE Intelligent Systems,* 21(3), 96–101.

Shafer, Keith. (November/December 1998). Mantis project provides a toolkit for cataloging. *OCLC Newsletter,* 21–23.

Spärck Jones, Karen, et al. (1996). Experiments in spoken document retrieval. *Information Processing & Management,* 32(2), 399–419.

Vizine-Goetz, Diane. (1997). From book classification to knowledge organization: Improving internet resource description and discovery. *Bulletin of the American Society for Information Science,* 24(1), 24–26.

Wang, Jue. (2007). Digital Object Identifiers and their use in libraries. *Serials Review,* 33(3), 161–164.

Weibel, Stuart. (1997). The Dublin Core: A simple content description model for electronic resources. *Bulletin of the American Society for Information Science,* 24(1), 9–11.

Wool, Gregory. (1998). A meditation on metadata. *Serials Librarian,* 33(1/2), 167–178.

Zeng, Marcia L., and Chan, Lois Mai. (2004). Trends and issues in establishing interoperability among knowledge organization systems. *Journal of the American Society for Information Science and Technology,* 55(5), 377–395.

Zeng, Marcia Lei, and Qin, Jian. (2008). *Metadata.* New York: Neal-Schuman Publishers.

Zhang, H. J., et al. (1995). Video parsing, retrieval and browsing: An integrated and content-based solution. *Proceedings of ACM Multimedia* (pp. 15–24). New York: ACM Press.

CHAPTER 4

Language in Information Representation and Retrieval

As briefly discussed in §1.3.3, language is a fundamental component in both information representation and information retrieval (e.g., in query formulation). Language in information representation and retrieval (IRR) assumes the form of either natural language or controlled vocabulary. Whenever there is a choice, a question arises as to which type of language one should use for representing and retrieving information.

4.1 Natural Language

Natural language is the language people speak and write. In natural language, no effort is made in IRR to limit or define vocabulary, syntax, semantics, and interrelationships among terms. What people use for representing information or forming a query without consulting a controlled vocabulary is called natural language.

Natural language is commonly used in three ways for IRR. One is to use terms taken from titles (e.g., KeyWord In Context [KWIC]), topic sentences, and other important components of a document for representation of information. Another is to use terms derived from any part of the document for information representation (e.g., derivative indexing). The third way is to use words or phrases extracted directly from people's questions for query representation, a topic discussed in Chapter 5.

Natural language basically consists of two kinds of words: significant words and function words. Significant words are those terms that carry substantial meanings or subject concepts, whereas function words include articles, prepositions, and conjunctions such as *an, a, the, and, for, of, to, this, that, her,* and *their.* When natural language is applied in automatic IRR, a stop-word list (or stop list for short) is usually compiled and stored in the system to prevent those words from becoming indexing or query terms. The stop list contains all possible function words plus those significant terms that are too general or common to be suitable representations. Such terms are sometimes called trade words. For example, the word *engineering* alone would be meaningless as either an indexing term or a query term in an engineering database. Terms of an ephemeral nature, known as buzzwords, are included in the stop list as well because they would not last long as candidates for indexing or query terms. Most buzzwords appear as technology related, such as *gopher* and *denial of service*. None of the terms on the stop list would be used for either representation or retrieval purposes. However, each IRR system should have its own stop list, created specifically for the system through consideration of its target audience and other factors.

As a counterpart of the stop list, a go list can also be created for natural language IRR (Rowley, 1992). All significant words, minus trade words and buzzwords, are eligible for membership on a go list. Like the stop list, the go list is machine-readable and can be checked against at the time of representation and retrieval. In general, the go list in natural language seems to be implemented less often than the stop list, for two reasons. First, the stop list is shorter and easier to manage, and this mechanism would generally check the usage of natural language in IRR. Second, go lists are mostly used for controlled vocabulary IRR in the form of thesauri, subject heading lists, and classification schemes.

In recent years, word lists as a semi-controlled vocabulary have increasingly been used in automatic IRR. Because word lists include, at most, synonyms and antonyms for terms contained in the documents and have little other vocabulary control, they appear to be another form of the go list. Some internet retrieval systems create and maintain a word list or go list for their own use.

4.2 Controlled Vocabulary

Controlled vocabulary is an artificial language, while its vocabulary, syntax, semantics, and pragmatics are limited and defined (Wellisch, 1995). The same word in different controlled vocabularies might have a different meaning given the orientation of the vocabulary. Controlled vocabulary must be constructed and maintained with specific subject area(s) in mind. Terms to be included in controlled vocabulary are selected by following the principle of either literary warrant or user warrant. Literary warrant means that terms to be included in the controlled vocabulary must be chosen from existing literature. Similarly, user warrant implies that terms to be selected for the inclusion in a controlled vocabulary must have been used in the past. Thesauri, subject heading lists, and classification schemes are the three major types of controlled vocabularies.

4.2.1 Thesauri

A thesaurus is a controlled vocabulary of terms in natural languages that are designed for post-coordination (National Information Standards Organization, 1993). Rowley (1992) further defined a thesaurus as follows:

a compilation of words and phrases showing synonyms, hierarchical and other relationships and dependencies, the function of
which is to provide a standardized vocabulary for information
storage and retrieval systems. (p. 252)

Post-coordination is manipulative and has a shorter history than pre-
coordinated languages such as classification schemes. Post-coordinated languages such as thesauri allow users to coordinate terms at the time of
representation and retrieval. The main drawback of post-coordination is
false coordination. One example is that the two words *computer* and *desk* can
be coordinated as either *computer desk* or *desk computer*, depending on what
the original intention is. If *desk computer* is intended, coordinated results
such as *computer desk* would be considered false coordination.

Standard notations are used in thesauri to specify the hierarchical, associative, homographic, and other relationships among the terms included.
USE and UF (*used for*) identify which terms in the thesaurus are preferred
descriptors, and SN (*scope note*) defines the meaning of a descriptor. NT
(*narrower term*) and BT (*broader term*) display the hierarchical relationships
among descriptors. The associative relationships among descriptors are
expressed by the notation of RT (*related terms*). Thesauri are usually displayed alphabetically and hierarchically. Rotated or permuted display, systematic or classification display, and graphic display are sometimes seen in
certain thesauri as well (Aitchison, Gilchrist, & Bawden, 1997).

Thesauri are the most commonly used controlled vocabulary in nonmonograph IRR because of their specificity, flexibility, and ability to handle
complex concepts. The thesaurus of the Educational Resources Information
Center (ERIC) descriptors is an example.

4.2.2 Subject Heading Lists

A subject heading list is a controlled vocabulary of terms in natural language
that are designed for both pre-coordination and post-coordination. Pre-
coordination, predominant before the 1940s, combines terms before they are
used for representation and retrieval. If one intends to, for example, represent or retrieve documents about *internet retrieval systems*, the three-word
phrase would appear exactly in a pre-coordinated language. Pre-coordinated
controlled vocabularies are thus nonmanipulative. Because subject heading
lists allow both pre- and post-coordination, they seem more flexible than
classification schemes but less so than thesauri.

Terms in subject heading lists are called subject headings and are
arranged alphabetically. Notations for subject headings include *See*, for
pointing from nonpreferred terms to preferred ones while *X*, meaning *See*

from, presents the reciprocal expression of the *See* statement, as in *handicapped* See *physically challenged*, and *physically challenged* X *handicapped*. Another set of notations for subject heading lists is *See also* and *XX*, which stands for *See also from*. *See also* indicates both the hierarchical and the associative relationships among the chosen subject headings. That practice, however, undermines the specificity of subject heading lists. Similar to the *X* notation, *XX* shows the reciprocal expression of the *See also* statement.

Generally, subject heading lists are used for both the representation and the retrieval of information, although they appear to be applied less frequently than thesauri for representing and retrieving nonmonograph information. Sears List of Subject Headings is one example of subject heading lists. Another well-known example is the Library of Congress Subject Headings, whose notations for the 11th edition, however, look more like those for thesauri.

4.2.3 Classification Schemes

A classification scheme is a controlled vocabulary of terms in alphanumeric form that are designed mainly for pre-coordination. Units in classification schemes are called classes, which are further labeled numerically, alphabetically, or alphanumerically. As the first type of controlled vocabulary developed, classification schemes witnessed and weathered changes during the past centuries. On the other hand, they have been updated and revised again and again with the passage of time.

Unlike thesauri and subject heading lists, classification schemes are built on an artificial framework of knowledge. For instance, Dewey Decimal Classification (DDC) chooses to present the world of knowledge on the basis of 10 classes. Exactly 10 classes are formed at each level within the scheme, which indicates the system's rigidity. The hierarchical relationship among classes is displayed using indentations or different lengths of classification notations. That is, the longer a classification notation, the deeper the class is located in the hierarchical structure. Associative relationships among the terms are indicated via the *See* and *See also* mechanism, which is used only occasionally.

Traditionally, classification schemes are most often selected for representing and retrieving monograph information. DDC and Library of Congress Classification (LCC) are two examples of classification schemes.

4.2.4 A Comparison of Thesauri, Subject Heading Lists, and Classification Schemes

Table 4.1 summarizes the features of each of the three types of controlled vocabularies (CV). In addition to what has been discussed, analysis method

Table 4.1 Comparisons of Controlled Vocabularies

CV / Feature	Thesauri	Subject Heading Lists	Classification Schemes
Term Component	Descriptors	Subject Headings	Classification Labels
Reference Notation	U, UF, SN BT, NT, RT	See, See also X, XX	See, See also
Analysis Method	Synthesis $\longleftrightarrow$ Enumeration		
Coordination Method	Postcoordination $\longleftrightarrow$ Precoordination		
Specificity	More $\longleftrightarrow$ Less		
Flexibility	More $\longleftrightarrow$ Less		
Target Document Type	Nonbooks	Books, nonbooks	Books

is another feature associated with controlled vocabularies. Enumeration, as an analysis method, means simply providing a list of terms without the ability to combine them to express something more complex. In contrast, synthesis allows some combination of terms to form more complex ones, at either the representation or the searching stage (Lancaster, 1986). Analysis method is closely related to the coordination method. That is, the pre-coordinate vocabulary is enumerative whereas the post-coordinate language is synthetic. Analysis and coordination methods also determine the specificity and flexibility of the controlled vocabulary. A synthetic and post-coordinate vocabulary appears more specific and accommodating than an enumerative and pre-coordinate language.

According to Table 4.1, thesauri seem to have more specificity and flexibility than classification schemes, and subject heading lists fall in between them on this spectrum, which explains why thesauri have been the most widely used controlled vocabulary in IRR.

4.3 Natural Language Versus Controlled Vocabulary

The preceding two sections have discussed the features and characteristics of both natural language and controlled vocabulary. It is now time to examine how they differ from each other and what they have in common as IRR languages.

4.3.1 Different Eras of Information Representation and Retrieval Languages

In the history of IRR, controlled vocabulary is a latecomer compared with natural language. Four different eras can be identified in the development of IRR language so far.

The first era refers to the time before any controlled vocabulary was introduced. Natural language was the only language applied while IRR was taking shape as a field. People began to realize the limitations (e.g., homographs and synonyms) of natural language when it was applied for representing and retrieving information.

The second era is signified by the introduction of controlled vocabulary to IRR. In the beginning, pre-coordination systems such as classification schemes were heavily used. Other types of controlled vocabularies, that is, subject heading lists and thesauri, were implemented later. The two kinds of IRR languages coexisted in this era, with a slant toward controlled vocabulary. Also, the debate on natural language versus controlled vocabulary started then and has continued ever since.

The third era is symbolized by the resurgence of natural language due to the keyword retrieval technique and the development of full-text systems. Controlled vocabulary is still applied for IRR but most often to bibliographic IRR systems. Will controlled vocabulary remain a viable IRR language? More debates have been provoked in this era regarding natural language versus controlled vocabulary.

The fourth era started when natural language interface was implemented in IRR and a vocabulary control mechanism was employed behind the scenes. Because the vocabulary control mechanism is invisible to the end user, Milstead (1995) called it invisible controlled vocabulary in a natural language retrieval environment. One example is to hide the controlled vocabulary behind the shell of natural language. Advances in natural language processing have also contributed significantly to this development. Some information retrieval systems, such as West's WIN (Westlaw is Natural), have begun providing retrieval services in natural language.

Although the boundaries between the different eras do not appear very obvious and clear cut, IRR language has apparently passed through the first two eras and now spans the third and fourth eras.

4.3.2 Why Natural Language or Why Controlled Vocabulary?

There must be reasons behind the coexistence of natural language and controlled vocabulary in information representation and retrieval. The reasons are nothing else but the complementary pros and cons of the two kinds of IRR languages.

4.3.2.1 The Synonym Issue

The issue of synonyms is one of the most cited arguments against using natural language in IRR. In natural language, synonyms are different terms that refer to the same entity. For example, *microcomputers, personal computers, PCs, desktops, notebooks, laptops,* and the like are all synonyms. But which term in this partial list of synonyms should be chosen and used for representation and retrieval purposes? This is an issue in the debate about IRR languages. When controlled vocabulary is the selected IRR language, synonyms are not a source of concern because one and only one term is chosen from the controlled vocabulary as the preferred term. The rest of the synonyms are treated as nonpreferred terms and cross-referenced to the preferred term.

4.3.2.2 The Homograph Issue

Homographs, the result of the phenomenon known as polysemy, seem to be another argument often presented in the debate on natural language versus controlled vocabulary. Homographs are terms that are spelled the same but carry different meanings in different contexts. Terms such as *record, subject, drug, spring, bank,* and *duty* are just a few examples of homographs. In natural language representation and retrieval, homographs, because of the lack of context, can produce problems such as ambiguity. Lancaster and Warner (1993) have pointed out that the retrieval problem of ambiguity caused by homographs is often more theoretical than actual because words that may be ambiguous on their own are no longer ambiguous when used in association with other words. It is true that homographs would not become ambiguous in meaning if used in conjunction with other words, but the conjunct usage may or may not happen in natural language representation and retrieval. By comparison, the context for interpreting homographs is always provided via assorted means in controlled vocabulary. One common method is to use parentheses to specify the context for homographs, as in *duty* (responsibility) and *duty* (tax).

4.3.2.3 The Syntax Issue

Language has syntax. But how can syntax be expressed when natural language is selected for representing and retrieving information? Suppose a document is represented by the three terms *USA, automobiles,* and *Japan* in natural language; this document can be about, for example, Japan exporting automobiles to the U.S., or the opposite—the U.S. exporting automobiles to Japan. It is unclear which country is the exporter when only these three terms are given, without any syntax information. This problem can be solved easily in controlled vocabulary with devices such as roles, which are symbols or numbers that indicate the syntax relationship between or among terms. In this example, we could define the number 1 as the role of exporter and then put it next to the term *Japan,* that is, *Japan* (1). Similarly, we can designate the number 2 as the role of importer and then assign it to the term *USA: USA* (2). The mechanism provided in controlled vocabulary allows people to tackle the syntax issue, whereas natural language cannot.

4.3.2.4 The Accuracy Issue

It is always desirable to have an IRR language that could accurately represent information and search queries. That objective appears attainable if natural language is chosen as the IRR language. The rationale for the statement seems twofold. First, no additional manipulation (e.g., explanation) is needed if natural language is used for IRR. Second, interpretation is unnecessary in natural language representation and retrieval because what the author or user uses will be the language for IRR. In comparison, controlled vocabulary is artificial and does not reflect the richness of the natural language used for composing documents and expressing search queries. Controlled vocabulary also lacks specificity as a result of the language manipulation process. Interpretation of controlled vocabulary seems indispensable, since the connotation and denotation of every term are defined with a particular target audience in mind. Such interpretation could inevitably introduce inaccuracy into IRR that relies on controlled vocabulary.

4.3.2.5 The Updating Issue

Natural language needs no updating while controlled vocabulary does. New terms can be used for IRR purposes as soon as they appear in natural language, but no change in controlled vocabulary can take effect until it goes through the rigid and lengthy updating process. Consequently, terms in controlled vocabulary are not always up-to-date. Requests that contain new terminology could hardly be satisfied if controlled vocabulary is chosen as the IRR language.

4.3.2.6 The Cost Issue

It takes time to create, maintain, and learn how to use a controlled vocabulary in IRR. The time needed for these activities will eventually get translated as a cost of IRR. In comparison, natural language is just the language people commonly use. Neither training nor maintenance is required for doing IRR in natural language.

4.3.2.7 The Compatibility Issue

There are times when an IRR system needs to change its language during the course of its development or when a user would like to perform multiple database searching. The compatibility issue thus emerges for controlled vocabulary IRR because each controlled vocabulary has its own unique features and characteristics. It seems impossible, for example, to use DDC to perform IRR tasks in an online public access catalog (OPAC) that has chosen LCC as its controlled vocabulary. If the systems are built on natural language, then switching or migrating from one system to another would typically be seamless because natural language should always be compatible with itself. This issue has been labeled the interoperability issue, borrowing the jargon used in computerized systems (Zeng & Chan, 2004). Similarly, knowledge organization systems (KOS) has become a new term for controlled vocabularies.

In summary, the strengths of controlled vocabulary in synonyms, homographs, and syntax are weak points for natural language. Likewise, the weaknesses of controlled vocabulary in accuracy, updating, cost, and compatibility are strong points for natural language. Just as Rowley (1994) reiterated in one of her writings:

> There is a general recognition that controlled vocabulary and natural language should be used in conjunction with one another, and there is some agreement as to the relative merits of each of these systems. (p. 116)

In other words, both natural language and controlled vocabulary have found their own places in IRR. But will this continue to be the case?

4.4 Language for Information Representation and Retrieval in the Digital Age

In the print world, controlled vocabulary and natural language are used in parallel for IRR. In the online world, close human involvement in IRR is still required, and controlled vocabulary has taken a dominant position as an IRR language. In the digital age, natural language has become the norm for IRR, while controlled vocabulary is used only occasionally or on a much smaller scale because of the unique features of digital information.

A large percentage of digital information is available on the internet, where a quality control mechanism is absent, the life expectancy of the information is short, and the magnitude of information increases exponentially. Any application of the costly controlled vocabulary in the digital IRR environment therefore requires justification and rationalization. The popular internet retrieval systems that undertake the bulk of IRR tasks on the internet make no use of controlled vocabulary. The use of word lists by a few internet retrieval systems appears to be the closest thing to vocabulary control in digital IRR.

However, natural language should not be the only IRR language in the digital environment because the lack of vocabulary control could be one of the major reasons for the poor results from internet retrieval systems. In general, the task of controlling vocabulary could shift from the shoulders of information professionals to that of end users when natural language is chosen as the IRR language. When controlled vocabulary is formally adopted, however, it is the information professional's responsibility to assume the task of vocabulary control. Otherwise, the end user must assume the role of vocabulary control informally, for instance, by thinking about synonymous terms needed in a search query. The increased interaction between the end user and the IRR system in the digital environment should not become an excuse for placing the responsibility for vocabulary control on the end user's shoulders, because even information professionals can only do a mediocre job in that respect.

So what will be the future of controlled vocabulary as an IRR language in the digital age? The answer does not seem certain at all. In retrospect, there appear to be four different ways in which controlled vocabulary can be used in IRR (Lancaster & Warner, 1993):

1. Controlled vocabulary for both representation and retrieval.

2. Natural language for both representation and retrieval but with the help of such controlled vocabulary devices as roles and pre-coordination.

3. Controlled vocabulary for representation only. The control for retrieval is done by means such as embedded or invisible controlled vocabulary in the system.

4. Controlled vocabulary for retrieval only. This approach is implemented by the use of a search-only thesaurus, which is also known as post-controlled vocabulary.

In consideration of the IRR features in the digital environment, the second approach appears more feasible than others. Both the third and fourth approaches store controlled vocabulary online for lookup or searching, which also seems to be a viable option for employing controlled vocabulary. On the other hand, the field of IRR in recent years has witnessed the emergence of such language frameworks as taxonomies, folksonomies, and ontologies. Although each of them possesses unique characteristics, they all have been developed for representation and retrieval purposes in the digital age.

4.4.1 Taxonomies

Briefly discussed in §2.2, the term taxonomy originates from the Greek *taxis* (order or arrangement) and *nomos* (law or science). Initially, taxonomy referred to the classification of living organisms (e.g., animals and plants). The term is, however, gaining a wider and more general meaning than before, now defined as the classification of all things and extending its connotation far beyond the previous coverage of living organisms. According to Gilchrist (2003), the earliest reference to the new use of the term appeared in 1997 in an article about Yahoo!, an internet retrieval system stemming from and well known for its taxonomy-based directory service.

Taxonomies actually find their roots in both classification schemes and thesauri. Like classification schemes, they express hierarchical relationships among categories—the basic units of taxonomy—with different levels of display; alphanumeric forms—the typical classification device—are not used in taxonomies. The associative relationships among categories are presented alphabetically at each level, mirroring one common thesaurus display in structure. Unlike classification schemes and thesauri, however, taxonomies provide no cross-referencing mechanism, which undermines the function a controlled vocabulary is supposed to provide.

Taxonomies, determined by their features, are in general utilized to categorize information and support browsing—one of the two retrieval approaches. They seem appealing particularly to enterprise information portals for their IRR needs (Gilchrist, 2003), besides their implementation on the internet. One reason behind this kind of interest is that taxonomies are able to accommodate the distinctive terminologies an enterprise may have. In addition, it is relatively easier and less costly to build and maintain a taxonomy than to have a traditional controlled vocabulary such as a thesaurus when mergers and acquisitions occur frequently in the realm of enterprises. Other potential prospects for taxonomies in IRR have been examined by Wang, Chaudhry, and Khoo (2006). The best known example of a taxonomy, nonetheless, is what is used for compiling the Yahoo! Directory (dir.yahoo.com).

4.4.2 Folksonomies

As described in §2.1.4, a folksonomy can be considered a taxonomy created by folks, or users (Vander Wal, 2007). On the other hand, a folksonomy appears closely related to social tagging and is essentially a by-product of social tagging because the former is built with tags that users choose during the tagging process.

Folksonomies commonly take the form of a tag cloud, which is a visual aggregation of tags generated at a tagging site based on tag frequencies. Tag clouds and folksomonies, strictly speaking, are synonyms. In contrast to taxonomies, folksonomies do not show any hierarchical relationships among their components, namely, tags. What is preserved in folksonomies is the associative relationship between tags, displayed in alphabetical order without any of the cross-referencing notation that is often applied in a traditional controlled vocabulary (e.g., a thesaurus). Folksonomies, therefore, cannot be treated in the same manner as other controlled vocabularies already discussed in terms of their composition, structure, and functionality.

In addition, all controlled vocabularies, from classification schemes to taxonomies, are conventionally developed by information professionals. By comparison, a folksonomy is a new type of IRR language, created exclusively by and for end users in the Web 2.0 movement, which has no boundaries in terms of subject, culture, or geography (Munk & Mørk, 2007). While tagging, users can choose tags from a folksonomy but also remain free to select any terms from their own vocabulary as tags. Because all tags in folksonomies are hyperlinked, this structure enables users to browse what is available at a tagging site via hyperlinked tags aside from searching.

The advantages and limitations of a folksonomy as an IRR language have been discussed extensively by many researchers (e.g., Noruzi, 2006; Speller, 2007; Spiteri, 2007; Trant, 2006) from the viewpoint of taxonomies alone or in reference to traditional controlled vocabularies. In summary, folksonomies inherit all the pros and cons of natural language with one added feature of controlled vocabulary, namely the alphabetical listing and frequency-based visualization of tags. In that sense, a folksonomy functions more as natural language than as a controlled vocabulary in the digital IRR environment. An example of a folksonomy can be found at Delicious.com when a tag cloud is visualized.

4.4.3 Ontologies

The term ontology, from the field of philosophy, is concerned with the study of being or existence. Researchers in artificial intelligence opted the term in the 1980s for knowledge acquisition and representation when one is conceptualizing a domain in the development of expert systems (Vickery, 1997).

Ontology in knowledge engineering, or, more broadly, in computer and information science, is usually defined as a formal, explicit specification of a shared conceptualization (Gruber, 1993).

Berners-Lee, Hendler, and Lassila (2001), on the other hand, adopted the term when envisioning the semantic web—a topic explored in §12.3. It is in this milieu that ontology truly departs from its origin in philosophy and is embraced as an IRR language. In their seminal paper, Berners-Lee, Hendler, and Lassila (2001), characterized ontologies as:

> Collections of statements written in a language such as RDF that define the relations between concepts and specify logical rules for reasoning about them. Computers will "understand" the meaning of semantic data on a Web page by following links to specified ontologies. (p. 38)

Ontologies can take a variety of forms. Uschold (1996) enumerated the following four, ranging from highly informal to rigorously formal, from the perspective of knowledge engineering. Highly informal ontologies are expressed loosely in natural language. Next on the spectrum are structured informal ontologies, which employ restricted and structured natural language to increase clarity and reduce ambiguity. The third form is called the semiformal ontology, which is expressed in an artificial, formally defined language. The last form on this continuum is rigorously formal ontologies, which meticulously define terms with formal semantics and theorems. Although a recognized description of ontology form in the light of semantic web is absent, the candidate presumably should be the rigorously formal type Uschold (1996) depicted.

The relations between concepts in an ontology include synonymy, antonymy, hyponymy (the "is-a" relation), and meronymy (the "part-of" relation). Those relations are frequently expressed in RDF graphs for the creation of the semantic web (Gilchrist, 2003). In addition, ontologies must specify logical rules for reasoning about the concepts and relations involved within as they, unlike traditional controlled vocabularies (e.g., thesauri), are not static. Rather, they must have the mechanism to reflect changes and perform updates automatically. Ontologies would, in conjunction with other semantic web constituents, make computers comprehend the semantics involved in web resources.

Furthermore, the functionality of ontologies is obviously not the same as that of traditional controlled vocabularies (e.g., thesauri and classification schemes). The former is intended more for conveying semantics from web resources to computers than for regulating term usage in IRR. Additional discussion of ontologies is offered in §12.3, a section devoted to the semantic web. WordNet (wordnet.princeton.edu) is often regarded as an example of an ontology.

Language for IRR in the digital age is certainly evolving, and research is actively being carried out to address the language issue in the field. Vocabulary switching, a mechanism for automatically changing from one IRR language to another across different subject domains, is being researched and explored as a promising scheme for resolving the debate over natural language versus controlled vocabulary. Once implemented, people will choose to use an IRR language at will, without being confined to a pre-designated selection and will not be limited to the vocabulary in a specific subject domain. Rather, users can break the bondage of their near specialties and effectively use the whole of scientific information in the research (Schatz, 1997). Vocabulary switching is different from the "invisible controlled vocabulary" in two aspects. First, vocabulary switching relies heavily on research in natural language processing. Second, vocabulary switching deals with IRR languages from multiple (many more than two) domains while invisible controlled vocabulary basically handles translation between natural language and one controlled vocabulary stored online. For example, Chen, Schatz, and their colleagues generated concept spaces for 10 million journal abstracts across 1,000 subject areas covering all engineering and science (Schatz, 1997). Furthermore, concept spaces have been found effective for interactive term suggestion and vocabulary switching (Chen, et al., 1997).

In short, automatic representation and retrieval with scalable semantics appear to be the future as far as the language issue in the digital age is concerned. The scenario would likely become a reality if the semantic web envisioned by Berners-Lee and his associates is developed.

References

Aitchison, Jean, Gilchrist, Alan, and Bawden, David. (1997). *Thesaurus construction and use: A practical manual.* 3rd ed. London: Aslib.

Berners-Lee, Tim, Hendler, James, and Lassila, Ora. (2001). The Semantic web. *Scientific American*, 284(5), 35–43.

Chen, Hsinchun, et al. (1997). A concept space approach to addressing the vocabulary problem in scientific information retrieval: An experiment on the Worm Community System. *Journal of the American Society for Information Science*, 48(1), 17–31.

Gilchrist, Alan. (2003). Thesauri, taxonomies and ontologies: An etymological note. *Journal of Documentation*, 59(1), 7–18.

Gruber, Tom R. (1993). A translation approach to portable ontology specifications. *Knowledge Engineering*, 5(2), 199–220. Retrieved November 20, 2008, from www-ksl.stanford.edu/kst/what-is-an-ontology.html

Lancaster, F. W. (1986). *Vocabulary control for information retrieval.* 2nd ed. Arlington, VA: Information Resources Press.

Lancaster, F. W., and Warner, Amy J. (1993). *Information retrieval today.* Arlington, VA: Information Resources Press.

Milstead, Jessica L. (1995). Invisible thesauri: The year 2000. *Online & CD ROM Review*, 19(2), 93–94.

Munk, Timme Bisgaard, and Mørk, Kristian. (2007). Folksonomy: The power law and the significance of the least effort. *Knowledge Organization*, 34(1), 16–33.

National Information Standards Organization. (1993). *Guidelines for the construction, format, and management of monolingual thesauri* (ANSI/NISO Z39.19–1993). Bethesda, MD: NISO Press.

Noruzi, Alireza. (2006). Folksonomies: (Un)Controlled vocabulary? *Knowledge Organization*, 33(4), 199–203.

Rowley, Jennifer E. (1992). *Organizing knowledge: An introduction to information retrieval.* Brookfield, VT: Gower.

Rowley, Jennifer E. (1994). The controlled versus natural indexing languages debate revisited: A perspective on information retrieval practice and research. *Journal of Information Science*, 20(2), 108–119.

Schatz, Bruce R. (January 17, 1997). Information retrieval in digital libraries: Bringing research to the net. *Science*, 275, 327–334.

Speller, Edith. (2007). Collaborative tagging, folksonomies, distributed classification or ethnoclassification: A literature review. *Library Student Journal*, 2(1). Retrieved November 15, 2008, from www.librarystudentjournal.org/index.php/lsj/article/view/45/59

Spiteri, Louise F. (2007). The structure and form of folksonomy tags: The road to the public library catalog. *Information Technology & Libraries*, 26(3), 13–25.

Trant, J. (2006). Exploring the potential for social tagging and folksonomy in art museums: Proof of concept. *New Review of Hypermedia and Multimedia*, 12(1), 83–105.

Uschold, Mike. (1996). Building ontologies: Towards a unified methodology. *Proceedings of the 16th Annual Conference of the British Computer Society*

Specialist Group on Expert Systems. Cambridge, England, December 16–18, 1996. Retrieved November 24, 2008, from www.aiai.ed.ac.uk/project/ftp/documents/1996/96-es96-unified-method.pdf

Vander Wal, Thomas. (2007). Folksonomy. Retrieved November 20, 2008, from vanderwal.net/folksonomy.html

Vickery, B. C. (1997). Ontologies. *Journal of Information Science*, 23(4), 277–286.

Wang, Zhonghong, Chaudhry, Abdus Stattar, and Khoo, Christopher. (2006). Potential and prospects of taxonomies for content organization. *Knowledge Organization*, 33(3), 160–169.

Wellisch, Hans H. (1995). *Indexing from A to Z.* 2nd ed. New York: H.W. Wilson.

Zeng, Marcia L., and Chan, Lois Mai. (2004). Trends and issues in establishing interoperability among knowledge organization systems. *Journal of the American Society for Information Science and Technology*, 55(5), 377–395.

CHAPTER 5

Retrieval Techniques and Query Representation

Now that the issue of language in IRR has been discussed in Chapter 4, it is time to move onto the next topic: retrieval techniques that should be considered in performing searches. Query representation, or query formulation, will be explained thereafter.

5.1 Retrieval Techniques

Retrieval techniques are designed to help users locate the information they need effectively and efficiently. A variety of techniques are available to users as information technology develops and as research on retrieval techniques advances. One group of retrieval techniques is called basic approaches, while the others are called advanced methods.

5.1.1 Basic Retrieval Techniques

Retrieval techniques such as Boolean searching, case sensitivity, truncation, proximity searching, and field search are basic approaches because they are generally supported by most information retrieval (IR) systems. In the following sections, the functionality and features of basic approaches will be examined one by one.

5.1.1.1 Boolean Searching

As described briefly in §1.1.2.1, Boolean searching was named after the Englishman George Boole, who conducted mathematical analyses of logic. Boole used three operators, namely, AND, OR, and NOT, to summarize the logical operations of the human mind: the addition (AND) of different concepts to form more complex ones, the separation (NOT) of complex concepts into individual simpler ones (Smith, 1993), and the inclusion (OR) of more concepts to expand their connotation. All these logical operations are also known as Boolean logic. When Boolean logic is applied to IR, the three operators, called Boolean operators, assume the following functionality:

- The AND operator for narrowing down a search

- The OR operator for broadening a search

- The NOT operator for excluding unwanted results

The AND operator combines two or more terms in a search statement and requires that all the terms be present in the documents found. For example, a search statement *filtering* AND *controversy* should get only results about filtering as a controversy. Any results about filtering in general or other controversies, such as gun control, would not meet the search requirement. The AND operator is especially helpful in searching for information covering complex concepts.

The OR operator expands a search by including more terms in the search statement. Terms being "OR'ed" together are in most cases synonyms or related terms. Documents that have any one of the terms are regarded as hits or anticipated results. For example, a search statement *filtering* OR *controversy* would turn out results about all kinds of filtering and all kinds of controversies in addition to documents on filtering as a controversy. Obviously, the OR operator aims to expand search scope and increase retrieval outcome.

The NOT operator is more restrictive if compared with OR. NOT limits the search scope by excluding term(s) listed after the NOT operator. For instance, a search query *filtering* NOT *controversy* would retrieve information about all kinds of filtering (e.g., *water filtering* and *air filtering*) as long as it is not a controversy. The NOT operator can be used purposely to exclude unwanted results at the time a search query is formed.

When only one type of Boolean operator is used in a single search statement, the process is called simple Boolean searching. When a single search statement includes more than one type of Boolean operator, the process is called compound Boolean searching; the natural order for processing the three Boolean operators in most IR systems is

- First, the NOT operator

- Second, the AND operator

- Third, the OR operator

For example, in the compound Boolean search statement *filtering* OR *censorship* AND *controversy* NOT *libraries*, the NOT operator (i.e., *controversy* NOT *libraries*) will be processed first to exclude any documents about controversies involving libraries. Then the AND operator will combine the two terms *censorship* and *controversy*, with the *library* concept "NOT'ed" out already. Finally, the term *filtering* will be OR'ed with the document set generated in the previous searches. If the search results do not meet the end user's expectations, he or she can use parentheses to change the natural order of processing or specify the intended order of processing. In the previous search statement, for instance, the end user could apply parentheses in this way: ((*filtering* OR *censorship*) AND *controversy*) NOT *libraries*. As a result, the order of processing for this statement would be OR, AND, and then NOT because processing would follow the rule that the innermost parentheses are processed first, the outer ones next, and so on. The retrieved documents will be about *filtering* or *censorship* as a *controversy* but not related to *libraries*. As shown, multiple pairs of parentheses can be used to specify a particular order of processing in a compound Boolean search statement. For this reason, compound Boolean searching is sometimes called nested Boolean.

As a retrieval technique, Boolean searching is by far the one used most often by all the existing retrieval facilities. However, it takes time and practice to master Boolean search techniques, especially the compound Boolean search technique.

5.1.1.2 Case-Sensitive Searching

For languages such as English, French, and Spanish, in which upper and lower cases make a difference, case-sensitive searching allows the end user to pinpoint exactly how a term is represented in a query and the system. For example, the words *Target* and *target* refer to two different entities. The uppercase *Target* refers to a retail store in the U.S., while the lowercase *target* is simply a generic term meaning aim, goal, and the like. Once the distinction between the two cases is made, the user can decide whether case-sensitive searching is needed. If one intends to look for information about a Target store, the uppercase *Target* should be chosen as a query term. Otherwise, the lowercase *target* can be used.

The application of case-sensitive searching is on a much smaller scale when compared with Boolean searching. However, case-sensitive searching accomplishes specific types of retrieval tasks that no other retrieval techniques are able to do.

5.1.1.3 Truncation

Truncation, known variously as wildcard, stemming, stripping, term masking, and conflation algorithm, is a technique for retrieving different forms of a term but all with one part in common. IR systems usually designate a particular symbol (e.g., question mark ?, or asterisk *) for the truncation purpose. For example, use of the truncated term *network** as a query retrieves documents on *networks* and documents on *networking*.

Truncating the term suffix, as just described, is called right truncation, which accounts for the majority of truncation practices. Truncation can also be done by taking away the prefix or infix (i.e., some characters in the middle of a term). Taking away the prefix is called left truncation, whereas taking away the infix of the term is called middle or internal truncation. Left truncation is rarely seen, and few IR systems now support it. Middle truncation can be used to handle terms obeying different spelling conventions. For instance, the truncated query term *col*r* will retrieve both *color* and *colour.*

Similarly, searching on *organi*ation* will get information on both *organization* and *organisation.*

It is important to truncate the correct portion of a term if one intends to apply this retrieval technique. At one extreme, too much truncation (e.g., truncating *catalog* to *cat**) can lead to a lot of unwanted information. At the other, truncating too little (e.g., truncate *catalogue* to *catalogu*) will not achieve the goal of truncation. To provide some control over truncation, many IR systems also allow the user to specify the exact number of characters to be truncated.

5.1.1.4 Proximity Searching

While the AND operator can indicate which terms should be included in search results, it cannot specify how far apart these search terms are positioned in a document. For example, with the Boolean search statement *filtering* AND *controversy*, the two terms *filtering* and *controversy* could appear next to each other, several hundreds of words apart, or anywhere in the target document. Proximity searching, also known as adjacency searching, allows the user to specify precisely the proximity or distance between two search terms and their relative positions by using the WITH and NEAR operators. Notations for proximity searching may vary from system to system.

The WITH operator implies that the two terms should appear in the system next to each other and in the same order as stated in the search query. For instance, the search statement *information* WITH *technology* indicates that documents retrieved by the query must contain *information technology* as a phrase and not anything else (e.g., *information and technology, technology information*). In addition, an extension of the WITH operator, nWITH, can request that the terms linked by the operator be within n (n = 1, 2, ... n) words of each other and in the order specified. For example, a search statement *information* 2WITH *technology* would yield documents about *information and technology, information and network technology,* and the like.

The NEAR operator functions in a similar way, that is, the two terms it links should be adjacent. But unlike the WITH operator, the terms linked by the NEAR operator can appear in any order as long as they are next to each other. For example, the search statement *information* NEAR *technology* would produce results on either *information technology* or *technology information.* The nNEAR operator requires that terms linked by the operator be within n (n = 1, 2, ... n) words of each other but in any order. Thus, documents containing the following sample phrases are all legitimate results of the search statement *information* 2NEAR *technology:*

- *information and technology*

- *information and network technology*

- *technology and information*

- *technology and business information*

Phrase searching, as opposed to word searching, is just one particular application of proximity searching if the original information gathered for IR systems is represented only by words (i.e., word indexed). To be more specific, the WITH operator can accomplish exact phrase searching while the rest of the proximity operators support searches using different juxtapositions of the terms specified in the search statement. The juxtapositions can also be extended beyond the range of n words but to the same field or paragraph in some IR systems. For example, DIALOG, an online IR system, allows a user to specify that search terms must appear within the same field (e.g., title field or abstract field) or paragraph.

5.1.1.5 Field Searching

Traditionally, document information is represented by attributes such as author, title, publication date, and document type. These attributes are called fields once they are represented in IR systems. When information or documents are represented by field, they can be retrieved later the same way. Field searching, by definition, restricts searches to one field or multiple fields instead of an entire document.

Field searching performs two functions. One function is to zero in on the information one is looking for if the field attribute (e.g., author's name) is known. For example, if we wish to learn about Hans Peter Luhn's work related to IR, we may search by the term *information retrieval*. But we would realize immediately that such a search would inevitably bring out much more information than expected because all the works on IR, including those by Luhn, will be retrieved as search results. If we conduct a search by the author's name, that is, search by the author field, we should be able to get all the publications by Luhn on IR as well as other topics. We can then use the AND operator to combine the previous search results with the term *information retrieval* to exclude Luhn's work in areas other than IR.

In addition to what we just depicted, field searching can also narrow down a search effectively. Assuming that a search on IR is conducted in a system created for information science, the outcome could contain several thousand records. Few users would be willing to go through search results of that magnitude. At this point, field attributes such as publication year, language type, or document type can help narrow the search effectively. Subject or concept searching (i.e., searching by the "aboutness" of information) followed by field searching (i.e., searching on the "ofness" of information) is a common way to refine retrieval results.

Most information available on the internet is not represented by field attributes in internet retrieval systems because of the reasons discussed in previous chapters. Therefore, field searching is generally not applicable to IR on the internet. Nevertheless, other basic retrieval techniques discussed in this section are either fully or partially supported by internet retrieval systems, a theme explored further in Chapter 8, "Information Retrieval Systems."

5.1.2 Advanced Retrieval Techniques

The basic retrieval techniques described earlier are implemented in most, if not all, IR systems. By contrast, advanced retrieval techniques are provided selectively in a small portion of existing IR systems after they have been tested in research laboratories.

5.1.2.1 Fuzzy Searching

Fuzzy searching sounds related to truncation but with a major difference. While truncation is intended to retrieve different forms of a term when they share some parts in common, fuzzy searching is designed to find terms that are spelled incorrectly at data entry or query input. For example, the term *computer* could be misspelled as *compter, compiter, comptuer,* or *compyter.* Optical character recognition (OCR) and compressed texts could also result in erroneous contents. Fuzzy searching is thus designed particularly for detection and correction of spelling errors or errors that result from OCR or text compression (Grossman & Frieder, 1998).

N-gram is one special technique for the implementation of fuzzy searching. Simply put, n-grams are a fixed-length, consecutive series of n (n = 2, 3, … n) characters in a term (Kowalski, 1997) or a term decomposed into word fragments of size n. Taking the term *fuzzy searching* as an example, we can have:

- Bi-grams (n = 2): fu uz zz zy se ea ar rc ch hi in ng

- Tri-grams (n = 3): fuz uzz zzy sea ear arc rch chi hin ing

Other types of n-grams (e.g., quart-grams or penta-grams) are also available. These n-grams, not necessarily representing the semantic meaning of the term, become the basic units for identifying possible errors. Matching algorithms are then used to determine whether a match exists between the representation and a query (Grossman & Frieder, 1998). If all the n-grams for a term match the query but one or two do not, an error is detected and the correct outcome can be presented. Another common technique for implementing fuzzy searching is dictionary comparison. That is, each query word entered into the IR system is compared against a dictionary, and any error detected would then be corrected.

In other words, fuzzy searching can tolerate errors made at the time of data entry or query input. Documents containing errors due to misspelling, OCR, or similar causes would not be retrieved without the fuzzy searching technique.

5.1.2.2 Weighted Searching

There are times when the user wishes to put different emphases on each term in a query. For example, in the search query *filtering* AND *controversy*, the user is more interested in the *controversy* aspect rather than *filtering* per se. Weighted searching is devised specifically for that purpose.

For weighted searching, weights are assigned to terms when a search query is composed to indicate proportionally their significance or the emphasis the user placed on them. Weights can be given in the form of either symbols (e.g., symbol * in the ERIC system denoting major descriptors) or numerals (both decimals and integers). The weighting scale (e.g., a weighting scale of 1 to 5, with 5 being the highest point) is also variously defined by individual IR systems. Of course, a prerequisite for conducting weighted searching is that weighting has been applied at the representation, or more specifically, the indexing stage. For instance, from executing the weighted search query *filtering3* AND *controversy6*, the user would expect to get documents in which these two terms are represented using the same weighting scale; that is, weights of 3 and 6 are assigned to the terms *filtering* and *controversy*, respectively.

Threshold, a concept closely related to weighted searching, can be used to specify when search results satisfy the weighted query. Assuming the threshold for the *filtering3* AND *controversy6* search is set to 9, then any results with a threshold less than 9 (e.g., a document on the same topic but with a weight of 3 for *filtering* and 5 for *controversy*) would not be regarded as hits in this case.

Obviously, determining a weight to be assigned to terms is crucial in weighted searching. There are different weighting algorithms in usage. Term location, term proximity, term frequency (tf), inverse document frequency (idf), and individual judgment are the major criteria for weight assignment. Of those criteria, however, mainly individual judgment or the deterministic method (Davis, 1997) can be practically implemented for weighted searching because the user, at the time of assigning weights to query terms, has no knowledge about the documents to be retrieved. Yet all the other criteria for weight assignment are dependent on the attributes of terms derived from the original documents. Therefore, weighting techniques based on term location and other criteria seem applicable only to weighted indexing.

Weighted searching based on individual judgment sounds very subjective. Nevertheless, its implementation actually relies further on a combination of such factors as information need, nature of IR systems, and kinds of results expected. In other words, the user decides the weights for query terms by taking into consideration those specific factors. The weight assignment at the time of query formation is therefore not merely an arbitrary exercise.

As indicated earlier, there are more weight assignment criteria to choose from for weighted indexing than for weighted searching. Among those criteria, term location refers to where the term appears in a document. As a rule of thumb, a term that appears in such places as the title, section headings, and topic sentences would receive a higher weight than those present in other parts of a document. Term proximity means the distance between indexing terms in a document. Generally speaking, the shorter the distance, or the closer the proximity between the terms under consideration, the higher the indexing weight the terms will be given. On the other hand, term frequency (tf) is defined as the number of times a term appears in a document. As discussed previously, terms with high frequency alone are not necessarily good indexing term candidates because they could be function words or words of insignificant meaning in retrieval. Rather, the best indexing terms, or terms that should be given high weights, are those that occur frequently in individual documents but rarely in the rest of the database (Salton, 1989). So the number of documents to which a particular term is assigned should also be considered in determining weights. This measure is known as inverse document frequency (idf) because the weights assigned are in reverse proportion to the document frequency. Namely, the fewer documents a term is assigned to, the higher weight it receives.

Because tf is often used in conjunction with idf to determine the weight to be assigned to terms, this practice is called the tf.idf weighting technique. Document length (dl) is also considered sometimes in combination with the tf.idf weighting technique, adding another parameter in determining term weights. If tf and idf are held constant, the longer the document that contains the term, the higher weight the term will receive. The tf.idf.dl weighting technique has been widely adopted in the Text REtrieval Conference (TREC) projects (Spärck Jones, 2000). Detailed discussion of the TREC series is provided in Chapter 11.

Other weighting techniques, such as probability approaches, are used in practice as well. Moreover, these weighting techniques are often implemented in various combinations with other methods. For example, term location could be applied jointly with term proximity in a weighting algorithm.

Weighted searching opens up another avenue for effective retrieval of information.

5.1.2.3 Query Expansion

Even if careful thought has been given to query formation, a topic explored further in §5.3, the user cannot guarantee that the search query needs no revision or expansion once it is formed. Query expansion is a retrieval technique that allows the end user to improve retrieval performance by revising search queries based on results already retrieved. Searches using query expansion are iterative and interactive, as shown in Figure 5.1.

Results obtained from searches after each query submission are examined to find out whether any information from the results can be derived and incorporated into a newer version of the query. Theoretically, the process of query expansion can be repeated until satisfactory results are obtained. Interaction between the IR system and the user during the query expansion process can help improve retrieval performance.

According to Resnick and Vaughan (2006), query expansion is one of the two methods commonly used in the context. The other technique is query contraction. Query expansion involves adding synonyms and other related words to a query to increase the number of matches that are identified, while query contraction aims to disambiguate any terms with multiple meanings in order to assure that only relevant matches are returned. Query expansion can further be categorized into three types based on the sources from which related terms for the expansion are selected (Gauch, Wang, & Rachakonda, 1999). Specifically, an expansion using terms chosen from a subset of the documents retrieved by a specific query is called query-specific expansion. If an expansion is conducted with terms identified through analyzing the contents of a particular full-text database, it is corpus-specific. If an expansion is made with terms found from online thesauri that are not tailored for any particular collection, it is referred to as language-specific.

Query expansion can be implemented manually and automatically. For manual query expansion, the user decides how the search results can be used

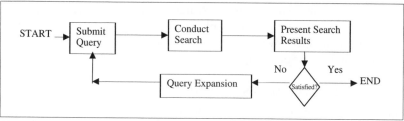

Figure 5.1 Process of Query Expansion

to modify the query. For automatic query expansion (also known as relevance feedback), the top-ranked documents in the search results are assumed relevant and thus included in query revision. The end user is not directly involved in the process of modifying the query (Grossman & Frieder, 1998; Salton, 1970). By this point, we can see that query expansion is not a very precise expression for describing this process because the query will not necessarily be expanded but will always get modified. Therefore, query modification appears to be a more appropriate term for this process.

Another technique for query modification is also advocated and actually employed by some IR systems: Terms are automatically listed on a drop-down menu as suggestions while the user is entering a query into the search box. Although some users may find this implementation distracting, others (e.g., White & Marchionini, 2006) argue that such a mechanism would truly support real-time query expansion.

The ranking of outputs, done by many IR systems, is a vital mechanism for relevance feedback or automatic query expansion. Similar to the weighting techniques discussed previously, ranking algorithms are based most often on criteria such as term location, term proximity, and term frequency (tf). Typically, each individual IR system implements its own ranking algorithms by choosing certain criteria. Such ranking algorithms are usually not published or in the public domain. A new ranking criterion called the backlink approach was introduced in 1998 by Google, an internet retrieval system, to rank web search results (Vidmar, 1999). The backlink approach judges the quality of a webpage by, among other things, counting how many other websites provide hyperlinks to it. More discussion on the backlink approach appears in Chapter 8, "Information Retrieval Systems."

Query by example is another implementation of query expansion where the term *example* refers to the results already retrieved; in other words, results that have been retrieved will be treated as examples for further queries. In sound and image IR, the example could come directly from the user, such as a hand-drawn sketch of a flower, rather than from information extracted from the search results. When searching on the internet, the user can do relevance feedback by simply clicking on hyperlinks such as "More like this."

Query modification is often needed in IR because it can help improve retrieval performance by revising the search query based on terms suggested at the search box or results already obtained. As a retrieval technique, query expansion, and especially relevance feedback, has wide application and great potential in IR in the digital age.

5.1.2.4 Multiple Database Searching

Multiple database searching, also known as federated searching, means searching in more than one IR system simultaneously. The term database here is customarily considered a synonym for system. The need for searching multiple databases is threefold. First, searching in a single IR system may not get what the user is looking for because every IR system has its own coverage, orientation, and features. In this case, other IR systems should be tried for the search. Second, multiple database searching can serve as a selection tool if the user is not sure which system(s) would be the best choice for a given query. Third, the results obtained from multiple database searching can also suggest or indicate suitable systems for the user to conduct further searches in.

In searching multiple databases, one must pay specific attention to the differences in query syntax, language, and search capabilities each system provides. A feature quite common and basic in one system may not be supported in others. Furthermore, the same feature supported in both systems may not be expressed in the same way. For example, the Boolean operator AND may be used in one system, while another system uses the plus sign. The languages used in multiple systems are likely dissimilar as well. Possibilities include natural language versus controlled vocabulary, different controlled vocabularies, and natural language used in different disciplines.

Another challenge that multiple database searching faces is how to handle data of different formats (e.g., ASCII, MAchine Readable Cataloging [MARC]) stored in multiple databases. Z39.50, a standard for Information Retrieval Service Definition and Protocol Specification for Library Applications, is set up to, among other things, handle data of all formats for retrieval tasks. Therefore, IR systems that are Z39.50 compliant can be searched simultaneously regardless of their format differences and geographical proximity (Michael & Hinnebusch, 1995). Approved by the American National Standard Institute (ANSI) and the National Information Standards Organization (NISO), Z39.50 is widely applied in web-based OPACs (WebPACs) and some other types of IR systems. With Z39.50, the end user can also retrieve information by using a uniform interface, no matter what interface an IR system originally had.

Growing out of Z39.50 to meet with current technological expectations, Search/Retrieve Web Service (SRW) and Search/Retrieve via URL (SRU) are two protocols intended to define a standard form for internet search queries as well as the structure of responses. When users submit the same query to multiple IR systems, the syntax expressing the query may be different, and likewise the structure of the responses. Each response contains not only search results but also formatting information. SRW and SRU, sometimes referred to as SRW/U in brief, address these problems by specifying the syntax for queries and results. Specifically, SRW/U allows users and IR system agents to query internet databases and return retrieved results seamlessly without the need for complicated metasearch protocols such as Z39.50 (Morgan, 2004). In comparison with Z39.50, SRW/U is less complex than but semantically equivalent to the classic Z39.50 (LeVan, 2003). SRW/U and related standards are promulgated by the Library of Congress (2008).

Aside from the aforementioned problems and challenges associated with multiple database searching, how to merge results retrieved from multiple databases poses another concern. For example, ranked outputs are becoming increasingly the norm in presenting search results. Yet ranking algorithms vary from one IR system to another. It is unrealistic to expect that a ranking of 0.90 for one document retrieved from one system is the same as a result with the same ranking from a different system. Data fusion, the combination of results from differing systems by the use of certain methods, appears a possible solution to this problem. Belkin and his colleagues (1995), for instance, suggested a group of techniques for merging results of multiple search strategies on multiple databases to produce the best possible response to a query. The Database Merging track of TREC, discussed in Chapter 11, is devoted to tackling the problem of merging data from heterogeneous sources to present a uniform output (Voorhees & Harman, 2000).

Multiple database searching is usually supported by IR services or vendors (e.g., DIALOG) that manage multiple databases rather than a single IR system. The so-called metasearch engines on the internet perform a similar function for retrieving information from various sources on the internet. This topic is discussed further in Chapter 8, "Information Retrieval Systems."

5.2 Selection of Retrieval Techniques

As shown in the previous section, there are different retrieval techniques for the end user to choose from for a given search task. Many factors need to be considered when selecting retrieval techniques. In this section, however, the discussion of the selection of retrieval techniques focuses on their functions and retrieval performance.

5.2.1 Functions of Retrieval Techniques

Each retrieval technique functions in certain ways so that the user can rely on it to achieve the right search objective. For instance, the use of truncation retrieves various forms of a term if they share a common portion in their spellings. In comparison, fuzzy searching accommodates spelling and OCR errors if some matches can still be found between the two different versions of a term. Therefore, the first question a user should ask when choosing a retrieval technique is what the retrieval technique (e.g., weighted searching) can accomplish. It is only after this question is answered that the user can know whether the retrieval technique under consideration is suitable for a given query.

5.2.2 Retrieval Performance

Retrieval performance is traditionally and most often measured by precision and recall although these two measures are continually the foci of controversial discussions. For clarity, the following discussion concentrates on precision and recall as retrieval performance measures, and the controversies surrounding them are examined in Chapter 11, "Evaluation of Information Representation and Retrieval."

Precision is, by definition, the ratio between the number of relevant documents retrieved and the total number of documents retrieved from a system. It measures the discriminating ability of an IR system, that is, the ability to separate the irrelevant from the relevant. If 100 documents are retrieved from a search and 35 of them are judged relevant, the precision ratio for this search is 35 percent. On the other hand, recall is defined as the ratio between the number of relevant documents retrieved and the total number of relevant documents in a system. It measures the retrievability of an IR system. Suppose that there are 100 relevant documents on a given topic in a system, of which 45 are retrieved; the recall ratio for this search would be 45 percent. For both precision and recall, the higher the percentage, the better the retrieval performance. But it is impossible to get search results high in both precision and recall because of the inverse relationship between the two measurements.

As far as retrieval performance is concerned, all the retrieval techniques discussed in §5.1 can be categorized as either precision improving (e.g., Boolean operator AND, weighted searching) or recall improving (e.g., Boolean operator OR, fuzzy searching). Therefore, the selection decision of retrieval techniques should also be made in consideration of the retrieval performance the user anticipates. If search results of high precision are expected, corresponding retrieval techniques need to be chosen and vice versa.

5.2.2.1 Retrieval Techniques for Improving Precision

Boolean operator AND improves precision by combining two or more terms in a search query for specifying the precise implication of a search request. For example, if there are three terms, *filtering*, *controversy*, and *web*, in a search request, precise results can be obtained by "ANDing" all three together. If only two of the terms are included in a search query, the results will increase in number but decrease in precision because the restriction on the third term is relaxed.

The Boolean operator NOT enhances the precision of a search by eliminating unwanted terms from a query. Suppose the user wants to search for documents on the filtering controversy with regard to web materials but not about TV programs. The NOT operator can be used to achieve that purpose.

Case-sensitive searching increases the precision of a search by differentiating upper- and lowercase spellings. The terms *Target* and *target* illustrate the point. If the user is interested only in finding materials on a Target store, case-sensitive searching should retrieve exactly what the user wants. If an IR system does not support case-sensitive searching, the user would have no way of making a distinction between the two different cases of the term. Consequently, documents on both *Target* and *target* will be retrieved as legitimate results, and the precision of the search will be negatively affected.

The WITH operator of proximity searching is also a method for improving precision because it specifies the order in which the search terms the WITH operator links appear in the original document or its representation. If a search statement reads *information* WITH *technology*, these two terms must appear exactly in the same order in the retrieval system. Any other combinations of the terms (e.g., *technology information, information and technology*) would produce, not precise results, but search noise. The nWITH operator functions similarly to the WITH operator in terms of precision improvement except that it allows variations within the range of n words between the two terms the operator links.

Field searching ensures the precision of a search by limiting it to a particular field. Each field is established to represent one attribute of a document. If a query is about one document attribute (e.g., author), the search will be more precise when it is restricted to that field than when it makes a comprehensive search in all the fields. It is possible that other fields contain the author's name for various reasons, but these fields are not intended to reflect the author attribute of documents.

Weighted searching, another precision-improving technique, assigns weights to query terms. By doing so, the user can specify the emphasis of a query and thus get results that match more precisely with expectations. Take the search statement *filtering* AND *controversy* as an example again. The user can put different emphases on the two terms by assigning different weights to them. If a higher weight is assigned to the term *controversy*, then the emphasis of this query is on *filtering* as a *controversy*. In other words, the user can be more precise about a particular query when using weighted searching.

In summary, the AND and NOT operators of Boolean searching, case sensitivity searching, the WITH operator of proximity searching, field searching, and weighted searching can all be used in their various capacities to improve the precision of retrieval tasks.

5.2.2.2 Retrieval Techniques for Improving Recall

The Boolean operator OR, as described earlier, requires only that either of the two terms it links appear in a retrieved document. Therefore, search results increase in number and also in recall, presumably. For example, if the query is *filtering* OR *controversy*, the query will get a hit when either *filtering* or *controversy* appears in the system. The restrictions on the OR search seem to be far fewer compared with the other two Boolean operators. The less the restriction a search has, the higher the recall it gets.

Truncation expands search results by allowing a specific part of a term to take various forms as long as all the results share one common component (e.g., a word stem). In that case, all the variations of a word stem are counted in the search. For example, a search query of *ejournal** will retrieve documents containing *ejournal* or *ejournals* or *ejournalism* or *ejournalist* or any other term that begins with *ejournal*. Obviously, the recall for this search is consequently higher than that for a search in which the query term is not truncated. When a search term is not truncated (e.g., *ejournal*), the search results will contain only those documents having the term spelled exactly as in the query.

The NEAR operator of proximity searching provides opportunity for retrieving more relevant results by permitting the terms the operator links to appear in either order in the system database. So a search on *information* NEAR *technology* will retrieve documents about either *information technology* or *technology information* and thus increase the possibility of improving recall. The nNEAR operator works in a manner similar to the NEAR operator but is even more accommodating by allowing variations within the range of n words between the two terms the nNEAR operator connects.

Fuzzy searching has the potential to improve recall by detecting and correcting errors that result from misspellings, OCR errors, and other sources. If a document is about *cellular phone* but the term is misspelled as *celluler phone*, a search using the fuzzy technique will still be able to retrieve the document. Recall for this search is thus increased.

Query expansion aims to retrieve more relevant results by modifying a query based on the previous batch of search results. This modification process can be repeated until enough relevant results are obtained. Recall, a measurement for the proportion of relevant documents retrieved out of all those that exist in a system, is clearly the parameter to be improved in query expansion. For example, the first round of a search retrieved only five documents relevant to the query *vector space model*. After viewing the results just obtained, Salton's name (e.g., *Salton, G.*) is incorporated into a new query for the second round of search. If six more relevant documents are retrieved as a result, recall has increased remarkably.

Multiple database searching offers another opportunity for improving recall because more databases are used in a search. When a query is searched in multiple databases, the chance of obtaining a larger number of relevant results becomes greater than from a search in a single IR system. Moreover, each single IR system can include only certain amounts and selected types of information. But a group of IR systems can undoubtedly cover a wider variety of information in larger quantity.

As shown, the OR operator of Boolean searching, truncation, the NEAR operator of proximity searching, fuzzy searching, query expansion, and multiple database searching can all expand searches in one way or another. Although more results would not necessarily result in higher recall for IR, they can increase the possibility of getting a more relevant outcome for a given query. In addition, knowing how each retrieval technique affects the recall and precision measurement of a search task, users can make educated decisions in choosing the right retrieval techniques for their searches.

5.3 Query Representation

An information need must be expressed verbally or in writing before a search can be performed to satisfy it. The expressed information need is called a search request or retrieval question, usually in natural language. The search request can then be transformed into a query using the IR system's facilities, such as query syntax, retrieval techniques, and controlled vocabulary if one is adopted. That transformation process is called query representation—the most critical factor in retrieval (Spärck Jones, 2000).

5.3.1 General Steps

Query representation is an intellectual exercise that typically consists of the following steps:

1. Conduct a concept analysis of the search request by decomposing it into concept groups or facets.

2. Think about synonyms, broader terms, and narrower terms of the concepts identified.

3. Translate these terms into controlled vocabulary if one is used.

4. Use Boolean logic to "OR" all the synonyms (terms) in every concept group, "AND" relevant facets, and then "NOT out" any unwanted facet(s).

5. Apply other retrieval techniques where needed.

Although these steps are not carved in stone, they comprise the essence of query representation. There could be some variations in practice. The following is a step-by-step discussion of the query representation process in consideration of its crucial role in IR.

5.3.1.1 Concept Analysis

The first step in query representation is to parse a search request into concept groups or facets. The search request, for example, is to locate documents discussing web filtering as a controversy rather than as an information technology. We find, after analysis, that there are three discrete concepts in the search request, as shown in Table 5.1.

In this case, the terms included in the request happen to be the same as the concepts involved. However, there are situations in which the two do not exactly match. For instance, a search request may contain the terms *buses* and *subways*, but the underlying concept is about *public transportation*. Therefore, *public transportation*, rather than *buses* and *subways*, should be used for representation purposes here. In addition, only nouns or noun phrases should be used to represent the concepts. Verbs, if there are any in the request, will be represented by Boolean operators. Other parts of speech should not be selected for representing concepts identified in a search request.

Table 5.1   Concept Analysis of a Search Request

Concept 1	Concept 2	Concept 3
Web filtering	Controversy	Information technology

5.3.1.2 Term Variations

Terms, in most cases, have synonyms, broader terms, narrower terms, and other variations. The objective of this step in query representation is to think about as many variations as necessary for the concepts previously identified so that the concepts will be represented comprehensively. Table 5.2 shows possible variations for the three concepts identified in the previous step.

As shown in Table 5.2, not all possible term variations are exhausted because of reasons such as popularity and brevity. Under Concept 1, for instance, we did not list *World Wide Web* as a variation for *web*. The decision on whether a particular term should be listed depends on several subjective

Table 5.2   Concept Groups for Query Representation

Concept 1	Concept 2	Concept 3
Web filtering	Controversy	Information technology
Filtering Censorship Filtering on the Web Filtering on the WWW Censorship on the Web Censorship on the WWW	Debate Dispute	Network technology Computer technology

criteria, such as anticipated recall and familiarity with the topic. While not all the term variations suggested will be included in the final query for a search, listing a number of possibilities can help select candidate query terms. This practice of listing term variations can also provide entry terms for choosing the right terms from a controlled vocabulary if one is used.

5.3.1.3 Term Conversion

If a controlled vocabulary is used as the IR language, the terms expressed in natural language in the previous step should be converted accordingly into the chosen vocabulary. Otherwise, the user can skip this step in query representation and move to the next one. The conversion requires familiarity with the controlled vocabulary in use and can take any of the following approaches:

- Exact equivalent: The term listed has an exact equivalent in the controlled vocabulary. This appears to be the easiest choice among all the conversion approaches.

- Synonyms or related terms: The term under consideration has only synonyms or related terms in the controlled vocabulary. Efforts should then be made to choose the one that is the closest in meaning to the term being converted.

- Broader terms: The term listed has only broader terms in the controlled vocabulary. Specificity of the original term will be negatively affected as a result of this conversion.

- Narrower terms: The term under consideration has only narrower terms in the controlled vocabulary. Breadth of the original term will be reduced as a consequence of this conversion.

- Unlisted terms: The term to be converted is either a proper name (e.g., corporate name, personal name, or place name) or a new term with no counterpart in the controlled vocabulary. In this case, a new term, called an identifier, has to be created for conversion purposes if the user happens to be an information professional. It is very likely in this case that the new term will be the same as the term being converted.

Except for the exact-equivalent approach, all other conversion approaches require the interpretation of terms. The accuracy of the interpretation determines the accuracy of the conversion practice.

5.3.1.4 Application of Boolean Operators

Suppose all the terms grouped under each concept in Table 5.2 are in the right form; the next task is to apply Boolean operators to link the terms and concepts identified previously according to the relationships among them. Although there might be some deviations in implementation, there are two general rules for applying the Boolean operators:

1. Link the terms in the same concept group (e.g., all the terms in a column in Table 5.2) with the OR operator.

2. Link every concept in a search request (i.e., in the row of Table 5.2) with the AND or the NOT operator, depending on the need.

Figure 5.2 illustrates this process symbolically with the concept groups enumerated in Table 5.2 for the search request example.

Apparently, a couple of points need to be clarified about Figure 5.2. First, how many terms from each concept group should be included in a query? In other words, how many terms should be OR'ed together to represent each concept identified? The answer relies mainly on the number of results the user expects to get. The more terms are OR'ed together, the more results one will receive. Likewise, the fewer terms are OR'ed together, the fewer results one will obtain. One common practice in making such a decision is to prioritize all the terms listed and then choose the first few terms in the list to be

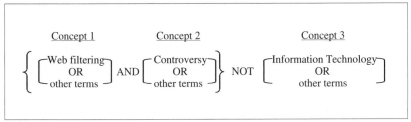

Figure 5.2   Application of Boolean Operators

OR'ed together according to one's need. In Figure 5.2, we do not specify how many terms to use to represent the corresponding concept. Rather, we only indicate that other terms are available for the OR operator.

The second point that needs to be explained in Figure 5.2 is the use of parentheses. In discussing Boolean searching in §5.1.1.1, we introduced the order of processing for compound Boolean searches. The example illustrated in Figure 5.2 is a compound Boolean search, which requires the use of parentheses to change the natural order of processing. If parentheses are not used, the search results will be anything but what the user intends for the search. Suppose we take away all the parentheses in Figure 5.2 and keep all the terms suggested in Table 5.2 as well as in the same order. The first term listed under Concept 3 (i.e., *information technology*) would be excluded from the result set created for the last term shown under Concept 2 (i.e., *dispute*). Other unexpected results would also be generated eventually. Therefore, parentheses have to be used if the natural order of processing is to be changed.

The importance of the Boolean technique in IR is self-explanatory, as Boolean logic has to be applied in query representation unless a search query contains only one single term. However, the application process of Boolean searching actually is more complex than it appears. For more discussion of the complexity and difficulties of Boolean searching, see Chapter 7, "Information Retrieval Models."

5.3.1.5 Use of Other Retrieval Techniques

There are many other techniques the user can apply to represent a query precisely and explicitly. For the *web filtering* search, for example (see Table 5.2), the end user might consider

- Whether case-sensitive searching is available to differentiate when *Web* refers to World Wide Web and *web* means spider web

- Whether the term *debate* should be truncated

- Whether proximity operators such as WITH or NEAR should be used to represent *information technology*

- Whether the search should be limited to certain fields, such as title field and descriptor field

- Whether the chosen IR system supports fuzzy searching

- Whether weights should be assigned to any of the terms selected

- Whether relevance feedback is supported by the system or whether query expansion should be applied manually

- Whether multiple databases should be searched

As indicated earlier, not many IR systems provide all the search facilities discussed so far. Therefore, this list of retrieval techniques serves more as a checklist than as a "must-do" list. By this time, the query should be fully represented and ready to be submitted for searching.

Query representation, as information representation, is a very complex process. Although we summarized these five steps to illustrate the major points of query representation, the actual practice may not consist of the same number of steps or follow the same order. For example, experienced users tend to combine some of the steps while novice users would be reluctant to take any shortcuts.

To sum up, Step 1 of query representation deals with the parsing of search requests into concepts. Step 2 and Step 3 are concerned with the translation of concepts into query terms. Step 4 and Step 5 focus on the application of various retrieval techniques.

Because each user, each search request, and each IR system is different, query representation should reflect this phenomenon by taking into consideration the uniqueness of the process.

5.3.2 Difficulties With Query Representation

Query representation, as discussed, is not a mechanical but an intellectual process, which requires thinking and judgment. In addition, there exist several difficulties in this intellectual exercise.

Concept analysis constitutes the first difficulty in query representation. The user should have the right knowledge, experience, and skills to identify and express the concepts contained in a search request. Subjectivity can easily slip into the process. Inaccurate analysis is not an uncommon phenomenon.

The second difficulty in query representation is the language. Natural language is rich, flexible, subtle, and sometimes vague, whereas controlled vocabulary is rigid, artificial, and hard to maintain. Yet a search request must be represented as precisely as possible in either language. This conversion can introduce discrepancies into the representation process and eventually affect retrieval performance. The use of controlled vocabulary increases the difficulty of query representation because it takes time and effort for the user to become familiar with it. On the other hand, the use of natural language in representing queries has its own drawbacks, as discussed in Chapter 4.

Applying the right retrieval techniques presents another difficulty in query representation. Each IR system defines its own specifications and implementation regarding retrieval techniques (e.g., the + sign in some internet retrieval systems means the Boolean operator AND while in others it is a weighting symbol). Mastering the usage of these techniques also takes time and needs practice.

These difficulties are all likely to cause an inaccurate representation of search requests, which in the end leads to mismatches between query representation and information representation. To overcome these difficulties, we can on one hand educate and train the user and, on the other, look forward to breakthroughs in research on automatic query representation.

5.3.3 The Automatic Approach

Automatic representation of queries is very desirable if it can actually be accomplished. The automatic approach, like automatic indexing and other automatic methods of text processing, relies largely on attributes such as keyword frequency, proximity, and location. Algorithms based on probability, linguistics, and artificial intelligence are also adopted sometimes. However, unlike automatic indexing, which includes both mechanical and intellectual activities, automatic query representation has only an intellectual component. Because computers still cannot think like a human being, it is not hard to imagine the difficulties that would arise if the intellectual task of query representation were turned over to them.

IR researchers have tried automatic query representation in the past. The automatic approach has also received close attention in the TREC projects. It was reported, for example, that automatically constructed queries from the topics did as well as or even better than manually constructed ones in TREC-1. There was no clear gain from manual query preparation (Spärck Jones, 1995). In TREC-4, a few automatic results were comparable with the manual ones for short queries. The trend in TREC-5 and TREC-6, however, is for manual query construction, normally done with long topics, to clearly outperform automatic query formation for the same long sources (Spärck Jones, 2000). More discussion of the TREC series is presented in Chapter 11.

Although the TREC results are not conclusive, they demonstrate the limitation of the automatic approach with the current status of research in this area. Further work is needed to improve the automatic method of query representation.

References

Belkin, N. J., et al. (1995). Combining the evidence of multiple query representations for information retrieval. *Information Processing & Management*, 31, 431–448.

Davis, Charles H. (1997). From document retrieval to web browsing: Some universal concerns. *Journal of Information, Communication, and Library Science*, 3(3), 3–10.

Gauch, Susan, Wang, Jianying, and Rachakonda, Satya Mahesh. (1999). A corpus analysis approach for automatic query expansion and its extensions to multiple databases. *ACM Transactions on Information Systems*, 17(3), 250–269.

Grossman, David A., and Frieder, Ophir. (1998). *Information retrieval: Algorithms and heuristics*. Boston: Kluwer Academic Publishers.

Kowalski, Gerald. (1997). *Information retrieval systems: Theory and implementation*. Boston: Kluwer Academic Publishers.

LeVan, Ralph. (2003). Z39.50 as a web service. Retrieved December 1, 2008, from staff.oclc.org/~levan/docs/srw-niso20030430.ppt

Library of Congress. (2008). SRU: Search/Retrieval via URL. Retrieved December 1, 2008, from www.loc.gov/standards/sru

Michael, James J., and Hinnebusch, Mark. (1995). *From A to Z39.50: A networking primer*. Westport, CT: Mecklermedia.

Morgan, Eric Lease. (2004). An introduction to the Search/Retrieve URL Service (SRU). Ariadne, 40 (July 2004). Retrieved December 1, 2008, from www.ariadne.ac.uk/issue40/morgan

Resnick, Marc L., and Vaughan, Misha W. (2006). Best interface and future visions for search user interfaces. *Journal of the American Society for Information Science and Technology*, 57(6), 781–887.

Salton, Gerard. (1970). Automatic text analysis. *Science*, 168, 335–343.

Salton, Gerard. (1989). *Automatic text processing: The transformation, analysis, and retrieval of information by computer*. Reading, MA: Addison-Wesley.

Smith, Elizabeth S. (1993). On the shoulders of giants: From Boole to Shannon to Taube: The origins and development of computerized information from the mid-19th century to the present. *Information Technology and Libraries*, 12(2), 217–226.

Spärck Jones, Karen. (1995). Reflections on TREC. *Information Processing & Management*, 31(3), 191–314.

Spärck Jones, Karen. (2000). Further reflections on TREC. *Information Processing & Management*, 36(1), 37–85.

Vidmar, Dale J. (1999). Darwin on the web: The evolution of search tools. *Computers in Libraries*, 19, 22–28.

Voorhees, Ellen M., and Harman, Donna. (2000). Overview of the sixth Text REtrieval Conference (TREC-6). *Information Processing & Management*, 36(1), 3–35.

White, Ryen W., and Marchionini, Gary. (2006). Examining the effectiveness of real-time query expansion. *Information Processing & Management*, 43(3), 685–704.

CHAPTER 6

Retrieval Approaches

Information retrieval can be accomplished by searching, browsing, or the two approaches combined. The selection of an appropriate retrieval approach depends on, among other factors, the kind of information need a particular user has. In this chapter, we explore the three different retrieval approaches along with their features and applications.

Koll (2000) made the following analogy when discussing information retrieval. He wrote that finding a needle (i.e., a document or information) in a haystack (i.e., IR system or database) can mean [emphasis in the original text]:

1. A *known* needle in a known haystack

2. A *known* needle in an unknown haystack

3. An *unknown* needle in an unknown haystack

4. *Any* needle in a haystack

5. The *sharpest* needle in a haystack

6. *Most* of the sharpest needles in a haystack

7. *All* the needles in a haystack

8. Affirmation of no needles in the haystack

9. Things *like* needles in any haystack

10. Let me know *whenever* a new needle shows up

11. *Where* are the haystacks

12. Needles, haystacks—*whatever*

In the above listing, different possibilities about the needle and the haystack are enumerated but not exhausted. Obviously, searching is a suitable approach for certain cases (e.g., No. 1), and browsing seems appropriate for other cases (e.g., No. 12). Some cases in the list (e.g., No. 5) may require the combined use of the two retrieval approaches.

6.1 Retrieval by Searching

Searching is a retrieval approach that has long been in use. It is also a topic always being covered in discussions of information retrieval (IR), where it might be called database searching, online searching, web searching, or the like. Once the query is represented, the user is ready to conduct the search for retrieving information from the system.

6.1.1 Characteristics of Searching

Searching, first of all, is intended to find out what would match the terms specified in the query, using the different retrieval techniques examined in Chapter 5. Searching can be conducted via either subject or nonsubject access points. Typical subject access points in IR systems include descriptors, identifiers, classification labels, subject headings, cited references in citation searching, and terms from titles, abstracts, or the text itself in full-text searching (Hjørland, 1997). Common nonsubject access points encompass language, publication year, document type, and the like.

Searching can be an effective retrieval method when the query is specific and the user knows exactly what to look for. If the user, for example, would like to find all of Salton's research published in the 1990s, a search by author field and publication year field should produce the anticipated results. If the user intends to learn about, for instance, all those who made contributions to the field of information retrieval, searching alone is unlikely to meet the need.

In the search approach, retrieval techniques such as Boolean logic allow the user to combine different facets in a search query wherever needed. With the exception of some internet retrieval systems, most IR systems support further modification of search queries with the help of appropriate retrieval techniques (e.g., field searching). All these tasks are completed by the system once they are submitted to it as part of queries. The process is straightforward and does not place a heavy cognitive load on the user.

Searching is a structured activity, however. There is little chance for serendipity (i.e., discovering something worthwhile but unexpected during a search) as the system only presents those results that match the query. In addition, searching skills do not come naturally. The user must learn how to search and must practice to master them. The cost for learning and practicing can be high if the IR system is fee-based.

6.1.2 Types of Searching

Searching can be categorized into different types according to search objectives. When the user has a particular document in mind, the search is called known-item search. Known-item search is generally conducted based on a known document attribute such as author and title. A close analogy of the known-item search is Koll's (2000) "known needle in a known haystack."

When people select research topics, they perform a literature search to find out whether other researchers have done any work in this area. The researchers are not surprised if they do not find anything germane to their query in a search. Rather, they are pleased to know that nothing has been published yet on the topic. This type of search is labeled negative searching (Stielow & Tibbo, 1988), or as Koll (2000) put it, the "affirmation of no needles in the haystack." Negative searching should be thorough and comprehensive so that the end user can be confident that no similar research is in existence.

To keep abreast of a research front or for other similar reasons, people like to find out what is new in a field by conducting literature searches. This kind of search has been named selective dissemination of information (SDI.) As explained in Chapter 1, Luhn (1961) designed the SDI method that has become widely used, especially in the business and scientific communities. For SDI searches, the query remains the same but is submitted to the IR system periodically. SDI searches can also be processed automatically. Koll (2000) portrayed SDI searches as "Let me know whenever a new needle shows up."

Subject or topical search stands for another searching type. The end user has an information need and would like to search for some relevant results. To formulate the search query, subject access points mentioned in §6.1.1 should be used, supplemented by nonsubject attributes (e.g., language and publication year). Different retrieval techniques should be considered in determining the recall and precision of the search. Koll (2000) gave several examples of subject search from the perspective of recall and precision when he made the following analogies:

- Any needle in a haystack: The search is low in recall but high in precision.

- The sharpest needle in a haystack: The search is high in precision.

- Most of the sharpest needles in a haystack: The search is high in recall.

- All the needles in a haystack: The search has perfect recall.

Other possibilities (e.g., searches low in precision but high in recall) apparently exist for measuring retrieval outcome with recall and precision. Compared with other types of searching, subject search seems to be the most complex and complicated, partly because the results obtained from the search have to be evaluated using the controversial criteria, recall and precision. As mentioned before, the controversies around precision and recall as retrieval performance measures will be examined closely in Chapter 11, "Evaluation of Information Representation and Retrieval."

Passage searching, briefly mentioned in §1.2.1 as passage retrieval, represents a different kind of search: Only the relevant passage (e.g., a paragraph) in a document, rather than the entire document, will be presented to the user. The filtering function is capitalized on in passage searching. Although emerging only in recent years, passage searching exhibits a great potential for helping the user reduce information overload and improve retrieval precision.

This section has described five different search types: known-item search, negative search, SDI, subject search, and passage search. Using a different categorizing criterion, Baeza-Yates and Ribeiro-Neto (1999) classified searches into two kinds: ad hoc and filtering. No matter how a search type is labeled, the objective is to decide which search techniques and search strategies should be adopted to satisfy a user's needs.

6.1.3 Search Strategies

Search strategies are the approaches people take when conducting searches. In the golden age of online searching, the following four types of search strategies were identified and illustrated (Fenichel & Hogan, 1981).

6.1.3.1 The Building Block Approach

The building block approach starts with single-concept searches. Single concepts, such as *web filtering* and *controversy*, listed in Table 5.1, are those that have been identified in concept analysis. After all the single-concept searches are completed, the resulting sets are combined using appropriate Boolean operators.

This strategy can decompose a complex search task into simpler ones. It also allows the user to make corrections or adjustments, if needed, in a timely fashion during the searches. The user does not have to redo an entire search because of, for example, a small typo made when entering the search statement. As a result, the building block approach puts less pressure on the user, who can then focus more on interacting with the system. For these reasons, this search strategy is highly recommended to users, especially novice users.

6.1.3.2 The Snowballing Approach

The snowballing approach, also known as the citation pearl-growing approach (Fenichel & Hogan, 1981), implies search results will increase in quantity, much like making a snowball in the snow. Obviously, this approach aims to improve recall. Using this search strategy, the user first conducts a search and then modifies the search query based on the results retrieved. The modification process includes going over the results, selecting relevant terms (e.g., title words and descriptors), and incorporating them in a revised version of the query. This process can be repeated until the user is satisfied with the search.

For example, if a search on *electronic book* retrieves documents that contain terms such as *Stephen King* and *ebook*, the user can adopt the snowballing approach by including these two terms in the revised search statement in order to expand search results. We know that Stephen King is the first popular author to publish electronically and that *ebook* is an abbreviated form of *electronic book*. The snowballing approach in essence is similar to the advanced retrieval technique, query expansion, discussed in §5.1.2.3. Korfhage (1997) named this practice citation processing. As shown, this snowballing approach is particularly useful when the user would like to identify related terms in order to expand a search.

6.1.3.3 The Successive Fraction Approach

The successive fraction approach appears to be the opposite of the snowballing approach. Starting a search with a broad concept, the successive fraction approach narrows the search by applying various limiting techniques. One type of limiting uses related Boolean and proximity operators when composing a search statement. As discussed earlier, the NOT operator narrows down a search by excluding certain terms. The AND operator achieves the same purpose by adding more requirements in a search. The WITH operator also narrows down a search by specifying the position of words in a search query. Another kind of limiting can be done by using nonsubject attributes such as language, document type, and publication year. Limiting by such nonsubject attributes seems more straightforward than limiting by operators.

Suppose a search was conducted on *filtering*, and the results include everything about *filtering* that is covered in the IR system. If our purpose is to find information on web filtering as a controversy but not as an information technology, we can use the successive fraction approach to reach our objective. For example, we would first add the term *web* to the search statement by using the AND operator. The term *controversy* can be added similarly. Then the NOT operator would be applied to exclude any results containing the term *information technology*. Further limiting can be accomplished by restricting the search only to documents published, for instance, after 1996.

As discussed, the successive fraction approach narrows down a search step by step using limiting techniques available from the IR system. This search strategy requires the user to be familiar with the system's limiting features and to stay interactive with the system during the search. If the successive fraction approach is chosen, cost may be a concern for the user of online IR systems (see §8.1) as it requires more processing time than other search strategies do. It is true that internet retrieval systems (see §8.4) do not impose charges on the user; however, the limiting facilities provided by such systems continue to be far from adequate.

6.1.3.4 The Most Specific Facet First Approach

The most specific facet first approach is applied to multiple-concept searches (Fenichel & Hogan, 1981). It assumes that the user knows all the facets or concept groups contained in a search and is also able to identify the most specific one. This search strategy can be very efficient because it begins a search with a term that should take the least amount of time to be processed. In addition, there will be no point in continuing the search if the number of results retrieved for the most specific facet seems unacceptable. For example, there are three facets in the statement "treatment and prognosis of neuroendocrine tumors in the lung," namely, *treatment and prognosis, neuroendocrine tumors,* and *lung.* Among the three facets, neuroendocrine tumors appears to be the most specific and will be searched first in this approach. If a search on *neuroendocrine tumors* retrieves only two documents, a search including all three facets will not likely produce more results than the two already located.

Besides its efficiency, implementation of this approach seems very sophisticated. As concept analysis alone is undeniably a daunting task, it becomes virtually impossible for a novice user to single out the most specific facet in a multiconcept search request. The most specific facet first approach thus is not recommended for neophytes.

One extension of the most specific facet first approach is called the next most specific facet first method, which takes the facet coming next in terms of specificity for conducting searches. However, neither approach is used often in the IR community. The lowest posting first approach, described in Fenichel and Hogan (1981), is simply a variation of the most specific facet first approach in that the most specific facet usually generates the lowest postings.

6.1.3.5 Toward a Quick and Convenient Approach

As pointed out in the beginning of this section, all the search strategies described were proposed and developed in the peak time of online searching. The retrieval environment (e.g., the emergence of internet retrieval systems) and the searchers themselves (e.g., end users as searchers without the assistance of intermediaries) have significantly changed since then. While the building block approach and the snowballing approach are still favored by some users, many people just type in a single keyword they would like to search on or enter several terms at once, leaving a space in between them, and make little use of the Boolean operators and other search facilities (e.g., Jansen, Spink, & Saracevic, 2000; Siegfried, Bates, & Wilde, 1993; Wallace,

1993). This approach can be labeled the quick and convenient approach. Few searchers today would try the successive fraction approach or the most specific facet first approach. On the other hand, some of the search facilities or devices (e.g., language types and Boolean operators) are now incorporated into the IR system's interface. The user can simply choose these options from search forms, predefined buttons, or drop-down menus without actually typing them into a search statement.

6.2 Retrieval by Browsing

Browsing is another major form of retrieval activity. In comparison with searching, browsing did not receive much attention in the IR community until the 1990s. With the development of CD-ROM systems, OPAC systems, and particularly the hyperstructured web, browsing gained popularity quickly and became economically feasible in information retrieval when the user no longer needed to worry about the connection charge as in the case of professional online IR systems. Today, users can retrieve information by browsing at their leisure.

6.2.1 What Is Browsing?

Browsing is seeking and selecting information by skimming, scanning, and other similar activities. In information retrieval, people like to browse

- To get information when a topic is not clearly defined

- To find information that is hard to specify explicitly

- To obtain an overview of the information the IR system offers

- To choose the right information from a mixture of relevant and irrelevant items

- To discover and learn new information

- When the IR environment encourages browsing

Additional reasons for browsing can be found in Marchionini (1995) along with thorough explanations. In cases such as "Needles, haystacks—whatever" (Koll, 2000), browsing should be a preferred retrieval method.

When browsing, the user does not need to represent a retrieval problem with specific terms, as required in the search process. In that sense, browsing is less demanding intellectually than searching. However, while browsing, people have to stay interactive with the IR system in order to examine and assess the information they are browsing and then make rapid relevance judgments (Marchionini, 1995). The cognitive load on the user in the browsing environment would therefore be greater than if searching is chosen as the retrieval approach.

Unlike searching, browsing can be done without any training and practice as a retrieval approach. According to Marchionini (1995):

> [Browsing] is natural because it coordinates human physical, emotive, and cognitive resources in the same way that humans monitor the physical world and search for physical objects. (p. 100)

People can browse as they are able to breathe. Nevertheless, there are few well-developed techniques to facilitate the browsing process. The user generally has few guidelines to rely on as to when to continue browsing for more information and when to stop browsing.

On the other hand, browsing can be a rewarding exercise: It might lead to serendipity, that is, finding something useful unexpectedly, because browsing allows the user to look for information randomly and in an unstructured manner. Retrieval by browsing is a method that has strengths as well as weaknesses.

6.2.2 Types of Browsing

Unlike searching, browsing does not appear to be a structured retrieval method. But different types of browsing are identified and discussed in the literature (e.g., Herner, 1970; Kowalski, 1997; Marchionini, 1995). Herner (1970) suggested that browsing could be directed, semi-directed, or undirected by judging if the user seeks a specific entity and depending on the browsing tactics used. Similarly, Marchionini (1995) classifies browsing into three categories: systematic, exploratory, and casual.

Directed, or systematic, browsing is done when the user knows clearly what to look for, e.g., a particular webpage on a website or a specific term in an online glossary. Users doing semi-directed, or exploratory, browsing have less specific or clear objectives for retrieval. They skim and scan to locate what they are seeking. For instance, a user may know that an important idea is discussed in a lengthy report. The user then has to browse the report to locate the right part in it. Undirected, or casual, browsing has the lowest predictability of the three types of browsing. With no particular information need, the user browses in the IR system. One example could be that a user jumps from one news item to another while scanning a web-based newspaper, hoping to find something interesting to read.

To examine browsing from a different perspective, Kowalski (1997) listed how people browse search results they obtain:

1. They browse by ranking. Because search results in the digital retrieval environment are normally presented in ranked order based on certain ranking algorithms, users can choose to browse, for example, results ranked high in relevance.

2. They browse by zone. The zone here refers to traditionally defined fields such as title and abstract. Titles and abstracts are some examples of content-rich zones for browsing.

3. They browse by highlighted area. Some IR systems highlight certain terms (e.g., search terms) and their contexts to help people locate what they are looking for efficiently. Those highlighted areas are good candidates for browsing.

In addition to the browsing types Kowalski described, two other kinds of browsing have become prevalent in internet retrieval systems. One is browsing by category, and the other is browsing by hyperlinks. Browsing by category is exemplified at the directory-based internet retrieval systems (e.g., Yahoo!). The information such internet retrieval systems collect is indexed and classified into categories (e.g., Computers, Education, Entertainment, Sports). For example, a user who intends to find a movie to watch would naturally browse the Entertainment category at Yahoo!. As for browsing by hyperlinks, the web with its hyperstructure makes this type of browsing not only feasible but also very inviting.

Hyperlinks are the nodes and pointers embedded in hypertext, which cleverly mimics the associative thinking of human beings. As Bush (1945) pointed out:

> The human mind ... operates by association. With one item in its grasp, it snaps instantly to the next that is suggested by the association of thoughts, in accordance with some intricate web of trails by the cells of the brain. (p. 106)

That kind of association has been vividly and thoroughly reflected on the web by the implementation of hyperlinks. The entire web consists of textual as well as multimedia information, intertwined by uncountable hyperlinks. Those links serve as guides for web users to browse, navigate, and locate digital information (Chu, 1997). Hyperstructured IR systems become one of the best, if not the best, environments for browsing.

Obviously, browsing can be categorized by applying different classification criteria. But the objective of browsing should always be the same in information retrieval: seeking information one intends to find.

6.2.3 Browsing Strategies

Browsing, like searching, can take different strategies. Marchionini (1995) wrote that there are four browsing strategies, namely, scan, observe, navigate, and monitor. Choosing the right browsing strategy can help people achieve their objective of browsing more effectively.

According to Marchionini (1995), scanning is a browsing strategy for seeking well-defined objects in a highly organized IR environment. The user knows what to look for and can scan information either linearly or selectively. To scan linearly is to browse in the information space sequentially, such as going over a list of retrieved results one by one. Selective scan means viewing only certain portions of the information (e.g., headings, hyperlinks, images, and contents of different colors at a website) out of all those being presented. Scanning seems to be the most basic strategy for systematic browsing.

In comparison, observation is the primary strategy used in exploratory or casual browsing (Marchionini, 1995). The user should be attentive to certain portions of what is being observed at the same time that other components in the IR environment (e.g., ads at websites) may distract one's attention. In other words, inputs of various kinds are sent to the user from different sources. The user has to stay focused on what is sought after and ignore noise and other distractions.

Navigation as a browsing strategy balances the influence of the user and the environment in that the environment restricts browsing by providing possible browsing routes while the user exercises some control by selecting which routes to follow (Marchionini, 1995). Navigation, also depending on the feedback of the IR system, can be used for either systematic or casual browsing. Observation is often applied in conjunction with navigation.

Monitoring is similar to scanning except that it tolerates poorly structured environments (Marchionini, 1995). While users are looking at the results retrieved by the system, for example, they can also pay some attention to a news report being broadcasted on the radio. Information-seeking activities take place in parallel. Monitoring is most often used in exploratory browsing.

In sum, browsing strategies seem subtler than the search strategies discussed previously. There are no concrete criteria to help the user determine whether the browsing should continue or end. There are no guidelines for the user to follow with regard to the change of browsing strategies. Instead, the user has to consider a number of qualitative factors (e.g., satisfaction and cognitive effort) for decision-making purposes. There is also no clear-cut line as to when to choose which strategy and under what circumstance. Does browsing as a retrieval method function better when used in conjunction with searching rather than being used alone? The next section attempts to answer this question.

6.3 Searching and Browsing Integrated in Retrieval

Searching and browsing are two distinct retrieval methods. About a half century ago, Luhn (1958) classified retrieval methods as:

1. Retrieval of information by look-up in an ordered array of stored records

2. Retrieval of information by search in a nonordered array of stored records

3. A combination of 1 and 2

The terminology and structure of the system database have undoubtedly changed over the years. However, it remains possible to see that the first category Luhn described represents browsing while the second denotes searching. The third type is the theme to be explored: the integration of browsing and searching.

6.3.1 Comparison of the Two Retrieval Approaches

The characteristics of both browsing and searching have been depicted in the previous sections. According to Cox (1992), browsing can be regarded as going from where to what. The idea is that the user knows where he or she is in the database and wants to know what is available there. Conversely, searching can be considered as going from what to where. The idea is that the user knows what he or she wants and wishes to find where in the database it is available. Marchionini (1995) stated that searching is the formal and analytical strategy while browsing is the informal and heuristic strategy. Aside from those distinctions, searching and browsing differ from each other in the following aspects.

6.3.1.1 Information Need

Information need is one major criterion that divides searching and browsing as retrieval methods. For a specific and known information need, searching appears the suitable choice as it would help the user obtain the "needle" from the "haystack" efficiently. In comparison, browsing can be used to perform retrieval tasks for users with broad and unspecified information needs. People can use different browsing tactics (e.g., scanning and navigation) to find out whether there is any information in the IR system that is relevant to their information need.

6.3.1.2 Efficiency and Potential for Improvement

Efficiency in retrieval and potential for improvement should be taken into consideration when comparing searching with browsing. Generally speaking, searching is quick, focused, and right to the point, whereas browsing could be time-consuming and is not intended as a focused activity. It also appears likely that the user may get distracted in the browsing approach. While various techniques are available for the user to broaden or narrow a search, browsing has few facilities to help improve its performance. In addition, the user can get information only from the portions of the system being browsed. Theoretically, browsing can go on and on if the user does not end it. Meanwhile the accuracy of browsing is likely diminished in such a prolonged process (Marchionini, 1995).

6.3.1.3 Cognitive Load

The entire search process can be divided into approximately three stages: representing the query, conducting the search, and evaluating results. Cognitive load on the user would be high at the first and third stage, and relatively low if the user does not try to be interactive during the search. Browsing, by contrast, is a highly interactive process throughout between the system and the user. Browsing becomes pointless if the user does not interact with the system and stay attentive to what is presented by the system. It is grueling for people to remain focused in the browsing approach for a long time because they have to constantly and rapidly assess the information they are browsing according to certain parameters. However, browsing relies on recognition of relevant information rather than recall from memory (Large, Tedd, & Hartley, 1999), which might lighten some cognitive load on the user.

6.3.1.4 Serendipity

The chance for serendipity in searching is virtually nonexistent because the system basically matches the query with what the database contains. It is neither feasible nor possible for the user to scan the whole system to discern additional information. By comparison, browsing provides opportunity for serendipity. The user would not be surprised to find something useful unexpectedly while browsing. This feature of browsing, however, could also easily become a source of distraction or disorientation, a limitation cited by researchers such as Marchionini (1995).

6.3.1.5 Efforts

Searching is a structured endeavor that requires people to learn and practice before they can perform it. Browsing, by contrast, is a retrieval approach natural to the user, who does not need to spend time learning it. Moreover, no query representation is involved in the browsing process, which can relieve the user from that highly sophisticated task and let the user simply focus on browsing.

Table 6.1 recapitulates the comparisons made between searching and browsing in five different aspects.

Table 6.1 Comparison of Searching and Browsing

Aspect / Approach	Information Need	Efficiency	Cognitive Load	Serendipity	Efforts
Searching	Specific & known	High	Light	Less	More
Browsing	Broad & uncertain	Low	Heavy	More	Less

6.3.2 The Integrated Approach

The comparison in Table 6.1 shows that searching and browsing each have strengths and limitations. Each retrieval approach works well in certain conditions and circumstances. Although there are occasions when one retrieval approach seems more suitable than the other, the integration of the two can lead to better retrieval performance in general. Searching may not be needed for every retrieval task. But browsing seems always necessary in judging the relevance of retrieved results.

Furthermore, IR systems have been designed to promote the integrated approach in the IR community. In IR systems developed earlier (e.g., DIALOG), menu and search options are provided simultaneously so that the user can choose browsing or searching as needed. For internet retrieval systems developed in the late 1990s, the norm is to have both a directory and a search mechanism side by side. Unlike the days when internet retrieval systems were first introduced to the public, these systems offered either a directory (e.g., Yahoo!) or a search mechanism (e.g., AltaVista), but not both. Fortunately, many internet retrieval systems quickly realized the advantage of supporting both browsing and searching within one IR system and subsequently changed their old practices. Today, there are hardly any internet retrieval systems that provide only one retrieval option for the user.

Users benefit from the integrated approach because they not only have the right apparatus for the right retrieval task but also get more out of the same IR systems. For example, Yahoo! supports searching within its browsable categories (e.g., Arts). Searching within a browsable category is therefore similar to searching a database that is specialized in an area the browsable category represents. That is to say, searching at Yahoo! within its Arts category is like conducting searches in an art database. Browsing and searching become integrated activities in this environment. Similarly, search results from an IR system (e.g., Clusty) are automatically grouped to facilitate browsing.

One plus one could be more than two if the combination is done wisely. This is true for the integrated retrieval approach covered here.

References

Baeza-Yates, Ricardo, and Ribeiro-Neto, Berthier. (1999). *Modern information retrieval*. New York: ACM Book Press.

Bush, Vannevar. (1945). As we may think. *Atlantic Monthly*, 176(1), 101–108.

Chu, Heting. (1997). Hyperlinks: How well do they represent the intellectual content of digital collections? *Proceedings of the 60th Annual Meeting of the American Society for Information Science*, 34, 361–369.

Cox, K. (1992). Information retrieval by browsing. In Ching-Chih Chen (Ed.), *NIT'92: Proceedings of the Fifth International Conference on New Information Technology* (pp. 69–79). West Newton, MA: MicroUse Information.

Fenichel, Carol H., and Hogan, Thomas H. (1981). *Online searching: A primer*. Marlton, NJ: Learned Information.

Herner, S. (1970). Browsing. In Allen Kent, Harold Lancour, and William Z. Nasri (Eds.), *Encyclopedia of Library and Information Science* (Vol. 3, pp. 408–415). New York: Marcel Dekker.

Hjørland, Birger. (1997). *Information seeking and subject representation*. London: Greenwood Press.

Jansen, Bernard J., Spink, Amanda, and Saracevic, Tefko. (2000). Real life, real users, and real needs: A study and analysis of user queries on the web. *Information Processing & Management*, 36(2), 207–227.

Koll, Matthew. (2000). Track 3: Information Retrieval. *Bulletin of the American Society for Information Science*, 26(2), 16–18.

Korfhage, Robert R. (1997). *Information storage and retrieval*. New York: John Wiley & Sons.

Kowalski, Gerald. (1997). *Information retrieval systems: Theory and imple-mentation.* Boston: Kluwer Academic Publishers.

Large, Andrew, Tedd, Lucy A., and Hartley, R. J. (1999). *Information seeking in the online age: Principles and practice.* London: Bowker-Saur.

Luhn, H. P. (1958). Review of information retrieval methods. Report No. RC-59. Yorktown Heights, NY: IBM Research Center.

Luhn, H. P. (1961). Selective dissemination of new scientific information with the aid of electronic processing equipment. *American Documentation,* 12(2), 131–138.

Marchionini, Gary. (1995). *Information seeking in electronic environments.* New York: Cambridge University Press. (Cambridge Series on Human-Computer Interaction 9)

Siegfried, Susan, Bates, Marcia, and Wilde, Deborah. (1993). A profile of end user searching behavior by humanities scholars: The Getty online search-ing project report no. 2. *Journal of the American Society for Information Science,* 44(5), 273–291.

Stielow, Frederick, and Tibbo, Helen. (Spring 1988). The negative search, online reference, and the humanities: A critical essay in library literature. *RQ,* 27(3), 358–365.

Wallace, Patricia. (1993). How do patrons search the online catalog when no one's looking? Transaction log analysis and implications for bibliographic instruction and system design. *RQ,* 33(3), 239–252.

CHAPTER 7

Information Retrieval Models

A model is defined as "a tentative description of a theory or system that accounts for all of its known properties" (Soukhanov, et al., 1984). Various models have been developed in information retrieval (IR) over the years. This chapter presents and explores some common IR models in order to facilitate the understanding and appreciation of the foundation of IR practices.

There are many levels at which IR procedures can be modeled. Theories and notions from other disciplines (e.g., Boolean logic, vector space, and probability) are drawn to form the bases for modeling IR activities. Different schemes have been suggested for classifying all the IR models developed so far (e.g., Baeza-Yates & Ribeiro-Neto, 1999; Belkin & Croft, 1987; Spärck Jones & Willett, 1997). Ingwersen and Järvelin (2005) extended the taxonomy of IR models that Belkin and Croft (1987) developed in both exact matching (see Figure 4.2a) and best matching (see Figure 4.2b) categories in their book. This chapter focuses on system-oriented models such as Boolean logic, vector space, and probability. Other IR models (e.g., the user-oriented cognitive model) will be examined in other chapters, where they fit more logically with regard to the subject content.

7.1 Foundation of All Information Retrieval Models: Matching

Matching is not a model in IR, but it lays the foundation for IR activities. As stated in §1.4.1, matching is the fundamental mechanism in IR. Matching can be made between terms or between similarity measurements such as distance and term frequency. Term matching is performed directly on terms derived from or assigned to queries, documents, or their representations whereas similarity measurement matching is conducted indirectly on measurements obtained by calculating, for example, distance between vectors, as in the vector space model. The following two subsections focus on discussing these two kinds of matching.

7.1.1 Term Matching

As explained in §2.1.1, terms used in information representation and retrieval (IRR) can be keywords, descriptors, or identifiers. Terms also include words, phrases, or other kinds of expressions. In addition, term matching can be done in one of the following four ways: exact match, partial match, positional match, and range match.

Exact match means that the query representation matches exactly with the document representation in the IR system. Case sensitivity search and phrase search are examples of exact matching. For example, *web filtering* is a term in a query, and the same phrase also appears in the system to be searched. Then an exact match is obtained as a result of searching.

In partial match, unlike exact matching, only part of the query term matches the document representation in the IR system. Truncation in searching is a typical example of partial matching. For instance, a search query of *information technolog** (where * is the truncation symbol) would retrieve documents containing *information technology, information technologies*, and *information technologists*, as a result of partial matching.

Positional match is done by taking into consideration the positional information in the matching process. Proximity searching is a case in point. If a search query reads *used* 1WITH *store*, the retrieved results would include documents containing phrases such as *used book store, used clothing store*, and *used furniture store*. Here the matching between the query and the document representation is done only with the first and last words given, while the word in the middle position is ignored during the matching process.

Range match is applicable to numeric expressions (e.g., sales amount) or expressions with a natural order (e.g., January, February, ... December). What is being matched in range matching is the upper limit of the range (publications before year 2002), lower limit of the range (e.g., publications after 1992), or both (e.g., publications between 1993 and 2001). Numeric databases and publication dates are conventional examples of range searching.

All these four different types of term matching deal with the original queries and document representations without any calculation or conversion. Term matching is most often seen in the Boolean logic model. In other IR models (e.g., vector space and probability), terms in query and document representations are not directly matched. Rather, they would be transformed as some similarity measurements before being matched.

7.1.2 Similarity Measurement Matching

Similarity measurement matching can be done in a number of different ways. In the vector space model, for example, matching is based on the distance between vectors or the degree of vector angle; the smaller the vector angle, the higher the degree of similarity between queries and documents. In the probabilistic model, similarity can be calculated based on term frequency to determine the probability of relevance between queries and documents.

In matching of this kind, a similarity measure other than terms themselves must be chosen. It is on this measurement that the matching is finally made. On one hand, similarity measurement matching provides additional approaches to accomplishing the retrieval task. On the other hand, such a practice can introduce mistakes and noise, particularly in the process of obtaining similarity measurements.

Regardless of the matching type, matching is the essential mechanism in IR. The IR models discussed here demonstrate how matching is done in different circumstances, along with the models' respective features, advantages, and limitations.

7.2 The Boolean Logic Model

The Boolean logic model is named after George Boole, who proposed Boolean logic in the mid-19th century. Boolean logic covers three logical operations: the logical product (x), the logical sum (+), and the logical difference (-). Three corresponding operators, AND, OR, and NOT, are used to express the logical operations in IR. In the early versions of some internet retrieval systems, the plus sign (+) was used to represent the AND operator, which might have caused some confusion to the user because it actually stands for the OR operator in Boolean logic.

The logical product, or AND operator, combines two or more terms in a search statement and requires that all the terms be present in the documents to be retrieved. The logical sum, or OR operator, links two or more synonyms or related terms in a search statement. Documents that contain any one of the terms specified in the search statement would be regarded as hits or anticipated results. The logical difference, or NOT operator, limits searches by excluding terms listed after the NOT operator in queries. Specific examples of Boolean operator usage were given in §5.1.1.1 when the Boolean search technique was presented.

As indicated in §1.1.2.1, Mortimer Taube introduced Boolean logic to IR. With the rapid development of computerized IR systems, Boolean logic has been increasingly adopted and used. As we move into the digital age, few IR systems do not support the Boolean model of searching. In fact, the Boolean logic model has become a widely applied mechanism in IR (Spärck Jones & Willett, 1997). This does not mean, however, that Boolean logic is an IR model without limitations. To the contrary, discussions about the strengths and weaknesses of the Boolean logic model can be found in many publications (e.g., Chowdhury, 1999; Cooper, 1988; Frants, et al., 1999; Korfhage, 1997; Spärck Jones & Willett, 1997).

7.2.1 Strengths of the Boolean Logic Model

The extensive application of the Boolean logic model in IR proves the value of the model. First, it supports the manipulation of different facets obtained by decomposing a query or document. The AND operator can combine two simple facets to form a complex one, thus narrowing down a search. The OR operator allows the specification of alternative facets of a query or document, thus broadening a search. The NOT operator can separate complex facets into individual simple ones, thus excluding unwanted facets from appearing in final search results. Such manipulations, if applied appropriately, can bring flexibility and effectiveness to IR at a level with which no other existing IR models can compete.

Second, Boolean logic IR systems are cost-effective and already indispensable to the user (Frants, et al., 1999). Thousands of Boolean logic IR systems are operational. The end user can make use of the Boolean operators to broaden, narrow, or eliminate certain results from a search. In that sense, the Boolean logic model is well established—although some researchers (e.g., Belkin & Croft, 1987) have commented that the model became established more through practice than through theory.

Third, the Boolean logic model is well understood (Spärck Jones & Willett, 1997) even though there is much less discussion about what the model can accomplish than what the model is unable to do, which might be a result of two factors. One is that the Boolean logic model is the oldest among all IR models. It is assumed that its strengths are so well appreciated that no further elaboration is needed. The other factor is that Boolean logic, as the oldest IR model, will have to be criticized whenever a new IR model is presented. It is natural for people to state that a new IR model is built to overcome the limitations of the old one. The system designer and user alike would prefer to work with a model that is well understood.

Fourth, Boolean IR systems are relatively easy to build because the algorithms involved appear simpler to implement than those based on other IR models. That may also contribute in part to the wide implementation of Boolean IR systems. Because of the aforementioned strengths (e.g., the manipulation mechanism and wide usage), the Boolean logic model always receives a lot of attention whenever IR retrieval models are scrutinized in detail.

7.2.2 Limitations of the Boolean Logic Model

The limitations of the Boolean logic model, as indicated before, have been examined and explored thoroughly in many publications (e.g., Chowdhury, 1999; Cooper, 1988; Frants, et al., 1999; Korfhage, 1997; Spärck Jones & Willett,

1997). The following discussion is a recapitulation of the shortcomings of the model.

First, it is difficult for the user to conduct Boolean searches without a fair degree of training and practice. The difficulty lies in two aspects: 1) It is difficult for the user to choose the right Boolean operator. There usually exists confusion about the AND and OR operators among users because these two words have different meanings in conventional sense or common semantics. The word *and* traditionally means *plus*, as in, for example, "They will search for this topic at AltaVista *and* Google," while the word *or* implies *either one*, as in, for instance, "They will search for this topic at AltaVista *or* Google." Literally, more sites will be searched in the former case than in the latter one. Some users customarily think the same when they form Boolean queries, that is, they use the AND operator when they want more results, and they use the OR operator when they want fewer. Boolean logic obviously does not work that way. That difference would likely lead the user to choose the wrong operators, namely, using AND and OR operators in the wrong places. 2) It is difficult for the user to correctly employ the order of processing in compound Boolean searching. As described in §5.1.1.1, compound Boolean searching involves more than one type of Boolean operator, and the natural order of processing is defined as follows: the NOT operator first, the AND operator second, and the OR operator last. However, the natural order of processing for compound Boolean searching can be altered by applying parentheses when needed. Such alteration is, nevertheless, complicated and demanding, especially for novices. The user would not be able to become comfortable with the artificial rules (e.g., the innermost parentheses being processed first) for changing the natural order of processing for compound Boolean searches until given adequate training and practice.

Second, it is difficult to express relationships other than the Boolean among terms (e.g., causal relationship) because such a mechanism is simply not provided in the model. Suppose a user would like to find some information about the application of computers in education. A search query is then formed using the Boolean operator AND: *computers* AND *education*. The term *application* is not included in the query because this relationship is supposed to be expressed via Boolean operators, but none of them has this function. Consequently, by conducting the search *computers* AND *education*, the user would get information on not only the use of computers in education but also education about computers. Boolean search statements can certainly get very complicated. But there are still only three operators available to the user to link the concepts involved. It is generally true that the more complicated a search statement is, the more likely it will cause misinterpretations due to the inability of the Boolean logic model to express relationships other than the relationships of Boolean logic among terms.

Third, no weighting mechanism is available in the Boolean logic model to indicate the relative importance of different concepts in a search query. All the terms or concepts in Boolean queries are assumed to have the same degree of significance, which is not always true in IR. For example, suppose the search query is *information access* AND *security*, and the user would like to place more emphasis on the term *security*. In other words, the user would like to get information about the security issue in information access rather than treating both terms as equal in importance. Within a Boolean IR system, however, the user's expectation would not be met because no weights can be assigned to the query terms.

Fourth, it is impossible to express partial relevance of search results in the Boolean logic model because it simply divides all the data in a system into two categories: either relevant, when there is a match between the query and document representations, or irrelevant, when there is no match. Nothing is left in between. Therefore, Boolean logic systems cannot present results in order of decreasing relevance. Since there is no ranked output, the user cannot specify, for instance, that the 15 top-ranked documents be retrieved. The user has to sift through all the results, sometimes numbering in the thousands or more, that the Boolean system presents in no particular order of relevance. In that sense, the user has no control over the size of output in Boolean searches.

Fifth, the user may get null output or output overload when doing Boolean searching. Null output is possible if the search query is very restrictive, as when, for example, several terms are linked together by the AND operator. On the other hand, output overload may occur if the search query is broad, as when, for instance, several terms are linked together by the OR operator. The user can modify the search query for increasing or reducing search output. However, the outcome then will not be what the user was initially looking for but the output of the modified query.

To cope with the limitations of the Boolean model, Cooper (1988) suggested some possible solutions, such as formulating queries free of Boolean operators to manage the unfriendliness of Boolean queries. An excellent example of Cooper's suggestion is the search form, although it was not widely implemented till the late 1990s. Furthermore, a good number of algorithms and methods, including IR models, have also been developed for providing ranked outputs, weighted inputs, and the like. However, "other retrieval models that may be more interesting theoretically have not, in practice, achieved results that are distinctly superior to those of Boolean retrieval systems" (Korfhage, 1997, p. 63).

7.3 Vector Space Model

The vector space model, also known as vector processing or vector product retrieval, was developed by Salton and his colleagues, who built the System for the Manipulation And Retrieval of Texts (SMART) to serve as the base for conducting extended series of IR experiments (e.g., Salton, 1968). A series of IR techniques (e.g., term weighting, ranked output, and relevance feedback) were also devised in the process of building the model. Apart from Boolean logic, the vector space model has had the most influence on the development of IR and of operational IR systems (Spärck Jones & Willett, 1997).

In the vector space model, each term is defined as a dimension while each query or document is expressed as a vector. A vector actually consists of a list of term values representing an item (i.e., a query or document). Term values in a vector could be either binary or weighted. The binary values could be 1 or 0, with 1 indicating the existence of the term in the item. The weighted values include real positive numbers (e.g., 1.5, 0.3, 2.4, 5.6). The weighted value for each term corresponds to the relative importance of that term in representing the item (Kowalski, 1997). The scheme used for term weighting in the vector space model could be objective (e.g., term frequency) or subjective (e.g., user's perception). The weighting methods discussed in §5.1.2.2 are theoretically applicable in assigning weights to terms in a vector. Each weighting algorithm has its pros and cons. Korfhage (1997) discussed in detail the term frequency-based approach and the user's perception-based method for assigning weights to terms in a vector.

The number of dimensions in a query or document vector is equal to the number of different terms representing the item. All query and document vectors constitute the multidimensional space. The complete set of term values in a vector thus describes the position of the query or document it represents in the space (Spärck Jones & Willett, 1997).

Conducting a search in the vector space IR system means checking the distance, shown as an angle, between the query and document vectors in the space. The vector space model judges the similarity between a document and a query (or between any two documents) by comparing their corresponding dimensions and by calculating such similarity measurements as cosine coefficient. If a query and a document are on a similar topic, the angle between their vectors should be small. If a query and a document are on different topics, the angle between their vectors should be large (Lesk, 1997). Similarity between documents can be measured likewise.

7.3.1 Strengths of the Vector Space Model

The vector space model, according to Spärck Jones and Willett (1997), provides a unifying basis for a wide range of retrieval operations, including indexing, relevance feedback, and document classification. The strengths of the model become quite obvious when contrasted with the limitations of the Boolean logic model.

First, the user is no longer required to understand and apply Boolean logic when conducting searches in a vector space IR system. Rather, what the user needs to do is simply select several terms based on his or her information need.

Second, the terms or concepts chosen to represent the query or document can be weighted to indicate their relative importance in the vector. For example, if a query or document is mainly concerned with the security issue in networking, a higher weight can be assigned to the term *security* and a lower weight to the term *networking*. In that way, these two terms will not be treated as having equal importance in the vector, and a more appropriate representation of the query or document can be made.

Third, the output of vector space searches are ranked in order of decreasing relevance because the model expresses the similarity or relevance between documents or between the query and a document on a scale (e.g., from 0.0 to 1.0 with 1.0 being the most relevant) instead of a binary division (i.e., either relevant or irrelevant) as done in the Boolean logic model. Therefore, the user can go over, for example, the top 10 ranked documents only and still be assured that the remaining, unexamined results would not be more relevant to the query than the 10 documents being viewed. The fact that the user can limit the size of the retrieval output is an improvement over the Boolean logic model. Ranked output saves the user's time and energy in the IR process because the user does not have to view all the documents, often in the thousands, before deciding which ones are the most relevant. The system is able to choose and present the most relevant documents to the user automatically.

Fourth, relevance feedback is a mechanism implemented in the vector space model for improving retrieval performance. Based on the relevant outcome previously retrieved, the vector space IR system would be able to automatically modify the query vector and present the user with more relevant results. Relevance feedback can be completed without the involvement of the user, and the process can be repeated as many times as necessary. The user can activate the process in internet retrieval systems by simply choosing the option labeled, for instance, "More like this" or "More similar results."

As seen in this discussion, the vector space model has overcome some of the limitations associated with the Boolean logic model. However, the vector space model also introduced some new problems to the field of IR.

7.3.2 Limitations of the Vector Space Model

The first limitation of the vector space model is the assumption of independence between the terms selected for describing a vector. When the Boolean logic model is examined, it is pointed out that the model cannot express other kinds of relationships beyond Boolean logic. However, the vector space model is unable to convey any relationship, including the Boolean relationships, between the terms. Rather, it requires the assumption that terms forming the basis for the vector space are orthogonal or independent of each other. That assumption is apparently incorrect. If terms are selected to describe a document vector, say *automobiles*, *export*, and *import*, how can we assume that there is no relationship at all between the terms listed? This limitation has been criticized the most among all those that pertain to the model.

The second limitation of the vector space model is the difficulty in specifying explicitly synonymous or phrasal relationships due to the absence of the Boolean and proximity operators. To be more specific, the model does not support Boolean and proximity operators. Consequently, the OR operator cannot be used to indicate synonyms (as in *cars* OR *automobiles*), and the WITH operator cannot be employed to form phrases (as in *information* WITH *retrieval*) in a vector. Yet in actual searches, there are always occasions when synonyms or phrases are needed to represent queries or documents. It is therefore hard for the user to conduct searches without the Boolean and proximity facilities in the vector space IR system when synonymous or phrasal relationships have to be represented.

The third limitation of the vector space model relates to its weighting mechanism, which can be subjective and complex. The weighting process is subjective when the user is asked to assign weights to terms, particularly query terms, based on his or her own perception and judgment. The user is supposed to estimate the relative importance a term would have in the search and then assign a weight to it. Subjectivity is inevitable during that process. On the other hand, weighting can be complex in that no weighting algorithm works without a flaw, and finding the best algorithm for a particular retrieval environment is not an easy task. In addition, databases in IR systems are dynamic, as they need constant updating. Term weights should thus be changed accordingly because the parameters (e.g., term frequency) on which a weighting scheme is based have changed. Kowalski (1997) outlined a number of approaches to deal with the dynamically changing databases and the impact on weighting algorithms. But, as pointed out by Kowalski himself, none of the approaches can be implemented without some concerns (e.g., cost).

Apart from the three limitations just described, the vector space model also needs several terms to represent a query or document so that the vector can be discriminating enough for good retrieval performance. In comparison, "only two or three AND'ed terms may suffice in a Boolean environment to obtain a high-quality output" (Spärck Jones & Willett, 1997, p. 259). Assigning more terms in the vector space model would result in more expense. In addition, the model lacks theoretical justification for some of the vector manipulation operations. For example, the choice of a particular measure for computing vector similarity in using the IR model is not prescribed by any theoretical considerations. Instead, it is left to the user (Salton, 1989).

Ideally, the vector space model should place document vectors in such a way that those documents jointly relevant to certain queries are clustered together and those never wanted simultaneously would appear well separated in the space (Salton, Wong, & Yang, 1975). However, matching a query against clusters of documents, coined as the cluster hypothesis, has not been possible (Spärck Jones & Willett, 1997).

The vector space model was not applied in many operational IR systems until the advent of internet retrieval systems. The SMART system, serving as its test bed, enables the model to grow and mature. The creation of the vector space model has greatly enriched research and development in the IR field.

7.4 Probability Model

The probability model was introduced by Maron and Kuhns (1960) and further developed by Robertson and other researchers (e.g., Robertson & Spärck Jones, 1976). According to Spärck Jones and Willett (1997):

> The rationale for introducing probabilistic concepts is obvious: IR systems deal with natural language, and this is far too imprecise to enable a system to state with certainty which documents will be relevant to a particular query (a situation that is in marked contrast to the unambiguous retrieval operations that are required for searching in numeric database management systems). (p. 259)

The model applies the theory of probability, that is, an event has a possibility from 0 percent to 100 percent (0.0–1.0) of occurring, to IR. It takes into consideration the uncertainty element in the IR process, that is, uncertainty about whether documents retrieved by the system are relevant to a given query (Bookstein, 1985). The model intends to estimate and calculate the probability that a document will be relevant to a given query based on some methods. The event in this context of IR refers to the probability of relevance between a query and a document. Unlike other IR models, the probability model does not treat relevance as an exact miss-or-match measurement. Rather, relevance is expressed in terms of probability. For example, the model might tell a user that Document D has a 35 percent probability of being relevant to Query Q.

The model adopts various methods to determine the probability of relevance between queries and documents. Relevance in the probability model is judged according to the similarity between queries and documents. The similarity judgment is further dependent on *term frequency*. Generally speaking, the more similarity that exists between queries and the documents, the higher probability that those documents are relevant to the queries. In a probabilistic IR system, the results obtained for any query are supposed to consist of documents that satisfy that query with a probability higher than a specified threshold (Korfhage, 1997).

7.4.1 Strengths of the Probability Model

In comparison with the Boolean logic model or the vector space model, the probability model has the following strengths.

First, the model provides "an important guide for characterizing retrieval processes, as well as theoretical justification for practices used previously on an empirical basis such as the introduction of certain term-weighting systems" (Salton, 1989, pp. 348–349). The retrieval processes are characterized with a degree of uncertainty when the relevance between queries and documents is judged. It is more realistic to express the probability of relevance rather than pure relevance alone between queries and documents. Furthermore, major operations of the model, such as the query–document similarity measurement, are determined by the model itself instead of by some arbitrary decision, as in the vector space model.

Second, the model includes term dependencies and relationships (i.e., the occurrence of one event will affect the occurrence of the other in its operations. Users no longer need to assume independence between terms, as they have in the vector space model, an assumption not supported in practice. The model also weights query terms and association between queries and documents so that users can specify the relative importance of the term or association in the retrieval task. Ranked output is also provided because the model assumes that the principal function of an IR system is to rank the documents in a collection in order of decreasing probability of relevance to a user's information need (Spärck Jones & Willett, 1997). This assumption is called the probability ranking principle. Under the probability ranking principle, the user can have some control over the size of retrieval output. Both the weighting and ranking are expressed in probability.

Third, the model is able to take advantage of feedback information to develop well-founded methods (Bookstein, 1985). Similarly, Kowalski (1997) pointed out that this model could accurately identify its weak assumptions and work to strengthen them. The self-improving feature adds another positive element to the probability model.

Fourth, the probability model in its original form does not employ the Boolean logic facility that many users find hard to apply. In that sense, IR systems based on the probability model are more user-friendly than Boolean-based IR systems.

7.4.2 Limitations of the Probability Model

The limitations of the probability model have also been scrutinized from different perspectives since its creation. A brief summary of them follows.

First, although the relevance value in this model is continuous instead of the dichotomous 0 or 1, as in the Boolean model, the probability model assumes that relevance has a binary property, that is,

$$Pr_{(nonrel)} = 1 - Pr_{(rel)}$$

where $Pr_{(rel)}$ is the probability of relevance, and $Pr_{(nonrel)}$ is the probability of nonrelevance. In other words, the value for the probability of irrelevance is fixed once the probability of relevance is computed, thus eliminating the intrinsic uncertainty factor from the IR process. Just as Robertson (1977) noted, the assumption of dichotomy is a strong one and almost certainly not generally valid.

Second, the probability model cannot greatly improve retrieval effectiveness. Results obtained using the probability model, although good, have not been sufficiently better than those retrieved from the Boolean logic or vector space systems. A question would naturally arise regarding the necessity of having an additional IR model when it would perform only as well as the existing models.

Aside from the two limitations just discussed, the model has other weaknesses. For example, sophistication in mathematics is required to understand and use the probability theory, which could affect the accessibility of the model. Moreover, the model has many variations. There are disagreements over which methods are the best and how to resolve various technical questions even though a consensus exists on the general model (Bookstein, 1985). Similar to the vector space model, the probability model was, until the emergence of internet retrieval systems, used for experimental purposes more than it was applied in operational IR systems.

7.5 Extensions of Major Information Retrieval Models

Boolean logic, vector space, and probability are in general regarded as the three major IR models. Each of them has some extensions. For instance, extended Boolean logic is an extension of the Boolean logic model and vector space model in combination. Fuzzy set is also based on the Boolean logic model but additionally introduces the set theory into IR. Latent semantic indexing is a derivation of the vector space model. It is designed to find a smaller set of dimensions and values that can be used as a substitute for the original matrix (Lesk, 1997). Inference network, an extension of the probability model, ranks documents in order of decreasing probability so that they satisfy the user's information need rather than the probability that they are relevant, as in the basic probability model (Spärck Jones & Willett, 1997).

Additional extensions of the major IR models can be found in the taxonomy of IR models presented by Baeza-Yates and Ribeiro-Neto (1999). Two of the better-known extensions, extended Boolean logic and fuzzy set, will be examined further in the following two sections.

7.5.1 Extended Boolean Logic Model

As mentioned earlier, the Boolean logic model has the disadvantage of not incorporating term weights, and the vector space model has the weakness of not being capable of expressing Boolean logical relationships. The extended Boolean logic model was developed to have weighted terms while keeping the Boolean structure. Although Bookstein and others have also conducted research on this topic (e.g., Bookstein, 1978), it was Harry Wu who, under the supervision of Gerard Salton, formally introduced the extended Boolean logic model when he was writing his dissertation (Salton, Fox, & Wu, 1983; Wu, 1981).

In the extended Boolean logic model, term weights are assigned based on any combination of the following parameters: proximity, location, frequency, and perceived relevance. Thanks to the term weighting feature, the model can also provide ranked output and thus control the number of retrieved documents. Meanwhile, the advantages of the structured Boolean query formation are preserved.

But, the extended Boolean logic model has not been widely implemented in IR due to the following reasons: First, it is hard to assign term weights effectively and accurately because of the same issues outlined in §7.3.2 regarding the limitations of the vector space model. Second, logically equivalent queries may fail to produce the same results when different weights are assigned to query terms (Korfhage, 1997). Normally, more documents will be retrieved for the term with a larger weight. Nevertheless, the model attempts to cope with the limitations of the Boolean logic and vector space models by combining their respective strengths. Some internet retrieval systems (e.g., Google) support extended Boolean logic searching.

7.5.2 Fuzzy Set Model

The fuzzy set model, initially proposed by Zadeh (1965), aims to overcome one limitation of the Boolean logic model (i.e., inability to express a partial relevance of search results) by generalizing the traditional set theory. In a traditional set, an object is either in the set or not in the set. Similarly, a document is either relevant or not relevant to a given query in the Boolean system. This sharp boundary separates members of a set from nonmembers, or relevant documents from irrelevant ones. But such a clear-cut line virtually is nonexistent in IR because the system and often the user cannot accurately tell whether a document is relevant to a particular query (Korfhage, 1997). Rather, partial relevance should be a more precise reflection of the judgment.

The concept of partial membership, in correspondence with the notion of partial relevance needed to improve the Boolean logic model, is known as fuzzy set theory. The model assumes that fuzzy documents and queries do not exist but fuzzy judgment can be made. For fuzzy sets, degrees of membership are identified in the range of 0.0 to 1.0, with 1.0 indicating full membership. An object can belong to a set partially by having a membership grade between 0.0 and 1.0. The boundary that divides members and nonmembers of a set thus becomes fuzzy.

For example, a set of top students is to be selected to form an honors class. The selection can be done in two ways. One is to use traditional set theory by exactly defining "top students" as those who hold a GPA of 3.9 and above. Any student who meets the specification will become a member of the honors class. All students whose GPAs are below 3.9 will not be admitted into or become a member of the class, even though some of them may have a GPA of 3.89. In contrast, the other method for selecting top students for an honors class employs the fuzzy set theory by assigning a membership grade to each student. Top students are therefore defined by the membership grades they receive. Those who have a GPA of 3.9 should be given a membership grade of 1.0 while students whose GPAs are, for instance, 3.5 or below will get a membership grade close to 0.0. Students with a GPA in between, say 3.8, will receive a membership grade of 0.8, for example. In that way, students who did not get a GPA of 3.9 can still be included in the set of top students, with their membership grades showing their connection with the set.

In application of the fuzzy set theory to IR, the relevance of documents should not be judged as relevant or irrelevant only, as done in the Boolean logic system. Instead, a membership grade can be assigned to a document to indicate how close it belongs to the set of relevant documents. Membership grades for the fuzzy set of documents are determined by the indexer during the indexing process (Bookstein, 1985).

The strengths of the fuzzy set model include the relaxation of the restriction in the Boolean logic model, namely, that documents are either relevant or irrelevant to a query, with no partial relevance allowed. In assigning the membership grade, the fuzzy set IR system can provide ranked output in decreasing order of relevance so the user can choose to view the top-ranked results. In addition, the Boolean query structure is preserved in the model for expressing logical relationships. Systems based on the fuzzy set model are good for exploratory retrieval.

The fuzzy set IR system is not as flexible as desired, however, because it does not assign weights to query terms as opposed to document terms. The retrieval values of the documents therefore depend only on the values of document terms (Salton, 1989). This statement is about the consequence of keeping the Boolean framework in the fuzzy set model. In such Boolean searches using the OR operator (e.g., A OR B OR C), a document D1 with only one query term (i.e., A) is assumed to be as important as document D2 containing all query terms (i.e., A, B, C). Obviously, the value or relevance for document D1 is judged on only one term (i.e., A) in this case, due to the fact that query terms are not weighted. As for queries using the AND operator (e.g., A AND B AND C), document D1 containing all query terms but one (i.e., A, B) is considered as useless or irrelevant as document D2 having no query term at all.

In addition, compared with the vector space model, the fuzzy set model provides no mechanism for query expansion. In contrast to the probability model, the fuzzy set model is less robust, at least theoretically. The model is applied only sporadically in the field of IR.

7.6 Information Retrieval Models: A Further Look

As indicated at the beginning of this chapter, the IR models and extensions illustrated up to this point are primarily system-based. Other IR models are built on different parameters. For example, the cognitive model takes into consideration the user factor in IR and will be discussed in Chapter 10.

7.6.1 A Review of the Major Information Retrieval Models

Verbatim descriptions of the three major IR models, i.e., Boolean logic, vector space, and probability, have been given in the previous sections. Table 7.1 is intended to summarize some important characteristics of these models.

The three IR models listed in Table 7.1 are reviewed from five different aspects: 1) Is Boolean logic supported? 2) Is term weighting provided? 3) Is output ranked? 4) Which matching criterion is used to determine similarity between queries and documents? 5) Any unique feature? These five aspects, to a large extent, determine the strengths and limitations of the IR models. For example, the availability of the Boolean search facility enables the user to compose structured queries. On the other hand, the same feature (i.e., Boolean logic) would also make an IR system user unfriendly because of the difficulty involved in conducting Boolean searches.

The Boolean logic model seems to be the weakest among the three listed in Table 7.1. It only supports Boolean searching, and matching is based on the presence of a term in the system. But the model is heavily used and applied widely in IR. The other two models appear similar on the surface in that they both, in their original form, do not include Boolean logic but provide the weighting and ranking mechanism. The criteria used by the vector space and probability models for weighting terms, ranking outputs, and measuring similarity are nevertheless dissimilar. In addition, relevance feedback is introduced as a unique retrieval capability in the vector space model. Efforts have been made to use the vector space or probability model to develop better IR systems. Such systems, however, have not been able to markedly outperform systems based on the Boolean logic model (Korfhage, 1997).

Table 7.1 Features of Three Information Retrieval Models

Feature \ Model	Boolean Logic	Vector Space	Probability
Boolean Logic	Yes		
Weighting		Yes	Yes
Ranking		Yes	Yes
Matching Criterion	Term presence	Vector distance	Term frequency
Unique Feature		Relevance feedback	

7.6.2 Information Retrieval Models Versus Retrieval Techniques

In Chapter 5 various retrieval techniques were presented and discussed. What is the relationship then between IR models and retrieval techniques? While there is no exact or explicit one-to-one association between the two, some of the retrieval techniques are clearly connected with the IR models from which they are derived. For instance, Boolean searching is no doubt an application of the Boolean logic model. Query expansion, particularly relevance feedback, is supported by the vector space model. Weighted searching can be based on algorithms developed in the probability model or other IR models, such as the extended Boolean.

Aside from those retrieval techniques, whose origins are evidently marked, the remaining ones are also backed by IR models. For example, proximity searching has its root in the extended Boolean model. Moreover, retrieval techniques do not have to come from the same IR model to be used together during the searching process. They could be applied side by side regardless of their sources of origin if an IR system is so designed. In fact, the building of multimodel IR systems should be encouraged, as discussed in §7.6.3.

Knowledge about the relationship between the IR models and retrieval techniques can help in choosing the right systems for retrieval tasks. One obvious example is that a Boolean system must be chosen if the user wants to do Boolean searches. If weighted searching is to be conducted, the user must choose an IR system based on, for instance, the vector space model.

7.6.3 Toward Multimodel Information Retrieval Systems

IR models, as demonstrated in this chapter, have their pros and cons. IR systems applying these models consequently can perform only certain retrieval functions as defined. To take advantage of the strengths different IR models possess, IR systems should be constructed by incorporating features from multiple IR models. A similar idea was expressed by Frants and others (Frants, et al., 1999), although they call systems using many IR principles "multiversion systems."

The current practices in the field of IR indicate that Boolean logic is the only model used in almost every IR system, while other models are gradually implemented in systems such as internet retrieval systems. Information queries can be very rudimentary as well as extremely sophisticated. IR systems for processing these queries should be designed accordingly by adopting a multimodel approach. Multimodel IR systems are increasingly seen on the internet, which is becoming a major platform for IR systems.

The remaining question about multimodel IR systems is how the various IR models should be integrated. Projects such as the Text REtrieval Conferences (TREC) can provide some guidance. The target users of an IR system should also be surveyed to better understand their information needs in this digital age.

References

Baeza-Yates, Ricardo, and Ribeiro-Neto, Berthier. (1999). *Modern information retrieval.* New York: ACM Book Press.

Belkin, Nicholas J., and Croft, W. Bruce. (1987). Retrieval techniques. *Annual Review of Information Science and Technology*, 22, 109–145.

Bookstein, Abraham. (1978). On the perils of merging Boolean and weighted retrieval systems. *Journal of the American Society for Information Science*, 29(3), 156–158.

Bookstein, Abraham. (1985). Probability and fuzzy-set applications to information retrieval. *Annual Review of Information Science and Technology*, 20, 117–151.

Chowdhury, Gobinda G. (1999). *Introduction to modern information retrieval.* London: Library Association Publishing.

Cooper, W. S. (1988). Getting beyond Boole. *Information Processing & Management*, 24, 243–248.

Frants, Valery I., et al. (1999). Boolean search: Current state and perspectives. *Journal of the American Society for Information Science*, 50(1), 86–95.

Ingwersen, Peter, and Järvelin, Kalervo. (2005). *The turn: Integrating of information seeking and retrieval in context.* Dordrecht, The Netherlands: Springer.

Korfhage, Robert R. (1997). *Information storage and retrieval.* New York: John Wiley & Sons.

Kowalski, Gerald. (1997). *Information retrieval systems: Theory and implementation.* Boston: Kluwer Academic Publishers.

Lesk, Michael. (1997). *Practical digital libraries: Books, bytes and bucks.* San Francisco: Morgan Kaufmann.

Maron, M. E., and Kuhns, J. L. (1960). On relevance, probabilistic indexing and information retrieval. *Journal of the ACM*, 7, 216–244.

Robertson, S. E. (1977). The probability ranking principle in IR. *Journal of Documentation*, 33, 294–304.

Robertson, S. E., and Spärck Jones, K. (1976). Relevance weighting of search terms. *Journal of the American Society for Information Science*, 27, 129–146.

Salton, Gerard. (1968). *Automatic information organization and retrieval.* New York: McGraw-Hill.

Salton, Gerard. (1989). *Automatic text processing: The transformation, analysis, and retrieval of information by computer.* New York: Addison-Wesley.

Salton, G., Fox, E. A., and Wu, H. (1983). Extended Boolean information retrieval. *Communications of the ACM*, 26, 1022–1036.

Salton, G., Wong, A., and Yang, C. S. (1975). A vector space model for automatic indexing. *Communications of the ACM*, 18, 613–620.

Soukhanov, Anne H., et al. (Eds.). (1984). *Webster's II new Riverside university dictionary.* Boston: Riverside Publishing Co.

Spärck Jones, Karen, and Willett, Peter. (Eds.). (1997). *Readings in information retrieval.* San Francisco: Morgan Kaufmann.

Wu, Harry. (1981). *On query formulation in information retrieval.* Unpublished doctoral dissertation, Cornell University, Ithaca, NY.

Zadeh, L. A. (1965). Fuzzy sets. *Information and Control*, 8, 338–353.

CHAPTER 8

Information Retrieval Systems

Tasks of information retrieval (IR) are accomplished in IR systems. Different types of IR systems have been developed since the 1950s to meet different kinds of information needs. Online systems, CD-ROM systems, online public access catalogs (OPACs), and internet retrieval systems are the four major categories of IR systems that have served users in various capacities to satisfy their information requests. In this chapter, each of the system types will be examined to show conceptually their features, functions, and capabilities in IR.

8.1 Online Systems: Pioneer Information Retrieval Systems

Online IR systems, also referred to as professional online systems, are often abbreviated as online systems or online databases. The word database is treated as a synonym for system in the latter case. They are the first kinds of IR systems that have applied computer technology. DIALOG and MEDLINE are two examples of online IR systems.

Online systems allow the user, with the help of the computer and telecommunication technology, to search databases located remotely. The systems initially supported only batch mode (i.e., an individual search request is not processed immediately after its submission but later, when a certain number of requests have been assembled) and later introduced real-time interaction between user and system. There are three stages in the development of online systems (Bourne, 1980):

- Feasibility studies and demonstration projects: 1950s

- Production with restricted user populations: 1960s

- National or multinational IR services: 1970s to present

Hahn (1996) presented a detailed account of the pioneers involved in the development of online systems. Bourne and Hahn (2003) narrated the developments of online systems between 1963 and 1976. After the advancements and improvements made since the 1950s, online systems have become a distinct group of IR systems in the digital age.

8.1.1 Features of Online Information Retrieval Systems

Online systems collected mainly bibliographic and some numeric information before the 1980s and eventually included full-text information. Multimedia information is not often seen in this type of retrieval system. Information included in online systems is selected and represented by professionals (e.g., indexers). Controlled vocabulary is extensively used for information representation and retrieval (IRR), and keyword searching is supported at the same time. Command language was the norm for users to interact with online systems until menu selection was introduced in the 1980s. Graphical interface was gradually employed in the 1990s, especially when online systems started adopting the web as their platform.

A great variety of retrieval techniques and IR models have been applied in online systems. Basic retrieval techniques, such as Boolean searching, case-sensitivity searching, truncation, proximity searching, and field searching, are available in almost every online system. Advanced retrieval techniques such as weighted searching, fuzzy searching, and query expansion, though not supported in all online systems, can be found in some applications. In fact, online systems prior to the mid-1990s served as test beds for IR research and development. They also functioned as showcases for new IR technologies before the emergence of internet retrieval systems. For example, DIALOG implemented ranked output by introducing the RANK command in 1993 (Basch, 1993).

In addition, online systems can be regarded as a laboratory for acquiring IR skills for several reasons. First, the system is constructed to allow structured practice and manipulation. Some online systems even set up special facilities (e.g., DIALOG's ONTAP files and workshops) to help train users. Second, online systems represented the only computerized IR systems at that time. Third, a wide range of retrieval skills can be tried and practiced in online systems. The fourth reason is nevertheless on the negative side: It is assumed that online system users must receive training before using it. The system is not intuitive and cannot be learned simply by trial and error. As a result, end users in online searching are generally information professionals who take up the role of search intermediaries between the system and the user with information needs.

8.1.2 Online Systems and Information Retrieval

Among the four types of IR systems identified in this chapter, online systems have the longest history and have had the greatest influence in IR. They implicitly set standards for others to follow. Whenever a new kind of IR system emerges, people always compare it with online systems to see how well the newcomer can do in the field. For example, Nahl-Jakobovits and Tenopir

(1992) investigated the factors of response time, coverage, content, and cost in both the CD-ROM and online versions of Psychological Abstracts and Sociological Abstracts. Hildreth (1988) contrasted OPACs with online IR systems and explored the incorporation of online system features in OPACs. Chu (1998) compared internet retrieval systems with online systems in aspects such as database structure, search capability, retrieval performance, output option, and user effort.

Online systems have apparently established themselves as the benchmark systems in IR. As mentioned previously, however, online systems are by no means perfect. High cost and user unfriendliness are attributes frequently ascribed to online systems. On the other hand, the pioneering role that online systems have played in IR is also widely acknowledged.

8.2 CD-ROM Systems: A Different Medium for Information Retrieval Systems

CD-ROM systems emerged from the application of CD-ROM technology in IR and have accomplished for the most part what they were designed to in the field of IR as web technology matures. They are described in this chapter chiefly to provide a complete picture of the IR system landscape. CD-ROM systems are usually searched locally and do not rely on telecommunication for access if the systems are not networked. PsycLIT from SilverPlatter was an example of a CD-ROM system.

CD-ROM systems can be regarded somewhat as online systems in the CD-ROM medium because these two kinds of IR systems share many features and because CD-ROM systems are modeled after online systems in many ways. Furthermore, CD-ROM systems were not implemented on a large scale until the 1980s, when online systems had already become very influential in the field.

There seem to be no obvious phases in the development of CD-ROM systems. One main reason for this phenomenon is that CD-ROM systems did not start from scratch but emerged rather as a marriage between CD-ROMs and the mature online systems, using the former as new storage medium. Therefore, the unique features of CD-ROM systems are determined to a large extent by the characteristics of the CD-ROM medium.

8.2.1 Features of CD-ROM Systems

Bibliographic, numeric, and full-text information remain the dominant information sources processed in CD-ROM systems. But an increase in multimedia information storage occurred as CD-ROM technology became more capable than online systems of handling such types of information. It is the multimedia CD-ROM systems that remain operational in some circumstances (e.g., encyclopedias). Controlled vocabulary is used for IRR in conjunction with natural language. Human involvement continues to be heavy in CD-ROM retrieval. Command language is seen less often in CD-ROM systems whereas menu selection is implemented more often. Graphic interface made its debut in the CD-ROM environment, and some systems even applied the hyperstructure in their implementations.

Basic retrieval techniques (e.g., Boolean searching and proximity searching) are supported in CD-ROM systems, and advanced search facilities (e.g., weighted searching and output ranking) are applied in a limited scope. It is not uncommon to see that one single system is stored on several CD-ROMs, which may restrict the application of some advanced retrieval technologies in the system.

Thanks to their high storage capacity and relatively small physical size, CD-ROM systems are theoretically portable because several disks can hold all the information needed in a database. However, the database alone cannot function as an IR system. Special equipment is required to run the system. On the other hand, it is more convenient for the user to search in CD-ROM systems, as they are not dependent on telecommunication technology to be functional. It is cheaper to conduct CD-ROM searches since they do not incur connection or other charges once the systems are purchased and installed. Users therefore can conduct searches without worrying if the clock is ticking and can concentrate more on the search itself.

The end user, rather than the intermediary, does most of the searching in the CD-ROM environment. One reason is that, according to the policy of fixed fee and unlimited access, CD-ROM systems usually impose no extra charges to the end user. Second, the interface of CD-ROM systems is friendlier than that of online systems as a result of the implementation of menu selection and graphic interfaces. Third, CD-ROM systems encourage browsing because online cost is not a concern to the end-user in this case. As discussed in Chapter 6, browsing and searching are the two major retrieval approaches, and the former is favored in some circumstances. By comparison, browsing in an online retrieval session is costly.

CD-ROM systems, however, have limitations in updating. Each update means the replacement of existing CD-ROM disks, which significantly limits the updating frequency. Typical update frequency for CD-ROM systems is quarterly or biannually. Yet the online counterparts of CD-ROM systems can be updated weekly, daily, or even continuously (e.g., Bridge World Markets News on DIALOG). Speed in searching CD-ROM systems can also be a problem, particularly when one system is spread over several CD-ROMs. CD-ROM systems also do not allow remote access if they are not networked. All these limitations contribute to the replacement of CD-ROM technology by the World Wide Web in this type of IR system.

8.2.2 CD-ROM Systems and Information Retrieval

CD-ROM systems have filled some voids that are not covered by online systems in IR by reaching out to the end user and by providing retrieval services to people for whom online systems might be too expensive or difficult to use. A large percentage of CD-ROM systems have corresponding online versions although their coverage and features may not be the same.

CD-ROM as a storage medium is gradually being replaced by the digital versatile disk (DVD), a more recent optical disk technology. With two layers on each of its two sides, a DVD holds up to 17 gigabytes of video, audio, or other information. In comparison, a current CD-ROM disk of the same physical size holds less than 700 megabytes of information (Tech Target, 2005). As DVDs represent a more advanced technology, they are replacing CD-ROMs as the medium for portable IR systems of multimedia information. Other functions of CD-ROM systems are gradually being taken over by web technology.

8.3 OPACs: Computerized Library Catalogs as Information Retrieval Systems

OPACs are traditional catalogs executed in a different medium (Malinconico, 1984). Before 1980, there were only some pioneering efforts, such as the Library Control System at the State University of Ohio. Since 1980, however, prototype and operational OPACs have been installed in a steadily growing number of libraries (Hildreth, 1985). Few libraries nowadays do not have an OPAC in their systems.

OPACs, either stand-alone or as part of an integrated library automation system such as Horizon from SirsiDynix, are an outcome of library automation. OPACs were first developed by both vendors and in-house teams. The latter option ceased to exist when library automation system vendors became more experienced and established. OPAC interfaces have been changed from command language to menu selection, form fill-in, and graphical presentations.

Hildreth (1984) classified OPACs into three generations to chart their recent history and predict their possible future design. The first generation of OPACs emulates more or less the card catalog approach to file content, organization, and access for mainly known-item searching. The second generation of OPACs adds enhancements in subject access points, search capabilities, and other aspects. OPACs of this generation resemble online systems in many ways. The third generation of OPACs, becoming a reality nowadays, makes the division between OPACs and online systems less visible by having expanded access. The user can search online databases and other resources via the OPAC of one's local library. Some other enhancements (e.g., integration of free text and controlled vocabulary search approaches) projected by Hildreth in 1984 for this generation of OPACs have also materialized.

The numbering of OPAC generations seems to have ended with the third one. Instead, OPACs different from those in previous generations are variously labeled as, for example, next generation and 21st-century OPACs (Antelman, Lynema, & Pace, 2006; Hildreth, 1995; Markey, 2007). The next generation of OPACs emerged by adapting to the digital environment of IRR and incorporating proven retrieval technologies (e.g., Antelman, Lynema, & Pace, 2006). Typically, the web becomes the platform for this generation of OPACs, enabling attainment of assorted features the web provides. For example, OPACs of this kind allow users to interact with the system via the web browser and interface. Consequently, no additional learning of this retrieval environment is necessary for OPAC users because they are already familiar with it. Links to other resources (e.g., ebooks and ejournal articles) can be created from OPAC records for seamless access in addition to having hyperlinked subject headings within the OPAC for modifying searches.

On the other hand, retrieval techniques established particularly in internet retrieval systems are introduced into OPACs, which include relevance feedback, ranking of search results, improved environment for browsing, and spell checking of search queries. The online catalog of the North Carolina State University Libraries (www.lib.ncsu.edu/catalog), implemented in 2006, is often cited as one example of the next generation OPACs (Antelman, Lynema, & Pace, 2006; Markey, 2007). This new generation of OPACs undoubtedly demonstrates improvements and enhancements over its predecessors; however, much of what Hildreth (1995) and Markey (2007) outlined in their wish lists for future OPAC systems remains to be achieved.

8.3.1 Features of OPACs

Changes and developments are made as OPACs evolve from one generation to another. But there are certain features that seem unique to OPACs as one type of IR system. First, OPACs contain bibliographic information about library resources for institutions at various levels (e.g., local, regional, and national). Although one OPAC is built for one library most of the time, there are occasions in which one OPAC includes resources for multiple libraries. In contrast, the other three types of IR systems do not limit their coverage to documents at one institution or more.

Second, OPACs can be considered as an extension of MAchine Readable Cataloging (MARC; i.e., a cataloging standard) records that are typically prepared by librarians using a set of rules and standards (e.g., classification schemes and cataloging rules) for the user population the library serves. Information representation in other kinds of IR systems cannot be done by using almost identical guidelines and with specific target users in mind. For example, DIALOG alone has hundreds of databases in its system. Each database is likely to be built and maintained using a different controlled vocabulary. While it is possible to define the user community of a library, it seems hard to clearly identify who would use an online system, let alone the apparently immeasurable and ever-changing internet retrieval systems.

Third, OPACs presently support at least field searching (e.g., author, title), keyword searching, and Boolean searching although library patrons make little use of the Boolean facility, for the reasons discussed in previous chapters. Known-item searching constitutes a significant portion of all OPAC searches, in part because OPACs are more likely than online systems to cover items "known" to the user. Advanced search features (e.g., weighted searching) are usually not provided for OPACs because good retrieval performance is possible to achieve even by using the basic searching facility and thanks to the well-defined library collection. In the so-called next generation OPACs, however, relevance feedback is often supported via such hyperlinks as "similar results." Users can also search within their retrieved results to locate more specific items, which is a feature newly added to this generation of OPAC systems.

Fourth, many present generation OPACs provide access to other resources, including online systems. In comparison, online systems cannot offer such gateway services due to their for-profit nature. With the help of Z39.50—a standard for retrieving information from different sources using a uniform interface—users can search other OPACs at different locations. As depicted in §5.1.2.4, Search/Retrieve Web Service (SRW) and Search/Retrieve via URL (SRU) together can supersede Z39.50 by providing similar functionality but with less complexity (LeVan, 2003).

Fifth, the design of OPACs encourages browsing, in that OPAC users can typically browse by access points such as author and title, whereas other types of IR systems usually present results chronologically or by relevance ranking. Browsing by call number in OPACs is particularly helpful to the user because the presentation order of the results bears a resemblance to the physical shelving order of library items. OPAC users thus are given the opportunity to locate related items shelved next to each other before going to the shelves in person.

However, OPACs are still hard to use despite the fact that most of the OPACs now belong to the third generation. Borgman (1986, 1996) attributed the negative end result to the design of OPACs, which fails to incorporate lessons learned from IR studies, and to insufficient understanding of searching behavior. The assumption that users without training should be able to use OPACs (Hildreth, 1988) is still not adequately supported today.

OPACs became the jewel in the IR system crown between the early 1980s and late 1990s, when they were compared with card catalogs and fee-based online systems. They are steadily falling from favor as internet retrieval systems evolve and improve in terms of retrieval capability and user friendliness. Literature published after the golden age of OPACs expresses serious concerns about their current state and future status, while Google, the increasingly popular internet retrieval system, not only dominates web searching but also expands its services beyond (e.g., Google Book Search and Google Scholar). Google's success in web searching, as well as its expansion into OPAC territory, seems to be the major source of such concerns (Marcum, 2006; Markey, 2007).

8.3.2 OPACs and Information Retrieval

The question about whether OPACs are library catalogs or online IR systems was asked in the past (Hildreth, 1985). The answer to this question today should be that OPACs are IR systems with their own characteristics. OPACs have been helping users locate materials in library collections and benefit from functionalities unheard in their predecessors, card catalogs. In addition, OPACs serve as a gateway to other IR systems by making linkages to them. As monographs are usually a major category of library materials, OPACs are the chief, if not the only, retrieval tool for accessing them. Without OPACs, library collections would become inaccessible in this digital age because other kinds of IR systems are not designed specifically for that purpose.

The creation of Google Book Search, as mentioned earlier, has changed and even challenged the dominant role OPACs play in locating book information. Google Book Search, initially named Google Print, started in 2004 with a group of publishers (e.g., Blackwell, Cambridge University Press, the University of Chicago Press) and two months later with libraries at several institutions (e.g., Harvard, University of Michigan, New York Public Library, Oxford, and Stanford) as its Library Project (Google, 2008a). The number of participants in this project has steadily increased since then. Books included in this project are searchable after being digitized. In addition, Google Book Search has such features as links to book reviews and citing sources (e.g., webpages) of the book being searched. Indisputably, Google Book Search facilitates book IR with an approach different from the OPAC method. Google Book Search, along with its web search system, also makes OPACs reexamine their own position, functionality, and performance in this digital age of IR (Marcum, 2006).

8.4 Internet Retrieval Systems: The Newest Member in the Family of Information Retrieval Systems

The exponential growth of the internet makes it possible for people to access large quantities of digital information regardless of time and geographical locations. Meanwhile, it becomes obvious that additional IR systems are needed for retrieving any particular "needles" from the internet "haystack." Individuals, companies, and institutions have subsequently developed a great number of internet retrieval systems, or IR systems for the internet, to cope with the information explosion on the internet.

As known, the phrase *web search engine*, or simply *search engine*, seems a more popular name than internet retrieval system when people make reference to systems for retrieving information from the internet. However, this book uses the latter because the former appears too narrow in meaning. First, the web is only one application, although currently the dominant one, of the internet. Information handled by other applications, such as file transfer protocol (FTP), is also covered by internet retrieval systems. Therefore, naming internet retrieval systems *web search engines* would imply that they deal only with information on the web and exclude information originating from other internet applications. Second, some internet applications had their own search facilities (e.g., Archie for FTP information)—although many have been phased out or have started using the web as the platform. Third, internet retrieval tools can be directory-based (e.g., Yahoo!) or search-based (e.g., AltaVista). It would then be inappropriate to refer to directory-based internet retrieval systems as web search engines because searching was not supported in their original design. The searching component now available in many directory-based internet retrieval systems is a result of the union between the two different types of systems, as will be discussed later.

More information will be presented in this book about internet retrieval systems than about other types of IR systems for two reasons. The first is that internet retrieval systems are newer than others in the family of IR systems. The second is that other systems have been studied in depth by many researchers over the years (e.g., online systems by Harter, 1986; Large, Tedd, & Hartley, 1999; Meadow, Boyce, & Kraft, 1999; Walker & Janes, 1999; CD-ROM systems by Chowdhury, 1999; Rowley & Slack, 1997; OPACs by Beaulieu & Borgman, 1996; Hildreth, 1985), but internet retrieval systems have yet to be examined thoroughly and systematically.

8.4.1 Taxonomy of Internet Retrieval Systems

Internet retrieval systems, though with a short history, come in great numbers and varieties. It has been impossible to enumerate how many internet retrieval systems are available on the internet since these systems began mushrooming in the mid-1990s. However, a categorization of internet retrieval systems by the following criteria is intended to provide an overview of the newest member in the IR family.

8.4.1.1 Classification by Retrieval Approach

Searching and browsing are the two major retrieval approaches described in Chapter 6. On the internet, retrieval systems based on searching are called search engines (e.g., AltaVista and Google) whereas IR systems based on browsing are called directories (e.g., Yahoo!). Directories are also often referred to as catalogs. Search engines let users compose their own search queries. By contrast, directories organize and present network resources under hierarchically structured categories. Users of directory-based internet retrieval systems can locate information by following a predefined path, that is, the hierarchy of categories developed for the system.

As discussed in Chapter 6, either searching or browsing as a retrieval approach has its limitations. For instance, search queries are difficult to formulate but are required in search-based internet retrieval systems. Internet users have to compose their own queries because information professionals usually do not act as intermediaries in this environment. Similarly, the number of results retrieved from the internet for most topics can easily exceed thousands, if not millions. But browsing, as a retrieval approach, has no mechanism for narrowing a retrieval problem. Consequently, internet retrieval systems attempt to surmount such difficulties by supporting both browsing and searching at the same site. The directory-based internet retrieval systems used to license search engines to provide the search component at their sites. The search-based internet retrieval systems likewise contracted with directory services to offer the browsing option at their sites. The partnerships between these two kinds of internet retrieval systems nevertheless changed constantly and eventually became a nonissue when major players in this area began developing both a search engine and a directory of their own systems.

The combination of browsing and searching at one site produces the third type of internet retrieval systems, namely, hybrid internet retrieval systems. In the hybrid environment, the user can search or browse at the same site without switching to another. Retrieval effectiveness is improved subsequently.

8.4.1.2 Classification by Application

Since the creation of the internet, many different applications have been developed: telnet, FTP, gopher, wide area information servers (WAISs), and the web or World Wide Web, to name a few. Each of these applications performs certain functions. For example, Telnet is for remote login from a local system so that resources (e.g., hardware and software) at the remote site can be used. FTP is for transferring files between remote systems and local ones seamlessly at high speed. The web is the largest information repository on the internet because of its friendly user interface and hypermedia feature. Gopher, an obsolete application today and completely superseded by the web, was designed for storing and retrieving resources on the internet with hypermenu interface. WAIS, on the other hand, was a Z39.50-compliant keyword search tool for internet resources. At one point or another, retrieval systems were built for all these applications except WAIS, because it consisted of a retrieval mechanism itself. Table 8.1 lists retrieval systems created for the major internet applications under the two different retrieval approaches.

As shown in Table 8.1, internet retrieval systems comprise more than just web search engines. Although many of the retrieval systems listed in Table 8.1 no longer exist today, they did play a distinguished role in retrieving information from the internet, particularly before the web-based internet retrieval systems were developed. To be more specific, Hytelnet provided a list of many telnetable resources via a hypertext interface. It also allowed automatic logins for the sites listed. Archie, developed by Alan Emtage, then a graduate student at McGill University in Canada, periodically scanned anonymous FTP hosts and compiled information (e.g., host name, directory name, and file size) for files available on those hosts. People were able to search "FTP-able" files by host name, directory name, and file name using Archie. Gopher enjoyed great popularity before the web became the star application on the internet. The retrieval systems designed for gopher information—Veronica, Jughead, and Gopher Jewels—are no longer in existence as gopher fades away from the internet. The life span of WAIS was relatively

Table 8.1 Major Internet Applications and Corresponding Retrieval Systems

Application	Search-based	Directory-based
Telnet	(Various)	Hytelnet
FTP	Archie	(None)
WWW	AltaVista, etc.	Yahoo!, etc.
Gopher	Veronica, Jughead	Gopher Jewels
WAIS	(Imbedded)	(Via Gopher)

short, in part because of its command language interface and the emergence of web-based internet retrieval systems. However, the uniform interface and the platform-independent Z39.50 implemented in WAIS have been carried on in many other retrieval applications (e.g., OPACs).

Portions of the retrieval tasks previously accomplished by non-web-based systems such as Archie have been incorporated into web-based systems. Other non-web-based retrieval systems (e.g., Veronica) are not available anymore because their retrieval mission is fulfilled. Information from such internet applications as Usenet (for many-to-many discussions about numerous topics) and lists (for one-to-many discussions on selected subjects) is also retrievable via general (e.g., Google at groups.google.com for Usenet information) or specific web-based retrieval systems (e.g., Tile.net at tile.net/lists for list information).

In sum, internet retrieval systems are at present all web-based or use the web as the platform. These retrieval systems include information coming from the web and other applications (e.g., FTP and Usenet) even though the web is currently the largest information repository on the internet.

8.4.1.3 Classification by Content

Internet retrieval systems can also be categorized by the content of the information they cover. Some of them maintain comprehensive coverage (e.g., Google) by gathering information from various sources and subject areas. By contrast, others may be built for only one particular field. One such example is Gateway for Educational Materials (www.thegateway.org) for education.

Some internet retrieval systems have evolved into portals by expanding the content coverage beyond searchable information. But search remains as the core in portals. Vortals, by comparison, are portals restricted to a vertical market (e.g., healthcare, insurance, automobiles, or food manufacturing). The market is vertical because it focuses on a relatively narrow range of goods and services, whereas a horizontal market is one that aims to produce a wide range of products and services (Tech Target, 2007). Roughly speaking, portals can be regarded as generic internet retrieval systems. Vortals, on the other hand, are specialized in retrieving information targeted for one vertical market. Both portals and vortals are hybrid internet retrieval systems that support browsing and searching.

In addition, there are retrieval systems devoted to retrieving special types of information on the internet. For instance, PhoneNumber (www.phonenumber.com) can be used for obtaining postal addresses and phone numbers. MapQuest (www.mapquest.com) lets users type in an address and retrieve, for example, a detailed, interactive map for that address.

This taxonomy of internet retrieval systems illustrates the variety and capacity of IR systems developed over the years. Internet retrieval systems, as a group, apparently have evolved and become the newest and yet the pre-eminent member in the IR family.

8.4.2 Features of Internet Retrieval Systems

Internet retrieval systems, particularly web search engines and directories, with the exception of WAIS, were not designed as part of internet development. Instead, they were created as an afterthought when internet users, facing an enormous amount of unprocessed information, were without any tools for retrieval purposes. For example, Archie was developed when FTP users wanted to find out whether any anonymous FTP sites hosted the information they needed. Web search engines and directories were built after web users found it increasingly difficult to locate what they wanted by just following hyperlinks embedded at websites. If the entire web had been treated as a library, the situation would have been comparable to having the library collection before creating a library catalog for it. Internet retrieval systems differ from the other types of IR systems in several additional aspects, discussed in the following sections.

8.4.2.1 Coverage and Source Information

Any information, before getting into online systems or OPACs, must go through editing, peer review, or similar checking procedures to ensure its quality. However, there are few quality control mechanisms in the information production process on the internet. Anyone can put any information onto the internet without its being checked for quality or suitability. Information of this kind would become the source information for internet retrieval systems.

Internet retrieval systems rely primarily on automatic harvesting devices such as robots, spiders, or crawlers for gathering information from the internet. These systems also allow people to submit information about their own sites although self-submission accounts for only a small percentage of all the information collected. Except for directory-based internet retrieval systems, it appears rare to have human beings manually select information from the internet. By comparison, information professionals are responsible for the data collection process in other kinds of retrieval environments.

When robots, spiders, or the like are dispatched for data collection, they are not all designed to copy the full content of a site. For example, Archie copied only the directory information of FTP sites. Some harvesting devices get the first 200 words or 20 lines of each site they visit. Others obtain just certain information (e.g., title, headings, and hyperlinks) from sites. Furthermore, websites, as the largest information storage on the internet, have networked hyperstructures. Few internet retrieval systems have the intent and resources to collect information from every hyperlinked document. For example, some may decide to copy the documents by following one level of hyperlinks, leaving information at other levels untouched. As a result, most sites have only part of their full information included in internet retrieval systems.

Besides the two factors just described, the so-called invisible web affects the coverage of internet retrieval systems. Invisible web refers to those components that are not accessible by common internet retrieval systems because of file formats (e.g., CGI scripts) or structures (e.g., databases mounted onto the web). Portable Document Format (PDF) files on the internet were not covered by any internet retrieval system until Google changed its practice in early 2001 to include them.

According to studies conducted by Lawrence and Giles (1998, 1999), internet retrieval system coverage relative to the estimated size of the publicly indexable web (i.e., 800 million pages as of February 1999) has decreased substantially since December 1997, with no system indexing more than about 16 percent of the estimated size of the publicly indexable web. In 1997, the coverage figure was about 33 percent. The conclusions were made after researchers examined six internet retrieval systems in one study and 11 in another, using real queries performed by NEC Research Institute employees. Others (e.g., Smith, 2000) have estimated that the top internet retrieval systems fail to index 70–75 percent of the pages on the web.

No matter what the actual coverage is, one thing becoming clear is that internet retrieval systems are able to process only a decreasing portion of internet information as the internet itself grows exponentially. The incomplete coverage of information and unselective practice of source information distinguish internet retrieval systems from their counterparts in other IR environments.

8.4.2.2 Indexing Mechanism

Automatic indexing algorithms based on word frequency and similar criteria dominate the indexing practice in the creation of internet retrieval systems. Limited human involvement is required in the indexing process even though some systems (e.g., Yahoo!) choose to manually categorize the information to be included in their databases. Controlled vocabulary is seldom adopted in indexing internet materials in consideration of factors such as cost, effectiveness, and the nature of the information on the internet.

There are some projects (e.g., intute at www.intute.ac.uk) that apply controlled vocabularies for organizing internet resources. A list of similar projects can be found at CyberStacks, a web-based virtual directory of many undertakings germane to library and information science (McKiernan, 2001). But these projects, strictly speaking, function more as OPACs for internet resources than as internet retrieval systems due to heavy human involvement in them.

Fields (e.g., author, title, and publication year) are identified and indexed when databases for online and OPAC systems are constructed. By comparison, internet retrieval systems consist of no field data in the traditional sense in their databases other than the fieldless index files for keywords and their corresponding locations in the system. Tagged information such as <title> ... </title> in HyperText Markup Language (HTML) or <price> ... </price> in eXtensible Markup Language (XML) can be treated at most as quasi fields because they are not uniformly assigned during the indexing process.

In short, the indexing mechanism for internet retrieval systems differs from that of other types of IR systems in that the former adopts the automatic approach based on keywords and does not index internet resources by fields.

8.4.2.3 Searching Facilities

As one type of IR system, internet retrieval systems provide virtually all the search facilities available in other retrieval environments. But there exist some points unique to internet retrieval systems, which are discussed here.

Boolean searching, taken for granted in non-internet retrieval systems, was not supported in every internet retrieval system in the past. On the other hand, the plus (+) sign was used widely as a surrogate for the AND operator in the early years of internet retrieval, but this is misleading because the + sign represents the notation for the OR operator or the logical sum, as explained in §7.2. Although that practice has been discontinued and the + sign has become the weighting symbol for weighted searching, using the + sign as the AND operator causes confusion for the end user, especially one who has not done Boolean searching before.

Proximity searching is essential in retrieving phrases (if database information is not phrase indexed) and specifying the relative positions of query terms. Online systems are particularly strong in supporting proximity searches. By contrast, proximity searching has not yet become a universal feature of internet retrieval systems. Among those systems that do support proximity searching on the internet, few provide the full range of proximity operators that are typically available in online and OPAC systems.

As for truncation, field searching, and case-sensitive searching, internet retrieval systems support them on a limited scale and with limited capabilities. Take truncation as an example: Other IR systems can get very specific by, for instance, limiting the number of characters to be truncated. But most internet retrieval systems can go only as far as unlimited right-hand truncation. Yet, automatic truncation is the default in some cases, generating more noise in search results. As mentioned in §8.4.2.2, there are only a few quasi fields (e.g., title and URL) in internet retrieval systems because such systems are in effect fieldless. There are not many opportunities for the user to limit a search by field in internet retrieval systems.

Weighted searching, not often seen in other kinds of retrieval systems, appears in the search facility repertoire of many internet retrieval systems. The plus (+) sign is used consistently among internet retrieval systems as the weighting symbol, meaning more weight for the term signaled. Weighted searching appears to override Boolean searching on the internet. For example, in a query on *tax* AND *penalty* with a weight assigned to *penalty*, the results might contain only the term *penalty*, whereas *tax* is totally ignored in the search.

Fuzzy searching, although not a common feature of other types of IR systems, does get implemented in some internet retrieval systems. For instance, if one intends to search for *Roosevelt Avenue* in Yahoo! Maps, an internet retrieval system specializing in map information, a misspelled phrase, *Roosvelt Avenue*, would still lead the searcher to the right location if other parts of the address (e.g., zip code) are correctly given. Google's "Did you mean: ..." feature, shown after a typo is made when entering a search query, is also an implementation of fuzzy searching.

Multiple database searching is not new to online systems. Databases suitable for performing such types of searching are usually set up or managed in one single system. For example, DIALOG is able to support multiple database searching by having several hundred databases that are similar in terms of structure. In the case of internet retrieval systems, cross-database searching would be a more appropriate term in this context because each singular retrieval system is constructed independently and is therefore different from others. They are not designed as subdivisions of a larger entity. Systems that can provide cross-database searching on the internet are called metasearch engines (e.g., Dogpile) or metaretrieval systems, to be consistent with the terminology used in this book. The number of individual retrieval systems each metasearch engine covers varies from one to another, normally in the range of half a dozen to two dozen. Usually single keyword searching works best in cross-database searching because there are more differences than similarities in terms of search syntax and semantics among those individual IR systems. Some internet metaretrieval systems remove duplicates before presenting results to the user.

Concept or meaning-based searching, rather than keyword matching, is particularly desirable on the internet because it is crucial in improving retrieval performance. Yet controlled vocabularies are not commonly used in internet retrieval systems. Some attempts have been made in this respect. For example, the IR system would automatically generate a list of concepts, based on input query terms, from which the user can choose. If the query is *book a flight*, for instance, the system presents a pull-down menu listing concepts such as *air travel, trip,* and *trajectory.* Then the user chooses a corresponding concept (e.g., *air travel*) in order to proceed with the actual search. Another example related to concept searching enables the user to conduct searches semantically. In this application, a particular word (e.g., *subway*) absent in a document would not exclude the possibility that the document is indeed conceptually relevant to the query on, for example, *public transportation.* Such implementations, strictly speaking, can be considered only as quasi-concept searching because their indexing does not appear to be concept-based—a prerequisite for concept searching. Rather, concepts are mapped onto keywords during searches using certain devices (e.g., a list of synonyms). In other kinds of IR systems, controlled vocabulary is almost universally applied, and concept searching is generally supported. In addition, internet retrieval systems that support concept searching typically become fee-based once they complete their beta testing on the internet. The semantic web, discussed in §12.3, should be able to provide concept searching unconditionally when it is established.

Peer-to-peer (P2P) searching is a feature new in the IR field and is closely related to the collaborative filtering approach used in commercial marketing. Search histories and bookmarks of previous users are examined when a new query is received in order to detect relevant information. When one joins a P2P network, that person's query will be searched against the sites visited and bookmarked by other people belonging to the same initial network. This process can be repeated by expanding the search scope to additional P2P networks of which those people are also members. Festa (2001) described P2P using Pandango, a project carried out by i5 Digital, as an example:

> Pandango … would determine relevance by examining a radiating network of "referrers." Once someone downloaded Pandango and joined its peer-to-peer network, that person's keyword search would examine the Web histories and bookmarks of an initial network of 100 referrers. From there, the application would search the Web histories of those 100 referrers' combined 10,000 referrers, and once again—so that the query would canvass the Web pages visited and bookmarked by 1 million people. (p. 1)

P2P searching is distributed, making use of search information generated by previous users instead of searching in a centralized database. Certain issues (e.g., privacy and security) would inevitably arise as a result of P2P searching on the internet. But they are beyond the scope of this book. P2P is also referred to as bonding in some publications (e.g., Schwartz, 2000). On the other hand, the emerging Web 2.0 movement is likely to supersede P2P searching with additional features. The impact of Web 2.0 technology on IR systems is explored in §8.5.

8.4.2.4 Ranking Techniques

Ranking mechanisms have been introduced to internet retrieval as an effort to help the user locate needles in the huge haystack more effectively. Algorithms commonly employed for ranking search results in all IR environments include, as depicted in §5.1.2.2, term frequency, term proximity, term location, and inverse document frequency. Whereas these algorithms rank search results according to the intrinsic attributes of documents (e.g., term frequency), three new ranking methods focus on the extrinsic features generated by people when they access target web documents or when they create their own sites.

The first new ranking technique, spearheaded by Google's co-founders Sergey Brin and Lawrence Page, is based on backlinks, that is, links pointing to a site to be retrieved (Brin & Page, 1998). Dubbed PageRank, the ranking technique assumes that the more times a site is pointed to by other sites, the more important it becomes. This practice appears very similar to citation analysis—an established method used for, among other things, evaluating the quality of scholarly publications. Borrowing some terminology from citation analysis, we can designate the site being pointed to as the *cited site*, while the site referring to the cited site becomes the *citing site*. In other words, Google has developed a mechanism for analyzing and ranking the links pointing to a cited site. The name PageRank is an algorithm pun because it is named after one of its creators—Lawrence Page—and refers to the target being ranked, namely, webpages. Other parameters, such as title, fonts, term proximity, and the importance of citing sites, are also considered in the rank computation (Brin & Page, 1998).

The second new ranking algorithm, known as the popularity approach, was developed by Direct Hit, which later became a part of Teoma. Teoma was subsequently acquired by Ask.com, another internet retrieval system. It ranks a site by the number of times users actually visit (thus the word *hit* in Direct Hit). If we regard AltaVista and similar search engines as author-controlled IR systems (i.e., the relevance of search results is determined by how well keywords match with document content), and if we call Yahoo! and similar directories editor-controlled IR systems (i.e., editors locate and catalog sites by examining them one by one), then Direct Hit represents a third kind of search mechanism: user-controlled IR systems, in which search rankings depend on the choices made by users (Frauenfelder, 1998). The more times a site is visited by others, the more popular that site becomes and the better ranking it receives. However, this particular algorithm did not get wide implementation.

The third ranking algorithm involves two steps. First, sites are ranked using the traditional ranking methods such as frequency and proximity for analyzing hyperlinks contained within and the text around them. Second, these hyperlinks are further scrutinized using the backlink method Google employs. This ranking method, called HITS (hypertext induced topic selection), was developed by Jon Kleinberg (1999) when he worked on IBM's CLEVER project. CLEVER aims to identify the following two kinds of websites: 1) authorities, the best sources of information on a particular topic, and 2) hubs, collections of links to those locations. The reiteration of these two steps locates and fine-tunes search results, which are eventually presented as pages of relevant links, separated into hubs and authorities. Hubs and authorities would receive higher ranking than regular sites. CLEVER is officially an IBM research project. So far it has offered only demo searches and research reports, but the HITS algorithm is increasingly integrated into many internet retrieval systems' ranking mechanisms.

The backlink method first adopted by Google and later by many other internet retrieval systems is not novel in the online retrieval environment. The Institute for Scientific Information (ISI) has built a series of databases (e.g., Science Citation Index) since the 1960s according to the citation principle, but citation frequency was not implemented as a criterion for ranking search results in citation databases until the introduction of the RANK command by DIALOG in 1993. Direct Hit's popularity method and Kleinberg's HITS algorithm, on the other hand, do not have counterparts in other retrieval environments where the ranking mechanism is still not widely available.

While traditional ranking methods may cause problems such as word stuffing (i.e., repeating some keywords deliberately to get a better ranking), or make little sense in situations such as pay for placement (i.e., ranking search results based on the amount of fees paid), the three techniques described here open up a new dimension for ranking and evaluating websites. However, they may bring further biases into the ranking process because new and unlinked sites would have an increasingly difficult time becoming visible in those retrieval systems (Lawrence & Giles, 1999).

The link-based ranking algorithms are not immune from abuses and criticisms. Tactics aiming to exploit the backlink approach include link farms and doorway pages. Link farms are collections of links that point to every other page at a given site in order to boost that site's backlink count, while doorway pages are webpages that consist entirely of links to achieve the same objective. The HITS method can be used to counterattack in part the problems link farms and doorway pages create. It is also because of those abusive tactics that more than 200 signals (i.e., factors) are used in ranking search results for a given query by Google (2008b). Other internet retrieval systems may not employ so many criteria as Google does in ranking their search results. Nevertheless, after learning about these types of abuses, no internet IR system would rely on any single link-based measure for ranking purposes.

Criticisms of link-based ranking are generally multifold: First, every link is counted as one vote for the linked page without differentiating among the links. Second, no efforts are made to identify the location of the webpage to which the link points. A link to the title of a page, for example, is treated the same as a link to the email address of the webmaster who may be responsible for the page's HTML coding only and not its intellectual content at all. Third, self-links, duplicate links, and links from interlinked databases and mirror sites are all counted as equal to regular links (Lewandowski, 2005). Such criticisms echo to a large extent those made of citation-based indicators in bibliometrics and scientometrics. Motivations for linking, like reasons for citing, are varied, complex, and difficult to identify because of the nature of the linking practice (Chu, 2005). In addition, Bharat and Hensinger (1998) indicated that well-connected hubs and authorities discovered by the HITS approach might not be about the original topic.

8.4.2.5 Search Modification

Modification of search queries or statements in online retrieval systems is well supported. The user can broaden or narrow a search with various facilities (e.g., truncation or field searching) available in the system. Compared with online systems, OPACs are less flexible in search modification although the situation improves in their next generation. Besides, the need for modifying searches in OPACs is relatively small because known-item searching makes up a significant portion of all OPAC searching.

By contrast, internet searches usually require modification because of the large amount of results each search produces and the difficulty in letting the end user compose a precise query. Yet it does not seem easy for users to modify their searches. First, no sets are created and stored for each search, while this is a common feature in online systems. Second, little modification mechanism is provided for refining searches. Google, for example, does permit users to conduct further searches within the results just retrieved by selecting the "Search within results" option. That is basically what the user can get in current internet retrieval systems with regard to search modification. The flexibility and diversification of search modification supported in other retrieval environments is still absent on the internet.

As controlled vocabularies are not commonly applied in processing network information, some systems (e.g., Gigablast) try, on the basis of the query a user enters, to suggest a list of terms for modifying searches. For example, when a query on *tulips* is made, Gigablast provides the following terms for further refining the search: *Holland*, *plant*, *spring*, *tulip bulbs*, and more. The user can choose which of the terms in the listing to use for the search modification. Even with such features implemented in some systems, it remains extremely difficult for internet users to narrow down a search to a desired level. Relevance feedback, the automatic approach for expanding a search, is available in systems such as Google, however. The user can do relevance feedback by simply clicking on hyperlinks labeled as "Similar pages" or "More like this," for example. At the same time, there is room for concern over how useful this approach is if the user already feels overwhelmed by the number of search results the system retrieved.

8.4.2.6 Interface

Command language and menu selection used to be the dominant interface modes in a large percentage of online and OPAC systems. That explains at least partially why some IR systems for nonweb applications (e.g., Archie and Veronica) had interfaces of similar kinds. As the web becomes a major internet application and popular platform for other applications (e.g., email), all internet retrieval systems tend to have web interface, which is graphical and hyperstructured. This uniformity in interface contributes to the user-friendliness of internet retrieval systems as a whole, a characteristic not intrinsic to other kinds of IR systems.

In summary, internet retrieval systems have unique features in coverage, source information, indexing, searching facilities, ranking methods, search modification, and interface when compared with online and OPAC systems. The searching of multilingual and multimedia information should also differentiate internet retrieval systems from other types of IR systems. That topic is covered in Chapter 9, "Retrieval of Information Unique in Content or Format."

8.4.3 Generations of Internet Retrieval Systems

Internet retrieval systems have grown into a new member of the IR family and become indispensable to many users (Fallows, 2008; Fallows, Rainie, & Mudd, 2004). A lot of changes and enhancements have been introduced to them since their inception. Although having only a short history of development compared with their counterparts, internet retrieval systems can be classified into three different generations based on the attributes presented in Table 8.2.

The first generation of internet retrieval systems refers to such pioneer systems as Yahoo! and WebCrawler. Text information was the major type of information those systems collected. No particular attention was paid to multimedia information processing when this generation of internet retrieval systems was built besides displaying the images already embedded

Table 8.2   Three Generations of Internet Retrieval Systems

Generation Attribute	1st Generation	2nd Generation	3rd Generation
Information Covered	Mainly text	Text or nontext	Multimedia
Retrieval Approach	Browsing & searching separated	Browsing & searching combined	Browsing & searching integrated
Indexing	Keyword	Keyword with concept mapping	Keyword & concept
Searching Capability	Basic	Basic & advanced	Precision improving
Search Modification	No	Limited support	More narrow-down features
Output	Not ranked	Ranked	Personalized

in the pages or sites, along with the text information retrieved. Directories and search engines were separated, and each system provided one retrieval approach, either browsing or searching. These systems did keyword indexing and supported, as one generation, basic searching capabilities (e.g., Boolean search, truncation, and proximity search). No search modification was possible with this generation of systems. Search outputs were not ranked, but users were given the opportunity to choose formats (e.g., title only or title with a brief summary) and the number of results (e.g., 10, 20, or 30) a system would present without refreshing the screen.

The second generation of internet retrieval systems was significantly larger than the first. Some systems represent improvements over their initial versions (e.g., Yahoo!) whereas others are new additions (e.g., Google). A considerable number of the second generation systems not only provide text IR services but also help in locating image, video, and MP3 files. The retrieval process is limited, however, to databases or files that contain a particular type of multimedia information. In other words, text information and multimedia information are processed separately in this generation of internet retrieval systems. Although powered by different companies in some cases, both the browsing and the searching mechanisms are presented at the same site so that the user can make a choice of retrieval approaches without switching to another site. Indexing is still based on keywords, but some efforts have been made to map concepts onto keywords using devices for concept searching (see §8.4.2.3). While basic searching continues to be supported by the second generation internet retrieval systems, advanced search facilities (e.g., weighted search) are introduced. Most internet retrieval systems offer two kinds of searching capability: 1) simple searching, which includes searches free of symbols or notations (e.g., operators), and 2) advanced searching, which accepts symbols and notations. Search forms are normally used for advanced searches. Searches can be broadened or narrowed in a limited number of ways, such as by date, by language, by searching within results, or by relevance feedback. Search results are ranked most of the time based on a ranking algorithm whose composition is usually kept secret. Choices of output number and display format gradually fade away in this generation of internet retrieval systems because of their diminishing significance to the user. As IR systems, the second generation has made a lot of progress in functionality and performance.

The third generation of internet retrieval systems should have further enhancements in attributes listed in Table 8.2. First, multimedia will not be treated separately from text information in the new generation of internet retrieval systems. Rather, techniques for processing and retrieving multimedia will be integrated with those for text information. Because the web is noted for its capability in presenting multimedia information and has become the major internet application, there is no reason why multimedia cannot be represented, processed, and retrieved together with the text information as research in multimedia IR advances. Second, directories and search engines are being integrated rather than simply offered at the same site. The user can search within a browsable category (as with Yahoo!), and search results are grouped into categories for browsing (as with Clusty). In addition to keyword indexing, concept indexing will be done when further progress has been made in research on natural language processing and representation. Search capabilities supported by previous generations will be improved and enhanced with a focus on improving precision. Additional search facilities (e.g., natural language searching) will be brought into the repertoire of retrieval capability the system maintains. The search modification mechanism should be oriented more toward effectively narrowing down searches because the user is usually overwhelmed by the huge numbers of results produced by internet retrieval systems. Search result presentation will ideally be ranked and customized according to the user's specification instead of the system's predefined options. For instance, Google, in its advanced search interface, allows the user to decide, among other things, whether offensive results should be eliminated or whether pages in a particular network domain should be presented. The third generation of internet retrieval systems should be able to show noticeable enhancement of retrieval performance.

As seen from these descriptions, internet retrieval systems have apparently passed out of their first generation and are evolving well into the second generation. The third generation is emerging on the horizon with great potential. Since the mid-1990s, we have experienced the change of generations in internet retrieval systems because of the rapid development of the internet for which those retrieval tools have been built. Their significance in the IR field and especially in the digital age cannot be overstated.

8.4.4 Internet Retrieval Systems and Information Retrieval

The internet has become not only a gigantic information warehouse but also a popular platform for accessing other kinds of IR systems. Internet retrieval systems no doubt are indispensable tools for retrieving information from the internet. They also function as gateways to other information sources. As more and more information is put onto the internet, the importance of internet retrieval systems in the field will increase in proportion.

In addition, internet retrieval systems are turning into the lab and showcase for new, advanced, and sophisticated IR techniques, a role that online systems have played in the past. To stay current with the most recent developments in the IR field, one should closely monitor internet retrieval systems instead of online or other kinds of systems. Changes occur constantly, if not on a daily basis, in internet retrieval systems. Internet-based newsletters and sites (e.g., Notess, 2008a; Third Door Media, 2008) are created to inform the user of the latest developments about them.

On the other hand, internet retrieval systems as a group are notorious for their low-precision search performance. Information retrieved from the internet may not be accessible because of factors such as broken and dated links, a consequence much less likely in other IR environments. The user must also be responsible for judging the quality of information since the quality control mechanism for information on the internet, if available, is at best very loosely structured (e.g., at the time of cataloging internet resources for directory-based systems).

Searching, according to Brewer (2001), is the most visible and important aspect of the internet after communication. Internet retrieval systems are designed specifically for retrieval purposes. Moreover, these systems are free of charge to end users if they already have internet access. It is therefore not an overstatement to say that internet retrieval systems hold a prominent place in the field of IR at present and will do so for a long time to come.

Although internet retrieval systems appear exceptionally promising in the field of IR, the challenges they face would still demand much more effort (Mayer, 2008). Marissa Mayer, Google's vice president for search products and user experience, believes that search doesn't conform to the usual 80-20 rule. Instead, as far as Google is concerned, it has solved about 90 percent of the search problem, but the last 10 percent of the search solution represents more than 90 percent of the work. Example problems in the last 10 percent include mobile search (including wearable devices), voice and natural language search, multimedia search that uses the content-based approach, and search results presented in media (e.g., images or video clips) that are the most appropriate to the user. From this perspective, internet retrieval systems as a group still have a long way to go in the field of IR.

8.5 Information Retrieval Systems: Some Trends

The past decades have witnessed the development and growth of IR systems in many dimensions. The digital age, especially network technology, has brought changes to IR systems, which no longer function independently of each other by system type. Instead, they not only work together within one category of IR systems (e.g., online systems) but also converge across their borderlines. The emerging Web 2.0 applications (e.g., social tagging and wikis), on the other hand, enable users to be contributors in IR so that they no longer merely stay at the receiving end in the IRR process. The next subsections are devoted to these two trends with regard to IR systems.

8.5.1 Convergence of Information Retrieval Systems

It can be seen from the descriptions and discussions in this chapter that each kind of IR system has its particular features, functions, and capabilities in IR, yet all are designed and maintained for IR purposes. Recently, various IR systems have begun to converge in order to provide better and more convenient IR services to users. Convergence may take any of the following forms.

The first form of convergence, chronologically speaking, is the loading of CD-ROM systems onto OPACs. Because OPACs are generally created for individual libraries that also house CD-ROM systems, many institutions consolidate these two systems after the latter fully complete their mission. Links are made from the OPAC to CD-ROMs, allowing the user to access two different IR systems at one place. Some institutions also establish links from their OPACs to online systems so that the otherwise separate connection procedure can be eliminated when the user conducts any online searches. This form of convergence takes place basically at the system connection level.

The second form of convergence occurs at the system database content level between OPACs and online systems. For example, an OPAC search reveals that a particular item is not in the library collection. The query for that item can then be submitted to the online system that the OPAC is linked with to see whether the item is in the online system. Document delivery systems (e.g., ProQuest) would very likely be used to obtain a copy of the item. But it is the linkage between OPACs and online systems that truly facilitates the retrieval process.

The third type of convergence happens when the hyperstructured web is increasingly being used as the platform for internet retrieval systems, as well as for online and OPAC systems. These IR systems become so interrelated that the boundaries among them are getting fuzzy. For example, field 856 of MARC, a cataloging standard, is allocated for recording URLs of internet resources. The end products of this practice would be, as indicated in §8.4.2.2, OPACs for internet resources. In addition, more and more books and journals are being published electronically on the web, integrated into library collections, and represented in OPACs. Therefore, information on the internet, previously the unquestionable target of internet retrieval systems, is included in OPACs, which in the past were reserved exclusively for representing and retrieving library collections. This practice has brought about the convergence of OPACs and internet retrieval systems. Another example of such convergence can be found where web documents list references or citations that are covered by online systems. Assuming a web document along with its references is located with the help of an internet retrieval system, the user can further search in the online system containing the hyperlinked references. The association between online systems and internet retrieval systems is seamlessly established.

From a broader perspective, the web is becoming the platform for using all different types of IR systems. From a narrower viewpoint, it is not unthinkable for a user to have access to a web-based library information system that includes all kinds of IR systems, namely, the library's OPAC, online systems the library subscribes to, and some internet retrieval systems the library chooses to present. Will the web become the only platform for IR systems in the future? Will a common platform catalyze further convergence among the IR systems? What will the impact of the convergence be on the user? We do not yet know the answers.

8.5.2 Web 2.0 and Information Retrieval Systems

The advent of Web 2.0 applications such as wikis and social tagging clearly has had an impact on IRR in general and on IR systems in particular. In §2.1.4, the Web 2.0 was mentioned as part of the discussion on social tagging (or tagging in brief) and its role in indexing. In the context of IR systems, blogging, tagging, and wikis have begun to demonstrate visible influence over the process of information retrieval.

Blogging is usually employed within the IR system so that a user can comment on, for instance, books a library purchased or articles retrieved from an online system. Blog messages of this type help fellow users to decide whether they should try to read a particular article or check out a particular book. Wikis are implemented in IR systems (e.g., SearchWiki of Google) to allow users to put their personal touch to what an IR system retrieves and presents by elevating results, adding new results, deleting ones already displayed, and posting comments (Notess, 2008b). This implementation, in a sense, leads us closer to customizing the presentation of search results, a part of personalized search. Determined by its unique nature, tagging is more and more included in IR systems as a means of providing additional access points from the user's perspective. IR systems that incorporate Web 2.0 applications are emerging. For example, 2collab at Elsevier, a major stakeholder in online systems, is an IR platform that allows its users to take advantage of tagging, wikis, and similar Web 2.0 applications while using its online systems (e.g., ScienceDirect). SOPACs (Social OPACs) are OPAC systems with Web 2.0 features (Blyberg, 2008; Stephens, 2007) although few implementations are in existence.

What the integration of IR systems and Web 2.0 technology will actually lead to in the field of IRR is uncertain. However, one thing is already apparent: Users seem truly enthusiastic about being able to contribute to IR, while system developers and informational professionals have begun to seriously consider how to make this integration valuable to all parties involved.

References

Antelman, Kristin, Lynema, Emily, and Pace, Andrew K. (2006). Toward a twenty-first century library catalog. *Information Technology and Libraries*, 25(3), 128–139.

Basch, Reva. (1993). Dialog's Rank command: Building and mining the data mountain. *ONLINE*, 17(4), 28–35.

Beaulieu, Micheline, and Borgman, Christine L. (Guest editors). (1996). Special topic issue: Current research in online public access systems. *Journal of the American Society for Information Science*, 47(7), 491–583.

Bharat, Krishna, and Hensinger, Monika R. (1998). Improved algorithms for topic distillation in a hyperlinked environment. In W. Bruce Croft, et al. (Eds.), *Proceedings of the 21st Annual International ACM SIGIR Conference on Research and Development in Information Retrieval* (pp. 104–111). New York: Association for Computing Machinery.

Blyberg, John. (August 16, 2008). SOPAC 2.0: What to expect. Retrieved October 7, 2009, from www.blyberg.net/2008/08/16/sopac-20-what-to-expect

Borgman, Christine L. (1986). Why are online catalogs hard to use? Lessons learned from information retrieval studies. *Journal of the American Society for Information Science*, 37, 387–397.

Borgman, Christine L. (1996). Why are online catalogs still hard to use? *Journal of the American Society for Information Science*, 47(7), 493–503.

Bourne, Charles P. (1980). On-line systems: History, technology, and economics. *Journal of the American Society for Information Science*, 31(3), 155–160.

Bourne, Charles P., and Hahn, Trudi Bellardo. (2003). *History of online information services 1963–1976*. Cambridge, MA: MIT Press.

Brewer, Eric A. (2001). When everything is searchable. *Communications of the ACM*, 44(3), 53–55.

Brin, Sergey, and Page, Lawrence. (1998). The anatomy of a large-scale hypertextual web search engine. *Computer Networks and ISDN Systems*, 30(1–7), 107–117.

Chowdhury, Gobinda G. (1999). *Introduction to modern information retrieval*. London: Library Association Publishing.

Chu, Heting. (1998). Internet search services vs. online database services. In Martha E. Williams (Ed.), *Proceedings of the 19th National Online Meeting* (pp. 69–75). Medford, NJ: Information Today.

Chu, Heting. (2005). Taxonomy of inlinked web entities: What does it imply for webometric research? *Library & Information Science Research*, 27(1), 8–27.

Fallows, Deborah. (2008). Search engine use. Pew Internet & American Life Project. Retrieved October 7, 2009, from www.pewinternet.org/~/media/Files/Reports/2008/P2P_Search_Aug08.pdf.pdf

Fallows, Deborah, Rainie, Lee, and Mudd, Graham. (2004). The popularity and importance of search engines. Pew Internet & American Life Project. Retrieved October 7, 2009, from www.pewinternet.org/~/media/Files/Reports/2004/P2P_Data_Memo_Searchengines.pdf.pdf

Festa, Paul. (February 26, 2001). Search project prepares to challenge Google. Retrieved October 7, 2009, from news.cnet.com/2/00-1023-253141.html

Frauenfelder, Mark. (September 25, 1998). The future of search engines. *The Industry Standard: The Newsmagazine of the Internet Economy*. Retrieved May 26, 1999, from www.thestandard.com/articles/article_print/0,1454,1826,00.html

Google. (2008a). About Google Book Search. Retrieved December 8, 2008, from books.google.com/intl/en/googlebooks/history.html

Google. (2008b). Technology overview. Retrieved November 30, 2008, from www.google.com/corporate/tech.html

Hahn, Trudi Bellardo. (1996). Pioneers of the online age. *Information Processing & Management*, 32(1), 33–48.

Harter, Stephen P. (1986). *Online information retrieval: Concepts, principles, and techniques.* New York: Academic Press.

Hildreth, Charles R. (1984). Pursuing the ideal: Generations of online catalogs. In B. Aveney and B. Butler (Eds.), *Online catalogs, online reference: Converging trends. Proceedings of a Library and Information Technology Association Preconference Institute* (pp. 31–56). Chicago: American Library Association.

Hildreth, Charles R. (1985). Online public access catalogs. *Annual Review of Information Science and Technology, 20*, 233–285.

Hildreth, Charles R. (1988). Online library catalogues as information retrieval systems: What can we learn from research? In P. A. Yates-Mercer (Ed.), *Future trends in information science and technology. Proceedings of the Silver Jubilee Conference of the City University's Department of Information Science* (pp. 9–25). London: Taylor Graham.

Hildreth, Charles R. (1995). Online catalog design models: Are we moving in the right direction? A report submitted to the Council on Library Resources. (Updated March 27, 2000.) Retrieved December 6, 2008, from myweb.cwpost.liu.edu/childret/clr-opac.html

Kleinberg, Jon. (1999). Authoritative sources in a hyperlinked environment. *Journal of the ACM*, 46(5), 604–632.

Large, Andrew, Tedd, Lucy A., and Hartley, R. J. (1999). *Information seeking in the online age: Principles and practice.* London: Bowker-Saur.

Lawrence, Steve, and Giles, C. Lee. (April 3, 1998). Searching the World Wide Web. *Science*, 280(5360), 98–100.

Lawrence, Steve, and Giles, C. Lee. (July 8, 1999). Accessibility of information on the web. *Nature*, 400, 107–109.

LeVan, Ralph. (2003). Z39.50 as a web service. [Presentation slides]. Retrieved December 1, 2008, from staff.oclc.org/~levan/docs/srw-niso20030430.ppt

Lewandowski, Dirk. (2005). Web searching, search engines and information retrieval. *Information Services & User*, 25, 137–147.

Malinconico, S. Michael. (1984). Catalogs & cataloging: Innocent pleasures and enduring controversies. *Library Journal*, 109(11), 1210–1213.

Marcum, Deanna B. (2006). The future of cataloging. *Library Resources & Technical Services*, 50(1), 5–9.

Markey, Karen. (2007). The online library catalog: Paradise lost and paradise gained? *D-Lib Magazine*, 13(1/2). Retrieved December 6, 2008, from dlib.org/dlib/january07/markey/01markey.html

Mayer, Marissa. (September 10, 2008). The future of search. Retrieved December 9, 2008, from googleblog.blogspot.com/2008/09/future-of-search.html

McKiernan, Gerry. (2001). Beyond bookmarks: Schemes for organizing the web. Retrieved January 19, 2009, from www.public.iastate.edu/~CYBER STACKS/CTW.htm

Meadow, Charles T., Boyce, Bert R., and Kraft, Donald H. (1999). *Text information retrieval systems*. Orlando, FL: Academic Press.

Nahl-Jakobovits, Diane, and Tenopir, Carol. (1992). Databases online and on CD-ROMs: How do they differ? Let us count the ways. *Database*, 15(1), 42–50.

Notess, Greg R. (2008a). Search engine showdown: The users' guide to web searching. Retrieved December 11, 2008, from www.searchengineshow down.com

Notess, Greg R. (December 4, 2008b). Customize your own Google results with SearchWiki. ITI NewsLink. Retrieved December 9, 2008, from newsbreaks.infotoday.com/nbReader.asp?ArticleId=51802

Rowley, Jennifer, and Slack, Frances. (1997). The evaluation of interface design on CD-ROMs. *Online and CDROM Review*, 21(1), 3–11.

Schwartz, Candy. (2000). Meeting review: Notes from the Boston 2000 Search Engine Meeting. *Bulletin of the American Society for Information Science*, 26(6), 26–28.

Smith, Ian. (2000). The invisible web: Where search engines fear to go. Retrieved December 12, 2000, from www.powerhomebiz.com/vol25/invisible.htm

Stephens, Michael. (2007). Web 2.0 & libraries, part 2: Trends and technologies. Chapter 3, Technology trends for a 2.0 world. *Library Technology Reports*, 43(5), 32–44.

Tech Target. (2005). Digital versatile disk. Retrieved December 6, 2008, from whatis.techtarget.com

Tech Target. (2007). Vortal. Retrieved December 9, 2008, from whatis.tech target.com

Third Door Media. (2008). Search engine land. Retrieved December 11, 2008, from searchengineland.com

Walker, Geraldene, and Janes, Joseph. (1999). *Online retrieval: A dialogue of theory and practice* (2nd ed.). Englewood, CO: Libraries Unlimited.

CHAPTER 9

Retrieval of Information Unique in Content or Format

Up to this point, the theme of information retrieval (IR) has been explored assuming that information is mainly text, is in English, and has a linear structure. This chapter focuses on the retrieval of information unique in content or format, that is, multilingual information, multimedia information, and hypertext or hypermedia information.

9.1 Multilingual Information

There are approximately 6,912 different living languages in the world, of which 2,092 are used in Africa, 1,002 in the Americas, 2,269 in Asia, 239 in Europe, and 1,310 in the Pacific (Gordon, 2005, p. 15). According to an estimation made in February 1999, the top three first languages in the world at that time were Mandarin Chinese (885 million speakers), Spanish (332 million speakers), and English (322 million speakers) (Sands, 2000). While in daily life, people can rely on their native language exclusively, the monolingual world is definitely disappearing in this digital age as far as information representation and retrieval (IRR) is concerned, because information is recorded and exchanged in multiple languages all over the world, including on the internet. The need for representing and retrieving multilingual information consequently becomes essential even though one language might be dominant in one setting if that language is what most people there use. In other words, the overall IRR environment must be multilingual to meet the information needs of various users who speak various languages.

English has been the major language for scholarly communication since World War II and remains in the leading position among all languages used on the internet to date. Even so, the gap between English and other languages (e.g., Chinese and Spanish) is quickly narrowing among internet users. According to Miniwatts Marketing Group (2009), for example, the top three languages used on the internet were English (28.7 percent), Chinese (21.7 percent), and Spanish (8.0 percent) in June 2009. In comparison, the percentage of information in English was much higher when the internet went public in the early 1990s. This change reflects the fact that at least the internet is becoming more multilingual.

Multilingual information must be coded for computer processing before it can be represented and retrieved digitally. Unicode is a standard specifically created for such purposes so that every character, letter, or symbol in any language can be coded with a unique number in byte regardless of platform or application (Unicode, Inc., 2008). In the time before Unicode, individual languages had their respective encoding schemes, making interoperability among them virtually impossible. For example, the well-known ASCII (American Standard Code for Information Interchange) is designed for coding English alphabets but cannot handle characters in other languages (e.g., Chinese). It has also become evident that Unicode is a must for internet development because of the multilingual information the global network handles (Lerner, 2003). Not only is Unicode necessary in coding multilingual information for further digital processing, but it also enables the web browser to detect whether an incoming webpage uses one of the common code schemes already installed on the user's computer (Coyle, 2005). In supporting the latter functionality, Unicode eliminates the need for the user to manually switch from one coding scheme (e.g., English) to another (e.g., Chinese) when viewing multilingual information such as search results.

9.1.1 Multilingual Information Retrieval in the Past

Before the advent of the internet and internet retrieval systems, multilingual information was included in online, CD-ROM, and OPAC systems on a selective basis. These systems usually adopt a selection policy with regard to the collection of multilingual information. For example, either translation or transliteration would be provided if information in a certain language is to be included. In multilingual IR, locating information using the same language in which the information is recorded (e.g., search Chinese information using queries in Chinese) does not seem widely supported although there are some exceptions. Generally speaking, foreign language information is transliterated for retrieval purposes in OPACs. Online and CD-ROM systems often use a first language to represent foreign language information (e.g., in indexing and abstracting), which can be retrieved later with the same first language.

There are systems designed for retrieving multilingual information directly instead of via translation and transliteration. For example, OPACs in China normally support two language modes: one for the Chinese language and the other for the so-called Western languages such as English and French. People can use, for example, Chinese to retrieve Chinese information and English for retrieving information in English. Multilingual IR systems of this kind should presumably produce better results than those based on translation and transliteration because multilingual systems can avoid introducing further discrepancies, which may be caused by translation or transliteration, into the retrieval process.

9.1.2 Multilingual Information Retrieval on the Internet

Although online, CD-ROM, and OPAC systems collect multilingual information, the need for multilingual IR in those environments does not appear as strong as on the internet, because of the following factors: First, the coverage of multilingual information in those systems is highly selective and restricted to quality information. Second, the internet is a global network of networks, naturally carrying much more multilingual information than other kinds of IR systems. Third, the absence of a quality control mechanism, as discussed in §8.4.2.1, also contributes to the boom in multilingual information on the internet.

It is apparent that the internet, as an IR environment, differs from other IR environments because of the composition of its users. Fallows (2007), writing for the Pew Internet and American Life Project, predicted that China would overtake the U.S. in total number for users within a few years. The prediction was confirmed even sooner than expected by the China Internet Network Information Center (CNNIC) when it reported that internet users in China reached 298 million in total at the end of December 2008 (CNNIC, 2008). The CNNIC report, along with data from the Miniwatts Marketing Group (2009) regarding the number of internet users from countries such as Japan, France, and Germany, indicates that the internet is evidently departing from its monolingual past. Internet retrieval systems address the issue of multilingual IR by either supporting multilingual searches or providing translation facilities developed by companies such as SYSTRAN (www.systransoft.com). AltaVista took the lead in both areas by collaborating with SYSTRAN, while many other internet IR systems (e.g., Google) followed suit, especially in the domain of multilingual searching.

When internet retrieval systems were initially developed, English was the only language that people could use for retrieval. At present, people can search the internet using more than two dozen different languages, including English, Chinese, French, German, Spanish, and Russian. Multilingual searching on the internet can be accomplished in two ways. One method is to conduct the search using an internet retrieval system specifically built for a particular language (e.g., Yahoo! in France), with search queries in that language. The other method is to restrict the search results to a specific language by selecting the chosen language listed on the homepage of an internet retrieval system. The search query remains in English, for example, but the results will be in the language specified (e.g., Spanish). Retrieval of this kind should, in a strict sense, be considered as cross-language IR, which is discussed in §9.1.3.

In addition to multilingual searching, multilingual information on the internet can be obtained by means of translation, thanks to the joint efforts made by internet retrieval systems and automatic translation software companies.

The collaboration between AltaVista and SYSTRAN is one such example. For instance, any results retrieved by AltaVista can be translated from English to Chinese, French, German, Italian, Japanese, Korean, Spanish, or Portuguese and vice versa using the SYSTRAN software—although the translation quality is not quite satisfactory due to the inherent limitations of automatic translation (Balkin, 1999).

9.1.3 Research on Multilingual Information Retrieval

The retrieval of multilingual information has attracted researchers' attention in recent years and became a track (i.e., a particular retrieval subproblem) in TREC-4 through TREC-6. The multilingual track investigated issues of IR in languages other than English. Spanish and Chinese, the two most widely used non-English languages (Gordon, 2005), were examined by more than 20 research teams from 1995 through 1997. Researchers found (Spärck Jones, 2000):

> The extension to Multilingual Spanish is relatively modest, but to Chinese is more demanding in covering a radically different script system. It therefore clearly raises the question of whether in practice, as opposed to broad principle, indexing and searching methods developed for English, e.g., those using statistical techniques, are readily transferred to and are effective for other, very different languages. (p. 46)

Indeed, different languages require IR systems with different capabilities for handling their distinctive features. For example, it is a very challenging task to automatically segment Chinese text into meaningful query terms because there is no space between words in Chinese writing until the end of a sentence. Therefore, the majority of research teams participating in the TREC-6 Multilingual Chinese track compared different segmentation methods (Voorhees & Harman, 2000). Case-sensitive searching, a basic retrieval technique for information in English, is not applicable to Chinese because there is no uppercase or lowercase in Chinese text.

An area related to multilingual retrieval is cross-language searching, in which documents cover several languages (e.g., English, German, French, or Italian) and queries are in each language. The Cross-Language Information Retrieval (CLIR) track was added into the Text REtrieval Conference (TREC) series in 1997, beginning with TREC-6 and running through TREC 2002. The focus of the CLIR track is to retrieve documents in one target language using queries written in a different language. In TREC-6, 13 groups participating in the CLIR track tried three major approaches to cross-language retrieval: 1) automatic translation, in which either the queries or the documents were translated into the target language; 2) the use of machine readable bilingual dictionaries or other existing linguistic resources; and 3) the use of corpus resources to train or otherwise enable the cross-language retrieval mechanism (Voorhees & Harman, 2000). As far as technical issues of CLIR are concerned, Kishida (2005) reviewed in detail translation techniques, methods for solving translation ambiguity, and matching strategies, among many other efforts CLIR researchers have made over the years.

Before TREC ended the CLIR track in 2002, two other major platforms for cross-language IR emerged. One is the Cross-Language Evaluation Forum (CLEF; www.clef-campaign.org), which aims to promote research and development in multilingual information access, mainly from the European perspective. The other platform is the National Institute of Informatics' Test Collection for IR Systems (NTCIR) Workshop, located in Japan (research.nii.ac.jp/ntcir/outline/prop-en.html). Mimicking the TREC series, NTCIR Workshops are designed to enhance research in information access technologies, including IR. Cross-language IR is one of the research tasks NTCIR Workshops undertake. Non-English languages regularly considered in those workshops include Japanese, Chinese, and Korean. Both CLEF and NTCIR actively explore problems in cross-language IR. Despite the establishment of TREC, CLEF, and NTCIR, concerns are being expressed regarding inadequate attention to many languages not covered in those projects and to the expanding multilingual web, as well as to literature other than news information (Gey, Kando, & Peters, 2005). To address those concerns, CLIR researchers are increasingly trying such natural language processing techniques as compound splitting and machine translation (e.g., Chen & Gey, 2004; Hollink, et al., 2004; Si, et al., 2008). Artificial intelligence seems to play a role in these endeavors.

In brief, multilingual searching means that target information and queries are in the same language whereas cross-language retrieval implies that target information and queries are in different languages. Limiting internet search results to one particular language, as mentioned in §9.1.2, is actually cross-language retrieval because the query has to be translated from one language into the language of the target information before the search is conducted. Regardless whether the retrieval is multilingual or cross-language, users should always pay attention to the features of the language in which the information is recorded because each language is unique. Only from this perspective can users successfully perform multilingual or cross-language retrieval.

9.2 Multimedia Information

According to a study by the School of Information Management and Systems at the University of California at Berkeley (Lyman, et al., 2000), the world produces between 1 and 2 exabytes (1 exabyte = 1 billion gigabytes) of unique information per year. Although the report did not specify multimedia information's percentage of that total, the amount of multimedia information (e.g., broadcast news, video conferences, reconnaissance data, audiovisual recordings of corporate meetings, and classroom lectures) is no doubt growing drastically because the web is able to store, transfer, and present multimedia information. For example, the publicly indexable web alone contained an estimated 180 million images, or 3 terabytes of image data, in February 1999 (Lawrence & Giles, 1999). As the web continues its rapid development and carries more multimedia information, the need to locate and obtain this information is also steadily increasing.

Multimedia was defined in Chapter 3 as any combination of sound, image, and text information, and Figure 3.1 presents a taxonomy of multimedia information. It should be noted that the term *image* is sometimes used loosely to refer to all kinds of multimedia because both still and moving images can contain textual information while moving images can also include sound information. Because textual information has been the subject of discussion in most parts of the book, the focus in this section is on nontextual information that consists of still images, sound, and moving images.

Numerous methods and algorithms have been developed for retrieving multimedia information, but they fall into two broad categories: the description-based approach and the content-based approach. Simply, the description-based approach manually employs captions, keywords, and other descriptions (e.g., artist and work size) of multimedia information for retrieval purposes. Human beings are directly involved in the retrieval process when this approach is used. The content-based approach, on the other hand, refers to techniques that are based on automatic processing of multimedia information itself.

The description-based and content-based approaches are used by two distinct research groups (Cawkell, 1992; Chu, 2001; Persson, 2000). It appears that people in the computer science field focus on the content-based approach while the information science community, including library science, concentrates on the description-based method (Cawkell, 1992; Rasmussen, 1997). This division occurs because of two factors. First, the academic background and training of the two groups of researchers are different: one in computer science and the other in information science. Second, the processing methods adopted for retrieving multimedia by the two approaches are dissimilar: one is automatic while the other is manual. The following sections examine how each approach has been applied in retrieving the three types of multimedia information: still images, sound, and moving images.

9.2.1 Still Image Retrieval

As indicated in §3.3.1, images include both still and moving images. Still images comprise pictures, photos, posters, document images (e.g., PDF—Portable Document Format files), and the like. Moving images, containing still images plus the moving attribute, can be subdivided into two categories: moving images with sound constitute videos or movies, and moving images without sound are animations or silent movies. For clarity, only still images are discussed in this section; moving images are discussed in §9.2.3.

Still images have their own meaning and properties that form the bases for the performance of retrieval tasks. In reference to Renaissance art, Panofsky (1955) identified three strata of meaning for images. The first stratum is pre-iconography, which describes primary or natural meaning of images and is further divided into factual and expressional facets; for example, for a picture of a bustling city, the city is the factual facet, and its bustling quality is the expressional aspect. Pre-iconographic descriptions of images require practical experience. For example, a city and a bustling scene are readily recognizable to those who have seen such entities before. The second stratum is iconography, identifying the secondary or conventional meaning depicted in the image (e.g., a picture of Rome as opposed to any other city). Iconographic identification requires knowledge of literary sources, for instance, familiarity with the features of Rome as a city. The third stratum is iconology, representing the intrinsic meaning or symbolic values of the image. The identification and interpretation of the intrinsic meaning of images, often unknown to the artist and maybe even emphatically different from what the artist consciously intended to express, require "synthetic intuition conditioned by personal psychology" (Panofsky, 1955, p. 41). Such meaning "is apprehended by ascertaining those underlying principles which reveal the basic attitude of a nation, a period, a class, a religious or philosophical persuasion" (Panofsky, 1955, p. 30). For example, to some people Rome could mean a city with a rich history, and to others it may denote the place in which the Vatican is located. The intrinsic meaning of images is apparently the most difficult to be interpreted. The interpretation would be highly subjective and dependent on one's experience and background.

Almost half a century after Panofsky, Eakins and Graham (1999) classified image attributes into three levels of increasing complexity. Level 1 image attributes are primitive features such as color, texture, and shape. An example of retrieval queries based on Level 1 image attributes is *red triangle*, where *red* indicates color and *triangle* suggests shape. Level 2 image attributes are logical features concerning the identity of objects depicted in the image. The objects could be general (e.g., an office building) or specific (e.g., Willis Tower, formerly the Sears Tower, in Chicago). Level 2 image attributes are more complex than Level 1 features in that the former make a logical reference to the identity of objects in an image or contain information beyond the primitive Level 1. For example, the image object is an office building rather than a particular shape or texture. Level 3 image attributes are abstract, involving a significant amount of high-level reasoning about the meaning and purpose of the objects or scenes depicted in an image (Eakins & Graham, 1999). These attributes concern the "aboutness" of images, for instance, the festive atmosphere depicted in a party scene.

Similarities can be found between Panofsky's three strata of meaning for images and the three levels of image attributes presented by Eakins and Graham (1999). The first layer in both cases deals with the "ofness," or physical attributes of images, except that Panofsky included the expressional facet of images in this stratum and did not analyze images down to pixels, a measurement created later for digital images. The second and third layers in both schemes cover the aboutness or subject attributes of images, dealing with their semantic contents. Some of the subject attributes can be objectively identified (e.g., differentiating Rome from other cities), while some can be ascertained only subjectively (e.g., Rome as a historical city or religious center). No matter how image attributes are categorized, they form the bases for retrieving still image information in both of the image retrieval approaches discussed next.

9.2.1.1 Description-Based Retrieval of Still Images

The description-based approach for retrieving still images, also known as the metadata-based, concept-based, or text-based approach, has to rely on descriptions provided by information professionals. Still images can be described by their ofness, or physical attributes (e.g., a picture of pandas), as well as their aboutness, or subject attributes (e.g., endangered animals). Such descriptions are often called metadata nowadays; Trant (2004) labeled this image IR approach as metadata-based. If the descriptions concern only aboutness, we can name the image retrieval approach concept-based (Rasmussen, 1997). If the descriptions are prepared with texts accompanying images, we can refer to the image retrieval approach as text-based (Goodrum, 2000). These descriptions then become the foundations for retrieving still images.

Both keywords and controlled vocabularies are adopted in retrieving still images. Keywords are mostly derived from captions or other textual information accompanying still images (e.g., an introduction to a photo exhibition). Users can also choose query terms themselves at the time of retrieval. Controlled vocabularies used in image retrieval include the Art and Architecture Thesaurus, ICONCLASS, and the Thesaurus for Graphic Materials. Further descriptions about these controlled vocabularies can be found in Rasmussen (1997). Taking it one step further, Jorgensen (2003) analyzed the attributes of these controlled vocabularies (e.g., objects and people) in terms of their frequency distribution to help users better understand their application. Visual thesauri, which use visual surrogates in addition to verbal expressions for image retrieval purposes, have also been tried in some cases (Mostafa, 1994; Rasmussen, 1997). This method appears similar to query by example, a retrieval technique briefly discussed in §5.1.2.3, Query Expansion.

Aside from retrieving images according to their aboutness, or subject attributes, many ofness attributes are available for accessing still images using the description-based approach. Date, size, and type of image are just a few examples. Searches of this kind do not differ much from field searching in text IR. Techniques developed for retrieving text information (e.g., Boolean searching and truncation) remain applicable in retrieving still images with the description-based approach. The major difference between text and image retrieval lies in the definition of fields. Fields in still image retrieval are defined in accordance with image attributes rather than features of text information.

However, the description-based approach to image retrieval inherits all the problems associated with human involvement in the process, such as inconsistency and high cost. Furthermore, the subjectivity in interpreting the aboutness of images is inevitable and of a higher degree than in text retrieval because the interpretation of the aboutness, or subject content, of images depends heavily on one's personal experience and background. For example, a glass of wine in a picture may be an indication of celebration to one person but a sign of drunkenness to another. Images themselves may not contain explicit cues for interpretation. The content-based approach was introduced to the area of image retrieval in part to cope with this problem of using the description-based method. Other factors that contributed to the emergence of the content-based approach include the development of technology and the growth of image information in the digital age.

9.2.1.2 Content-Based Retrieval of Still Images

The content-based approach for still image retrieval is implemented by automatically processing image attributes specified in search queries. These attributes are derived from image contents, thus the name of the content-based approach. As discussed in §9.2.1, image attributes can be categorized into different levels or strata (Eakins & Graham, 1999; Panofsky, 1955). However, image retrieval systems using the content-based approach at present operate most effectively only at Level 1, that is, primitive image features such as color, texture, and shape (Eakins & Graham, 1999).

Matching is the fundamental mechanism in any retrieval process, and the retrieval of still images with the content-based approach is no exception.

Image attributes specified in the query must match those represented in the image retrieval system before any results can be produced. The principal matching or retrieval mechanism for still images based on color, texture, and shape is explained clearly and thoroughly in Eakins and Graham (1999) although specific implementations may include some variations.

Color retrieval of still images is based on color histograms. Each image included in the system is analyzed to compute a color histogram, which shows the proportion of pixels of each color within the image. The color histogram for each image is then stored in the system for future use. The user can, at search time, either specify the desired proportion of each color (e.g., 30 percent white, 30 percent blue, and 40 percent orange) or submit an example image (i.e., query by example) from which another color histogram is calculated. Either way, the matching is performed to retrieve those images whose color histograms match those of the query most closely. The results obtained from some image retrieval systems by color can look quite impressive (Eakins & Graham, 1999).

Texture retrieval of still images is based on textual properties such as contrast and directionality. A variety of techniques have been used for measuring textual similarity between query and stored images. First of all, these techniques calculate the relative brightness of selected pairs of pixels from each image. Then other measures of image texture are computed, such as degree of contrast, coarseness, directionality, regularity (or periodicity), and randomness. Texture queries can be formulated in a manner similar to that for color queries by selection of examples of desired textures from a palette or by supplying an example query image. The system retrieves images with texture measures most similar in value to the query. Image retrieval by texture is particularly useful in distinguishing between areas of images with similar color (e.g., sky and sea or leaves and grasses).

A mechanism closely related to the texture retrieval of still images is described by Stix (2006). Each image in the image IR system is first analyzed by computers for distinctive features that consist of dark areas surrounded by light areas or vice versa. Some of the features are then bundled into groups of three, based on a calculation of how far one is from the other. Each feature represents the center point of a 10-by-10 square patch of pixels. The grouping of three patches is called a triplet. The location of each triplet is stored as an entry in a huge table that is designed to minimize the amount of computation required to search any individual entry. A query image is also separated into triplets via a method similar to that for processing target images. These triplets of query image are at last matched with those in the table during the retrieval process.

Shape retrieval of still images is based on object shape but independent of size or orientation. A number of features characteristic of object shape are computed for every object identified within each stored image. Two main types of shape features are commonly used: 1) global features, such as aspect ratio and circularity, and 2) local features, such as sets of consecutive boundary segments. Queries to shape retrieval systems are either an example image or a user-drawn sketch. Queries are then answered by computing the same set of features for the query image and retrieving those stored images whose features most closely match those of the query.

The content-based approach by color, texture, and shape appears to be capable of delivering useful results, although some of the features have proved much more effective than others (Eakins & Graham, 1999). It is generally accepted that color retrieval and texture retrieval yield better results than shape matching (Faloutsos, et al., 1994). Yet shape is a well-defined concept and easily recognizable in identifying natural objects embedded in images. Part of the problem with shape matching lies in the difficulty of automatically distinguishing between foreground shapes and background detail in a natural image. The Query By Image Content (QBIC) research group, for example, has developed some methods to tackle this problem (Flickner, et al., 1995).

Content-based image retrieval (CBIR) at higher or semantic levels, although unable to be performed satisfactorily at this time, is in demand by users. Breakthroughs in this area again depend largely on advancements in artificial intelligence research or will be made when computers can truly mimic the intellectual activities of human brains. Retrieval of images based on the semantic and subject attributes still requires the involvement of human beings, which implies the indispensability of the description-based approach for the time being.

9.2.1.3 Integration of the Two Image Retrieval Approaches

The content-based approach deals with image properties that can be processed automatically, but it works effectively at present only with primitive image features such as color, shape, and texture (Eakins & Graham, 1999). The higher levels of image attributes discussed earlier cannot be successfully handled for retrieval purposes because computers are still not able to perform intelligent analysis of images. In addition, the CBIR approach sometimes fails miserably (Stix, 2006). By comparison, the description-based approach could process higher or semantic levels of image properties by manually identifying and describing the images and objects therein in terms of what they are and what they represent. However, primitive feature matching (e.g., a particular shape of roof on a building) that can be done easily in CBIR would be an impracticable task in the description-based method. Each approach obviously holds its own place and has its own strengths in image retrieval (Chu, 2001).

Research in image retrieval is growing and expanding, especially in the content-based domain. The content-based approach, the more recent of the two, appears to be used in research projects more often and more extensively than the description-based approach (Chu, 2001). Nevertheless, the description-based approach remains the primary choice for operational systems (e.g., Graham, 1999).

The need for the integration of the two approaches becomes increasingly apparent as time passes and until automatic means for processing the semantic content of images are found (Cawkell, 1992). Eakins and Graham (1999), calling the description-based approach the keyword method, believed that the use of keywords and image features in combination would prove to be desirable. They listed several reasons to support their proposition. First, keywords can be used to capture the semantic content of images, while primitive feature match can usefully complement this by identifying image attributes (e.g., color or texture) that are hard to name using the description approach. Second, higher precision and recall scores can be achieved when, for example, text and color similarity are used in combination than when either is used separately. Third, retrieval by a combination of methods using different cognitive structures is likely to be more effective than by any single method (Ingwersen, 1996). Enser (2008) has referred to this integrated approach as semantic image IR.

Indeed, some researchers from the content-based community have tried to incorporate textual and semantic information with visual attributes of images into their research, signifying a promising start of the integration of the two methods (Chu, 2001). Reports linking the two distinct research approaches (e.g., Barnard, et al., 2003; Chang, et al., 1997b) were also published in recent years. In addition, Eakins and Graham (1999) noted in their study that the barriers between different research communities of the field are gradually coming down. The integration of the two approaches would bring about better and more efficient access to still images, as well as other types of multimedia information.

9.2.2 Sound Retrieval

Sound, also referred to as audio, includes nonverbal music and verbal speech, in addition to other natural or artificial sounds (e.g., birds chirping and traffic noise). Music and speech are the two major types of information explored in sound retrieval.

Music IR (MIR) has gradually become a distinct research area, with workshops, panels, and symposia specifically devoted to the topic (Downie, 2003). Like language—a major constituent in IR—music has hidden meaning. Yet music is even more complex than language in that each rendition of it adds a layer of complexity (Lippincott, 2002). Music has its own semantics, and a melody can convey meaning that words may or may not be able to describe. Similar to images, the same piece of music can be interpreted differently by people with different backgrounds and in different settings. In addition to musical attributes such as composer, style, and performer, used in description-based MIR, music possesses unique features (e.g., pitch, harmony, and timbre) based on which type of content-based MIR is performed. However, MIR faces daunting challenges in either retrieval approach due to the very nature of musical information itself (Byrd & Crawford, 2002; Downie, 2003).

Speech is in many ways a richer form of communication than written text because of the additional sound component. For example, the sound of a voice can help determine the speaker's identity (Oard, 2000). Speech is often referred to as spoken documents. Broadcast news, conference talks, and telephone conversations are some examples of spoken documents. Because sound information cannot be skimmed or scanned during the retrieval process, people have to listen to it from the beginning to the end when attempting to locate a particular segment. In general, listening to speech takes far more time than scanning text. Sound information obviously needs retrieval methods different from the ones for text retrieval.

9.2.2.1 Description-Based Retrieval of Sound Information

The description-based approach was the only method for sound IR before the emergence of the content-based approach. People can search music by, for example, composer, style, instruments used, or even music theme (Lesk, 2005). Speech information can be retrieved by, among other access points, speaker, location, date, media that recorded the speech, and speech topic. The main problems in using the description-based approach for sound retrieval are time and accuracy. Since sound information is not browsable, it is extremely time-consuming to prepare descriptions about sound information for retrieval purposes. If sound information attributes are categorized into two kinds, ofness and aboutness, the aboutness of sound information, as with any other type of information, is difficult for human beings to judge accurately. This seems especially true for nonverbal sound information, such as music that may not be intended for verbalization.

9.2.2.2 Content-Based Retrieval of Sound Information

Research on content-based music retrieval borrows from three fields: traditional IR, musicology, and music perception (Lippincott, 2002). Common attributes considered in content-based MIR include pitch, duration, harmony, and timbre. Specifically, pitch refers to how high or low the sound is. Duration deals with how long a note lasts. Harmony means two or more pitches sounded at the same time whereas timbre defines tone quality (Byrd & Crawford, 2002; Downie, 2003). These attributes are analyzed automatically for identification of music themes (Birmingham, et al., 2002) or discrete units of melodic information (Downie, 2000), which become the bases for content-based MIR. For example, Downie (2000) proposed the retrieval of music information by the n-gram intervals (i.e., distance between notes) contained within melodies. N-grams (see also §5.1.2.1) form discrete units of melodic information in much the same way as words form discrete units of language. Birmingham, et al. (2002), on the other hand, found that hidden Markov models worked well in the MusArt music retrieval system they developed. Algorithms for content-based MIR are in fact far more numerous than the two just mentioned. There seem to be as many automatic algorithms for music retrieval as there are users (Downie, 2000).

In a content-based MIR system, both database information and queries are processed using a particular algorithm for matching purposes. The end user can enter a query by singing, humming, or using a musical instrument (e.g., Birmingham, Dannenberg, & Pardo, 2006). But research on music retrieval, in contrast to that on text IR, is scarce even though annual conferences (e.g., the International Symposium on Music Information Retrieval) have been organized in recent years particularly for music retrieval. Operational content-based MIR systems are still rarely seen.

By comparison, far more research on content-based speech retrieval has been reported (e.g., Goodrum & Rasmussen, 2000; Spärck Jones, et al., 1996), and a track was created for spoken document retrieval (the SDR track) in the TREC series from TREC-6 through TREC-9 (Voorhees & Garofolo, 2000). The first step in speech retrieval is to separate nonspeech segments from speech segments. Nonspeech segments or speech constraints include nonspeech events (e.g., loud breath and tongue clicks), disfluencies (e.g., partially spoken words, pauses, and hesitations), functional events or components (e.g., *and* and *in addition*), and music or noise overlaid on speech. After these nonspeech segments are removed, the speech segments can be further analyzed by various speech attributes.

Speech segmentation is a challenging but necessary step in speech retrieval. While it is possible to directly transcribe the continuous stream of speech information without any prior segmentation, partitioning offers several advantages over the straightforward solution. First, interesting information can be extracted (e.g., the division between speakers and speaker identities) during the segmentation. Second, prior segmentation can avoid problems caused by linguistic discontinuity as the speaker changes. Third, eliminating nonspeech segments and dividing the data into shorter segments substantially reduce the computation time and simplifies decoding at a later stage (Gauvain, Lamel, & Adda, 2000).

A variety of algorithms have been developed for speech recognition and speech understanding. Recognizing who is talking is a slightly different problem from recognizing what is being said (Lesk, 2005). Speech recognition depends on speech understanding, which relies further on natural language processing (NLP), a topic discussed in Chapter 12. Pitch, speed, and intensity (i.e., longer pauses between sentences than between words) are among the attributes commonly used for sound retrieval. In addition, the speaker's gender, word usage statistics, and keywords characterizing each segment are employed in conjunction with a vocabulary specifically created for speech recognition and understanding (Kubala, et al., 2000; The SRI MAESTRO Team, 2000; Wactlar, et al., 2000). Established retrieval techniques such as weighting are also applied in speech retrieval (Spärck Jones, et al., 1996). The speech is automatically transcribed by the creation of corresponding text that will be used for matching during the retrieval process. Queries can be issued in the form of speech if a speech recognition mechanism is provided on the search end.

According to Lesk (2005), there are four parameters that strongly affect the difficulty of speech recognition:

1. Speech continuity: Continuous speech is more difficult to understand than speech with pauses between words and sentences.

2. Number of speakers: If all the speakers involved in a speech should be recognized, the task would be more difficult than if only one speaker is the subject of analysis.

3. Content of the speech: The content of a speech could range from anything without a fixed topic to a specific theme with a well-defined vocabulary, and it is much easier to perform speech recognition in the latter case than in the former one.

4. Speech environment: Many possibilities exist for speech environment. At one extreme the speaker uses a quality microphone in a quiet room (e.g., a conference speech), and at the other the speaker talks on a noisy street without a good microphone (e.g., an on-site interview). The former environment is the ideal one for speech recognition while the latter is not.

Besides the four factors, the speaker's accent could add to the complexity of speech recognition as well.

9.2.3 Moving Image Retrieval

Retrieval of moving images, because of their compositions, is built on the still image and sound retrieval just discussed. Moving images, comprising still images plus the moving attribute, can be accompanied by sound or not. Videos, movies, and television programs are examples of moving images with sound, whereas animations or silent movies represent moving images without sound.

The description-based approach has been exploited in retrieving moving images. Typical descriptions for moving images include such aspects as movie director and year of production, which are traditionally selected for reflecting ofness and aboutness. Moving image retrieval using this approach is, however, prone to the same problems (e.g., high cost and low efficiency) that are often present in retrieving other types of multimedia information.

Moving image retrieval using the content-based approach essentially involves three major tasks, although the retrieval may be conducted with some variations. The first task is to separate the sound component, if there is one, from moving images and process the sound information. The second task is to segment moving images into still images by shots or other attributes. The third task is to process the still images. In other words, moving image retrieval ultimately can be reduced to sound and still image retrieval. What really differentiates moving image retrieval from sound and still image retrieval lies in the segmentation of moving images. Because sound retrieval and still image retrieval have been considered in the previous sections, this discussion will concentrate on the segmentation of moving images for retrieval purposes.

Moving images must be segmented or decomposed before they become retrievable. Scenes or events are commonly used semantic units for segmenting moving images. They are identified by automatically detecting changes in such parameters as color distribution, texture, cuts, fades, dissolves, and camera flashes. A scene in turn comprises multiple shots that can be further decomposed into several frames each. So the breakdown can be done by scene, shot, or frame.

Segmenting moving images by shot is known as shot boundary detection (SBD). Most SBD techniques compute similarity between adjacent frames and flag a likely shot change when that similarity drops below a given threshold (Smeaton, 2004). These techniques work reasonably well if moving images have clear shot bounds, where the first frame of a new shot follows directly from the last frame of the previous shot. However, many moving images contain gradual transitions from one shot to another (e.g., fade-ins and fade-outs, dissolves, morphs, and wipes) to make them aesthetically more pleasing. It is such cosmetic effects in moving images that defy easy SBD. In comparison, some SBD techniques (e.g., edge detection) tend to handle gradual transitions well but are more likely to produce false positives during soft or out-of-focus shots (Smeaton, 2004).

As previously noted, a shot is made of frames grouped together on some common attributes. The frame that is representative of each shot is called the keyframe. Choosing a keyframe means locating the frame that best represents the average set of frames in a shot. The keyframe can be at the beginning of the shot, at the end, or any position in between. Nevertheless, no studies have been conducted to date to determine which techniques for keyframe selection are the most successful in practice (Smeaton, 2004). Rather, keyframe selection is often regarded as a "black art," and the most common approach involves choosing the keyframe from the middle of a shot.

A group of keyframes can then be put together to form a storyboard of annotated still images for representing each scene. Although automatic grouping of shots into logical scenes via keyframes is currently attracting much attention, efforts of this kind have proven difficult except in well-structured domains of moving images (e.g., broadcast TV news, which typically involves anchor personnel, introductory credits, and a series of separate stories). In addition to the keyframe method, video skimming is used to produce a series of short video clips, each capturing the essential details of a single sequence or a series of semantically meaningful shots (Eakins & Graham, 1999). Those entities form the basis for moving image retrieval. A sequence of moving images generally provides more information than keyframes do for retrieval purposes. Moving images themselves could serve as queries if short video clips are extracted and available in the IR system. Query-by-motion-example is one case in point (Chang, et al., 1997a).

Another approach, perhaps the simplest and most common, is to match the text of a user's query against a transcript of the spoken content extracted from the moving image. In spoken-document retrieval, this technique can still be very effective, even with a word error rate as high as 50 percent (Spärck Jones, et al., 1996). As one implication of this research finding, moving image retrieval based on recognized speech seems promising. The best example of a video-retrieval system that supports transcript searching or searching through closed captions is the landmark Informedia Digital Video Library project (www.informedia.cs.cmu.edu) developed at Carnegie Mellon University (Hauptmann & Witbrock, 1997). Sometimes, the speech information contained within moving images can be employed to resolve the ambiguities in the segmentation and interpretation of moving images. The reverse also holds true (Wactlar, et al., 2000).

From this brief description, it can be seen that automatic segmentation of moving images is not an easy task. Rather, the segmentation is a complex and multistep process. For example, a video can first be composed by story, then by event, shot, and frame (Boykin & Merlino, 2000; Smeaton, 2004). While the breakdown by shot and frame appears straightforward, the segmentation by story and event requires human efforts or artificial intelligence. This is another reason the content-based approach should be combined with the description-based method in multimedia retrieval, given the current status of retrieval technology (Wan & Liu, 2008).

9.2.4 Multimedia Retrieval on the Internet

The web of the internet is well known for its capability of handling multimedia information. Consequently, a good number of internet retrieval systems (e.g., Google) support multimedia searching, either alone or in collaboration with companies specialized in multimedia information management, allowing the end user to have access to the wealth of multimedia on the web.

Three different description-based methods are available to end users retrieving multimedia information from the web:

1. By keyword: Users can retrieve multimedia information by keyword just as they do when in search of text information. This method works particularly well at sites that are designated for image searches, such as Picsearch (www.pic search.com).

2. By multimedia type: Multimedia is a collective name for various kinds of nontext information, such as image, MP3, and video. These multimedia types can serve as access points in the retrieval process. Some internet retrieval systems (e.g., AltaVista) implement radio buttons or other similar mechanisms for people to choose the type of multimedia they would like to retrieve.

3. By filename extension: Filenames in the digital environment normally have up to three letters in their file extension to specify a file type. In the case of multimedia files, for example, *gif* and *jpg* are typical file extensions for still images. Sound files usually end with *au, wav, mp3*, or the like. File extensions for moving images include *mpg* and *mov*. These file extensions can be included in the query to retrieve the type of multimedia information specified (e.g., *greatwall.gif* as a search query).

The content-based approach is also available on the internet for retrieving multimedia information. Some internet retrieval systems support both approaches. For example, users can begin a search with the description-based keyword approach and then expand it with content-based attributes such as color and shape. Image search at Bing.com allows users to get more images similar to the one retrieved using keywords by simply clicking the "more similar images" link (Schwartz, 2008). Other systems are designed to deal only with content-based retrieval of multimedia information. Systems of this type (e.g., Convera's Visual RetrievalWare), however, are available to internet users only when the systems are undertaking the beta test. Once the testing is over, these systems become fee based and no longer in the public domain. Others might cease functioning due to the lack of promotion or proper management.

Multimedia IR on the internet is becoming easier than ever before, thanks to technology developments and researchers' efforts. But multimedia retrieval on the whole still has a long way to go before satisfactory performance is achieved. Lesk (2005) once summarized the state-of-the-art in multimedia retrieval as follows:

> We can classify pictures very roughly by color, texture and shape; this is not enough to deal with collections of millions of photographs. We can do speech recognition well enough to be of some use in analysis of voice recordings; we have little technology for searching music. We have various tricks for compressing and browsing video but only limited technology for searching it. (p. 115)

9.3 Hypertext and Hypermedia Information

The prefix *hyper* in hypertext means "extension into other dimensions" (Cornejo, 1994). In that sense, hypertext consists of nodes of information and links between them in a multidimensional space. Hypermedia is conceptually and structurally the same as hypertext except that hypermedia contains not only text but also sound and image information.

Nevertheless, both hypertext and hypermedia are different from text and multimedia in the following aspects. First, hypertext and hypermedia take a network structure rather than the linear and flat formation of text and multimedia. Second, linkages among hypertext and hypermedia exist physically while connections among nonhyperstructured documents are merely conceptual. Third, linkages among hyperstructured documents are established for the user whereas the user has to make connections among nonhyperstructured documents whenever necessary. The unique features of hypertext and hypermedia lead to new ways of IR in the hyperstructured environment.

Browsing, rather than searching, should be the major approach one uses in retrieving hypertext and hypermedia because, as discussed in §6.2.2, the hyperstructure environment encourages browsing activities. Access points or query terms are provided as hyperlink names in this retrieval process, eliminating the need for the user to choose them. Query term selection may sound easy to the trained information professional. To the end user, however, it is a complicated and demanding task that involves concept analysis and consideration of term variations. Moreover, the user is able to move automatically in this multidimensional IR space by just clicking on hyperlinks that connect various nodes of information. When searching is chosen as the retrieval approach, link names are evaluated as more important than regular terms in weighting and ranking if such a mechanism is available. For example, many internet retrieval systems rank a particular retrieved item higher than others if the query term matches a link name contained within the document.

On the other hand, retrieving hypertext and hypermedia by browsing has potential problems due to the hyperstructure. First, users may get lost in the hyperspace when browsing by simply following hyperlinks. Second, users may find it difficult to gain an overview of the information they are looking for because their attention can be sidetracked easily by so many other linked documents. Third, users might have difficulty finding specific information even if they know the information is present in the system. Site maps created at certain websites could be helpful in this respect. But they are not available in all hyperstructured IR systems, and if available, they might not be as detailed as desired.

Introducing the search approach in the hyperstructured environment facilitates the retrieval of hypertext and hypermedia. In fact, searching appears to be able to overcome all three problems enumerated for browsing as an approach to hypertext and hypermedia retrieval. While hyperstructured documents encourage browsing, searching would surmount any retrieval problems associated with browsing in a hyperspace. The integration of searching and browsing approaches, therefore, seems to be the best way of retrieving hypertext and hypermedia.

References

Balkin, Ruth. (1999). AltaVista's automatic translation program. *Database*, 22(2), 56–57.

Barnard, Kobus, et al. (2003). Matching words and pictures. *Journal of Machine Learning Research*, 3, 1107–1135.

Birmingham, William, Dannenberg, Roger, and Pardo, Bryan. (2006). Query by humming with the VocalSearch system. *Communications of the ACM*, 49(8), 49–52.

Birmingham, William, et al. (2002). The MusArt music retrieval system. *D-Lib Magazine*, 8(2). Retrieved December 19, 2008, from www.dlib.org/dlib/february02/birmingham/02birmingham.html

Boykin, Stanley, and Merlino, Andrew. (2000). Machine learning of event segmentation for news on demand. *Communications of the ACM*, 43(2), 35–41.

Byrd, Donald, and Crawford, Tim. (2002). Problems of music information retrieval in the real world. *Information Processing & Management*, 38(2), 249–272.

Cawkell, A. E. (1992). Selected aspects of image processing and management: Review and future prospects. *Journal of Information Science*, 18, 179–192.

Chang, Shih-Fu, et al. (1997a). VideoQ: An automated content based video search system using visual cues. *Proceedings of ACM Multimedia, Seattle, WA*, 313–324.

Chang, Shih-Fu, et al. (1997b). Visual information retrieval from large distributed online repositories. *Communications of the ACM*, 40(12), 63–71.

Chen, Aitao, and Gey, Fredric C. (2004). Multilingual information retrieval using machine translation, relevance feedback and decompounding. *Information Retrieval*, 7(1/2), 149–182.

Chu, Heting. (2001). Research in image indexing and retrieval as reflected in the literature. *Journal of the American Society for Information Science and Technology*, 52(12), 1011–1018.

CNNIC (China Internet Network Information Center). (January 2009). Statistical report on internet development in China. [In Chinese.] Retrieved January 20, 2009, from www.cnnic.net.cn/uploadfiles/pdf/2009/1/13/92458.pdf

Cornejo, J. G. (1994). *Hypertext: Its use in the documentary treatment of data*. Santiago, Chile: REDUCE-CIDE.

Coyle, Karen. (2005). Unicode: The universal character set. *The Journal of Academic Librarianship*, 31(6), 590–592.

Downie, J. Stephen. (2000). Access to music information: The state of the art. *Bulletin of the American Society for Information Science*, 26(5), 23–25.

Downie, J. Stephen. (2003). Music information retrieval. *Annual Review of Information Science and Technology*, 37, 295–340.

Eakins, John P., and Graham, Margaret E. (January 1999). *Content-based image retrieval: A report to the JISC Technology Applications Programme.*

Retrieved December 17, 2008, from www.jisc.ac.uk/uploaded_documents/jtap-039.doc

Enser, Peter. (2008). The evolution of visual information retrieval. *Journal of Information Science*, 34(4), 531–546.

Fallows, Deborah. (2007). China's online population explosion: What it may mean for the internet globally … and for U.S. users. Pew Internet & American Life Project. Retrieved October 9, 2009, from www.pewinternet.org/~/media/Files/Reports/2007/China_Internet_July_2007.pdf.pdf

Faloutsos, C., et al. (1994). Efficient and effective query by image content. *Journal of Intelligent Information Systems*, 3, 231–262.

Flickner, Maron, et al. (1995). Query by image and video content: The QBIC system. *IEEE Computer*, 28(9), 23–32.

Gauvain, Jean-Luc, Lamel, Lori, and Adda, Gilles. (2000). Transcribing broadcast news for audio and video indexing. *Communications of the ACM*, 43(2), 64–70.

Goodrum, Abby. (2000). Image information retrieval: An overview of current research. *Informing Science*, 3(2). Retrieved January 21, 2009, from inform.nu/Articles/Vol3/v3n2p63-66.pdf

Goodrum, Abby, and Rasmussen, Edie. (2000). Sound and speech in information retrieval: An introduction. *Bulletin of the American Society for Information Science*, 26(5), 16–18.

Gordon, Raymond G., Jr. (Ed.). (2005). *Ethnologue: Languages of the world*. 15th ed. Dallas, TX: SIL International.

Graham, Margaret E. (May 1999). *The description and indexing of images: Report of a survey of ARLIS members, 1998/99*. Retrieved February 1, 2000, from www.unn.ac.uk/iidr/ARLIS

Gey, Fredric C., Kando, Noriko, and Peters, Carol. (2005). Cross-language information retrieval: The way ahead. *Information Processing & Management*, 41(3), 415–431.

Hauptmann, Alexander G., and Witbrock, Michael J. (1997). Informedia: News-on-demand multimedia information acquisition and retrieval. In Mark T. Maybury (Ed.), *Intelligent multimedia information retrieval* (pp. 213–239). Menlo Park, CA: AAAI Press.

Hollink, Vera, et al. (2004). Monolingual document retrieval for European languages. *Information Retrieval*, 7(1/2), 33–52.

Ingwersen, Peter. (1996). Cognitive perspectives of information retrieval interaction: Elements of a cognitive IR theory. *Journal of Documentation*, 52(1), 3–50.

Jorgensen, Corinne. (2003). *Image retrieval: Theory and research*. Lanham, MD: Scarecrow Press.

Kishida, Kazuaki. (2005). Technical issues of cross-language information retrieval: A review. *Information Processing & Management*, 41(3), 433–455.

Kubala, Francis, et al. (2000). Integrated technologies for indexing spoken languages. *Communications of the ACM*, 43(2), 48–56.

Lawrence, Steve, and Giles, C. Lee. (July 8, 1999). Accessibility of information on the web. *Nature*, 400, 107–109.

Lerner, Reuven M. (2003). At the forge: Unicode. *Linux Journal*, 2003(107). [Article No. 8, html file].

Lesk, Michael. (2005). *Understanding digital libraries*. 2nd ed. San Francisco: Morgan Kaufmann.

Lippincott, Aura. (2002). Issues in content-based music information retrieval. *Journal of Information Science*, 28(2), 137–142.

Lyman, Peter, et al. (2000). How much information? Berkeley, CA: School of Information Management and Systems, University of California at Berkeley. Retrieved January 21, 2009, from www.sims.berkeley.edu/how-much-info/summary.html

Miniwatts Marketing Group. (2009). Internet world users by language. Retrieved October 8, 2009, from www.internetworldstats.com/stats7.htm

Mostafa, Javed. (1994). Digital image representation and access. *Annual Review of Information Science and Technology*, 29, 91–135.

Oard, Douglas W. (2000). User interface design for speech-based retrieval. *Bulletin of the American Society for Information Science*, 26(5), 20–22.

Panofsky, Erwin. (1955). *Meaning in the visual arts: Papers in and on art history*. New York: Doubleday Anchor Books.

Persson, Olle. (2000). Image indexing—A first author co-citation map. Retrieved January 21, 2009, from www.umu.se/inforsk/Imageindexing/imageindex.htm

Rasmussen, Edie M. (1997). Indexing images. *Annual Review of Information Science and Technology*, 32, 169–196.

Sands, Stella (Ed.). (2000). Languages. *Kids Discover*, 10(3), 3.

Schwartz, Barry. (2008). Search pictures with pictures at Live Search. Search Engine Land. Retrieved December 24, 2008, from searchengineland.com/ search-pictures-with-pictures-at-live-search-15666.php

Si, Lou, et al. (2008). An effective and efficient results merging strategy for multilingual information retrieval. *Information Retrieval*, 11(1), 1–24.

Smeaton, Alan F. (2004). Indexing, browsing, and searching of digital video. *Annual Review of Information Science and Technology*, 38, 371–407.

Spärck Jones, Karen. (2000). Further reflections on TREC. *Information Processing & Management*, 36(1), 37–85.

Spärck Jones, Karen, et al. (1996). Experiments in spoken document retrieval. *Information Processing & Management*, 32, 399–419.

SRI MAESTRO Team. (2000). MAESTRO: Conductor of multimedia analysis technology. *Communications of the ACM*, 43(2), 57–63.

Stix, Gary. (2006). A farewell to keywords. *Scientific American*, 295(1), 91–93.

Trant, Jennifer. (2004). Image retrieval benchmark database service: A needs assessment and preliminary development plan. A Report Prepared for the Council on Library and Information Resources and the Coalition for Networked Information. Retrieved December 18, 2008, from www.clir.org/pubs/reports/trant04/tranttext.htm

Unicode, Inc. (2008). What is Unicode? Retrieved December 13, 2009, from www.unicode.org/standard/WhatIsUnicode.html

Voorhees, Ellen, and Garofolo, John. (2000). The TREC Spoken Document Retrieval track. *Bulletin of the American Society for Information Science*, 26(5), 18–19.

Voorhees, Ellen, and Harman, Donna. (2000). Overview of the Sixth Text REtrieval Conference (TREC-6). *Information Processing & Management*, 36(1), 3–35.

Wactlar, Howard D., et al. (2000). Complementary video and audio analysis for broadcast news archives. *Communications of the ACM*, 43(2), 42–47.

Wan, Gary, and Liu, Zao. (2008). Content-based information retrieval and digital libraries. *Information Technology & Libraries*, 27(1), 41–47.

CHAPTER 10

The User Dimension in Information Representation and Retrieval

The user is a crucial factor that must be taken into consideration in all activities and efforts of information representation and retrieval (IRR) since the ultimate objective of IRR is to satisfy the user's information need. For example, information is represented so that users can retrieve it when needed. Various retrieval approaches and techniques have been developed so that users can choose appropriate ones based on their specific information needs.

The user dimension in IRR is vital regardless of the perspective one may take. From the system designer's viewpoint, for example, it is for the users to satisfy their information needs that IRR systems are constructed. Although users in information representation are most likely information professionals, different from the end users in information retrieval (IR), they share many similarities as users in IRR activities. This chapter examines users and their information needs and then explores the user-oriented cognitive approach in IRR. Finally, the interaction between the user and the IRR system is discussed along with some related issues.

10.1 Users and Their Information Needs

Users are individuals, each with distinctive characteristics. However, it is obviously impractical to study every single user for IRR purposes. Rather, researchers group users by applying common criteria such as gender, age, occupation, economic status, culture, personality, and educational background. It is based on these general features that we get to know the needs of various user groups better, even though we understand that user needs are affected by many other factors as well (e.g., information sources).

Take age as an example: Users of different ages have different information needs. On the whole, users of school age or at work normally have needs for education- or work-related information while other age groups tend to need general information most of the time. Occupation is another criterion that determines user needs. For instance, scientists usually form the so-called invisible colleges to exchange information (e.g., Crane, 1972; Price, 1963) while engineers in research and development labs rely on gatekeepers to communicate with the outside world (e.g., Allen, 1970). Chowdhury (1999) enumerated the information needs of users in different areas of activity (e.g., business and enterprises). More studies on users' information-seeking behavior, a newer term adopted by researchers in the field to replace the older expression information needs and uses, have been summarized by Case (2006, 2007) in his extensive survey of information seekers (i.e., users) by occupation (e.g., scientists or managers), role (e.g., patients or students), and demographics (e.g., age and ethnic group).

The digital age, especially the proliferation of the internet, has indeed redefined users and their information needs in the IRR process. Search histories, search preferences (e.g., file type, language, network domain, and country), and other search contexts are increasingly being explored in related research of IR on the internet (e.g., Komlodi, Soergel, & Marchionini, 2006; Rose, 2006). Meanwhile, the user should remain in control of how much context is included in the search query, both for privacy reasons and because current algorithms might sometimes incorrectly interpret context (Resnick & Vaughan, 2006). As the digital age is certainly upon us and here to stay, how this might affect future generations is becoming a research topic. For instance, Rowlands, et al. (2008), investigated the impact of digital transition on the information behavior of the Google generation (i.e., those born after 1993). The study claims that although young people demonstrate an apparent ease and familiarity with computers, they rely heavily on search engines, view rather than read, and do not possess the critical and analytical skills to assess the information they find on the web.

Understanding users and their needs facilitates IRR activities. A great many studies (e.g., for searchers, Borgman, 1989; Buente & Robin, 2008; Fenichel, 1981; Marchionini, et al., 1993; Zhang & Chignell, 2001; for indexers, Farooq, et al., 2007; Kipp & Campbell, 2006) have been conducted to explore the impact of user attributes on IRR in the digital age. Our knowledge about the user in IRR has undoubtedly increased thanks to research of this kind.

Information need, however, is a vague concept in that it is not well-structured but messy and disorganized. For this reason, Belkin and his colleagues dubbed it ASK, for anomalous state of knowledge (Belkin, Oddy, & Brooks, 1982). In addition, information needs have other features, including changing over time, varying from user to user, and depending on environment. Moreover, information needs often remain unexpressed or poorly expressed (Chowdhury, 1999). Indeed, users often have difficulty articulating their information needs at all, let alone expressing them accurately. It is not uncommon to get the following statement from users when they are asked what they are looking for: "I'll know when I see it." Information professionals often conduct reference interviews, a step in assisted searching, to help ease this problem.

Aside from user characteristics, Paisley (1968) identified four other factors affecting users' information needs:

1. Information sources: The array of information sources available to users has some effect on their needs. Users have different expectations when they are provided with, for example, information from a localized system as opposed to information from a system with national coverage.

2. Purpose: For what purpose do users need the information? If users want information only for answering some factual question (e.g., What is the world's tallest building?), their information needs are simple and straightforward. If users want information for a research project, their information needs clearly fit into another category.

3. External factors: Social, political, economic and other external factors can powerfully affect users and their information needs.

4. Outcome: What consequences do users get as a result of information use? For instance, positive outcomes (e.g., an increase in productivity) serve as rewards to the users and will encourage them to do more in that regard.

In short, users themselves, along with information sources, purpose, external factors, and outcome, constitute the five factors that influence their information needs. Although Paisley's work on information needs was published in 1968, it remains relevant today when we discuss the topic in the context of digital IRR.

As information needs are affected by so many factors, it is anticipated that there are different types of information needs. One common classification is to divide information needs into two categories: known-item need and subject need (Lancaster & Warner, 1993), or, in another set of terms, concrete information need and problem-oriented information need (Frants & Brush, 1988). Known-item need and concrete information need represent similar concepts, and the same holds true for subject need and problem-oriented information need. One category is specific and concrete while the other is not. It generally takes much more effort to meet a subject, or problem-oriented, information need. Other criteria (e.g., timeliness of information) for classifying information needs are applied less often. For example, users in hard sciences usually need current information whereas users from soft sciences may be more interested in retrospective and comprehensive information.

As pointed out earlier, IRR activities should be dictated totally by the information needs of users. Since it is the user who has information needs, the importance of the user dimension in IRR is manifest. Because of this reason, researchers try to adopt a user-centered approach to model development in IR.

10.2 The Cognitive Model and Other User-Centered Models

When the focus is on the user in IRR, researchers developing new models and approaches draw theories and methods from disciplines relating to human beings, such as psychology, sociology, and anthropology. The cognitive model of IR, for example, is a framework that draws heavily from cognitive psychology, while IRR in context is based on fundamentals of sociology, anthropology, and communication (Rogers, 2004). The following sections describe the cognitive model and other user-centered models in the field.

10.2.1 The Cognitive Model

Cognition is the mental faculty or process by which knowledge is acquired, or gained, as through perception, reasoning, and intuition (Soukhanov, et al., 1984). The cognitive model, different from other IR models, concentrates on users' cognitive activities during the IR process. For example, how is a user's information need formed? How does a user judge the relevance of results retrieved? These questions are obviously difficult ones, and researchers have been working on them over the years.

The IR models described in previous chapters focus on the information and system aspects of IR. For instance, how should information or queries be represented? What IR techniques should be supported? Which IR techniques work better than others? However, these models are still significantly limited in that little consideration is given to the social and cognitive contexts in which representation and retrieval tasks are carried out (Ingwersen, 1992). According to Ingwersen's (1996) cognitive model of IR interaction, there are three major elements (information objectives, IR system setting, and social or organizational environment), in addition to the user's cognitive space, which includes current cognitive state, problem or goal, uncertainty, information need, and information behavior. The user's cognitive process is emphasized in the cognitive model.

The cognitive model has many different implementations. For example, Belkin, Oddy, and Brooks (1982) designed an interactive IR system (e.g., question-answer) to find out the user's information need. The analysis of thinking-aloud protocols is another technique applied in understanding the cognitive activities of users when they search for information (e.g., Gorman, et al., 2002; Ingwersen, 1982). Pettigrew, Fidel, and Bruce (2001) described cognitive approaches to research on information-seeking behaviors at length even though their definition of cognitive frameworks is much broader than the one used in this book. The greatest strength of the cognitive model lies in its focus on the user's cognition, which is a determinant for the IR process. How is an information need formed? How is it transformed into a search query? How are retrieved results evaluated? All these questions relate to the user's cognition, and the cognitive model is designed to provide answers to such questions.

The cognitive model is user-oriented, which distinguishes it from IR models that emphasize the information or system components of the IR process. Users are dynamic. So are their information needs. Different users have different information needs. The same user's information need will be different at different times and locations and may change even during the interaction with the system. Again, only the cognitive model is able to deal with the dynamics of users with regard to their cognitive activities in IR. IR should be user-centered. Therefore, the orientation toward the user in the cognitive model can help build flexible and friendly IR systems.

Although the cognitive model appears very promising for improving IR performance, people's understanding of cognitive activities remains limited. As Ingwersen (1996) pointed out :

> Computers (or books for that matter) hold predefined and fixed presuppositions, whilst those of human beings are individually unpredictable, formed as they are by episodic, semantic and emotional experiences. (p. 6)

Users' cognitive activities in IR are unpredictable due to the nature of cognition and because we are yet to fully comprehend the cognitive process. Ingwersen (1996) suggested the poly-representation of the user's cognitive space and the information space of IR systems (e.g., providing cognitively overlapping access points, such as keywords, descriptors, and citations for retrieval purpose) as one method of tackling the uncertainty and unpredictability problem of cognition. The same suggestion was reiterated by Ingwersen and Jarvelin (2005).

In addition, cognition has some internal restrictions. For example, the capacity of people's short-term memory is seven chunks, plus or minus two (Miller, 1956). A chunk is a measurement for the smallest unit of meaningful information. A telephone number within a country, for example, consists of three chunks of information: area code (e.g., 212), region code (e.g., 333) and last four digits (e.g., 1819). The immediate implication of Miller's finding on users in the IR process is their limited capability to process information. If an IR system presents a dozen different choices simultaneously, users will have difficulty because the amount of information presented exceeds the capacity of their short-term memory. Therefore, IR systems should not have, for example, a menu with more than nine selections. On the other hand, a user may also feel tired, bored, or anxious when presented with many possibilities. All these factors can affect the user's cognitive ability. The cognitive model in IR must take such factors into consideration.

Human beings are the most complex creatures in the world. The least understood aspect of human beings is their cognition. Yet the cognitive model tries to attack the IR problem from the cognitive perspective. The approach is significant, and right on target, but it faces great challenges as well.

10.2.2 Other User-Centered Models of Information Retrieval

Research on information needs and users has flourished in recent years. According to Julien and Duggan (2000), studies of information needs, seeking, and use made up approximately 8 percent of research literature in library and information science at the time of their study. The percentage could have likely increased since then. Of these publications, many are devoted to user-centered models and conceptual approaches in IR (e.g., Bates, 1989; Belkin, et al., 1995; Dervin, 1992; Kuhlthau, 1993; Wilson, 1999). Extensive reviews of them can be found in Case (2007), Ingwersen and Järvelin (2005), Spink and Cole (2006), and Wilson (1999), in which the authors surveyed, contrasted, and explored numerous user-centered models in considerable detail.

Those user-centered models of IR are not only abundant in quantity but also have been formed with diverse orientations and from different perspectives. Researchers thus attempt to categorize such models using certain criteria in order to help others gain a better understanding of them. For example, Jarvelin and Wilson (2003) suggested that some models are of a summary type (e.g., Ellis, 1989; Ingwersen, 1996) and others are more analytic (e.g., Belkin, Oddy, & Brooks, 1982; Bystrom & Järvelin, 1995). Spink and Cole (2006), on the other hand, clustered user-centered models under three headings: the problem-solution perspective (e.g., Belkin, Oddy, & Brooks, 1982; Kuhlthau, 1993; Wilson, 1999), everyday-life information seeking and sense making (e.g., Dervin, 1992; Huotari & Chatman, 2001), and information foraging (e.g., Bates, 1989; Pirolli & Card, 1999). Regardless of how individual models are later examined, they all possess one feature in common, namely, keeping the user in the center of the model being created.

In retrospect, Wilson (2008) indicated that the development of user-centered IR research has led to a division between the needs of academia for theoretically grounded work and the needs of practitioners for service improvement guidance. Wilson further pointed out that a disconnection between research and practice comes to a significant extent: Early research was undertaken by practitioners, but presently research done by academia dominates the scene. This disconnection, nevertheless, should cause concerns in the field because a user-centered model would be worthless if it has few practical implications in IR, no matter how elegant it might sound. Disengagement between research and practice tends to produce results of no significance in the IR field. In addition, it is perhaps time to ponder the user-centered models already created and find out how they can be applied to assist users to perform better in the process of information seeking and retrieval. While some researchers (e.g., Case, 2007; Ingwersen & Järvelin, 2005; Wilson, 1999) have made good efforts in this respect, more work is definitely needed in this rapidly evolving area.

10.3 User and System Interaction

User interface is a term created to specifically take account of the user dimension in IRR. Interface is what the user sees, hears, and touches in interacting with the system (Shaw, 1991). The term interface, however, sounds static and focuses on just one point of the user-system interaction. For this reason, the term *user-system interaction* or simply *interaction* will also be used in this book to refer to the dynamic activities going on between the user and the IRR system. Another term that should receive some clarification in this chapter is human-computer interaction, or computer-human interaction. Neither term is used in this book because both *computer* and *human* are broader in meaning than the *system* and *user* dimensions of IRR that this book aims to cover.

10.3.1 Modes of User-System Interaction

User and system interaction in IRR can take place in any of the following modes: command language, menu selection, graphical operation, form fill-in, hyperlinks, and natural language dialog. These individual modes can also be applied simultaneously or in parallel for IRR.

10.3.1.1 Command Language

Chronologically speaking, command language was the first form developed for user-system interaction, and it dominated IR systems, particularly online systems such as DIALOG, in the early times of IRR. In this mode, command language (i.e., an artificial language specifically designed for retrieval purposes) is keyed in by the user to instruct the system to perform certain functions (e.g., starting a search). Command language terms are short; an example is *logoff* for ending a search and quitting the retrieval system. Another advantage of command language is speed of interaction (Large, Tedd, & Hartley, 1999). Compared with other interaction forms, command language is much faster at getting responses from the system because there are no extra steps (e.g., translating the menu selection into an instruction for the system) to be taken. In that sense, the interaction between the user and the system is direct. The speed is also valuable in an environment where charges for IR depend largely on connection time. In addition, users have flexibility in choosing which commands to use and are not limited by the choices listed, for example, in a menu. As a result, users have direct control of the interaction.

Command language as a mode of interaction, however, is not friendly to the user. The user has to learn, practice, and employ it on a regular basis due to its artificiality. The meaning of a command is sometimes not obvious and explicit to the user. For example, *select* stands for *search for* in DIALOG's vocabulary. Moreover, there is little uniformity among command languages in terms of syntax and semantics. The command language for ending a search session could be *exit* in one system and *logoff* in another. Interaction based on command language by and large offers little help and guidance to the user regarding what to do. The system may prompt, for example, "Enter a command" but give no hint as to which command to enter. Because of these difficulties, command language is mostly an interaction mode between the IR system and intermediaries (e.g., librarians and professional searchers) rather than between the IR system and end users.

10.3.1.2 Menu Selection

Menu selection is an interaction mode created, in part, to overcome the limitations of command language. CD-ROM systems and OPACs were the first two kinds of IR systems to employ the menu selection mode of interaction. The user interacts with the system by choosing from available options listed on the menu, which takes advantage of people's greater capacity for recognition than for recall. Therefore, in the menu selection mode, the user no longer needs to memorize commands and practice with them, as in the command language mode. Menus are also specific to the retrieval process. The menu choices shown, for example, during a search session and at the time of viewing search results are different. By contrast, the user has to figure out when to use which command in the command language mode. Furthermore, help in the form of a menu choice appears readily available to the user in the menu selection mode of interaction.

As an interaction mode, menu selection is more user-friendly than command language is. However, menu selection does not have the speed of command language in that the user has to interact with the system via the menu, and making a menu selection takes more time than typing in a command, especially when several levels of menus are provided in the system. Memory overload on the user is likely to occur if the number of menu choices exceeds the capacity of short-term memory (i.e., Miller's magic number 7, plus or minus 2, discussed in §10.2.1). Users also lose flexibility in directly interacting with the system because their selection is limited to what the system can supply. For novice users, however, menu selection is a preferred mode when interacting with IR systems.

10.3.1.3 Graphical Mode of Interaction

Graphical operation for user-system interaction is implemented by means of icons, buttons (including radio buttons), windows, and clickable maps. The user interacts with the system by operating (e.g., pointing and clicking) on such visual representations. The graphical mode of interaction is symbolized in internet retrieval systems. This mode of interaction uses representations of real-word objects (e.g., a printer icon for printing and a disc icon for saving files) and concept labels (e.g., a button labeled for searching) as the interface between the user and system. Windows can be opened, resized, and closed, depending on the need for interaction. Clickable maps allow the user to retrieve information by just clicking on the point that represents it. For example, a click at New York City on a national map of the U.S. would lead to the display of the city's map. The zoom in or zoom out features, if supported, are extremely helpful in using clickable maps.

The graphical mode of interaction can take different forms, but this mode collectively puts users at ease when they interact with it. The visualization of activities involved in retrieval tasks avoids overburdening the user with cognitive loads (e.g., choosing from a long list of menu items). The user may find enjoyment in the vivid and often colorful graphical mode of interaction. The multiplicity embedded in this mode enables the user to complete the retrieval task more efficiently. For instance, the user can choose icons for dealing with concrete objects in IR (e.g., print) while selecting buttons for abstract entities (e.g., Boolean searching).

The difficulty involved in developing the graphical mode of interaction should not be underestimated, however. Some operations in IR (e.g., go to the top of a document) cannot be represented appropriately by icons. In addition, graphical interaction may be unnecessary for certain IR activities (e.g., entering a query). The meaning of graphical representations, if not chosen properly, can be misleading or misunderstood. Graphical designs of interaction occupy more screen space and may thus force valuable information offscreen (Shneiderman & Plaisant, 2005). The time needed for interaction in the graphical mode is much longer than in the command language or menu selection mode because of the graphics. IR in this mode can thus be slow and cumbersome, which may not concern the user because the connection time accounts for little in computing the retrieval cost in such IR systems (e.g., internet retrieval systems).

10.3.1.4 Other Modes of User-System Interaction

Forms are a mode of user-system interaction in which the user fills in contents such as search terms and sets up search limits on a form the system provides. The form fill-in mode actually incorporates features of pull-down menus and buttons. OPACs and internet retrieval systems are two kinds of IR systems that often support this interaction mode. The user conducts a search by going over and filling out the form. There are no difficult decisions for the user to make. Rather, the system guides the user through the process of query formation and submission. The obvious limitation of this mode is its inflexibility in user-system interaction because the user is restricted to what is listed on the form.

Hyperlinks represent another form of interaction. There is some similarity between hyperlinks and menu selection; users interact with them by clicking on a menu item or a link that leads to another entity (e.g., another menu or a document). But hyperlinks do not have to be presented in groups, as in the case of menu selection. Hyperlinks can be created wherever they are needed, alone or with other hyperlinks. As discussed in §6.2.2, the hyperlink structure encourages browsing. Hyperlinks, therefore, are widely implemented in IR systems focusing on browsing. Yahoo!, the directory-based internet retrieval system, is an excellent example of the hyperlink mode of interaction. The user performs retrieval tasks by browsing through the hyperlinked categories Yahoo! develops. The main drawback of hyperlinks as an interaction mode lies in their networked structure. The user may get lost easily when interacting with the system by following the links because hyperlinks take up the network structure. The internal structure of hyperlinks often resembles a maze rather than a well-organized collection of links. Undoubtedly, the more hyperlinks there are in a retrieval system, the more confusing it becomes for the user.

Natural language is beginning to be applied in user-system interaction, and submitting queries in natural language to an IR system seems to be one of the major efforts in this respect. For instance, Ask.com (formerly Ask Jeeves) allows the user to enter queries using complete sentences (e.g., What is natural language processing?). The biggest advantage in using natural language in user-system interaction is its directness; any query representation would inevitably introduce distortion and alteration in meaning. The user in natural language mode would then have no need to interpret the meaning of the representations created for interaction purposes (e.g., command language, icons, and menu items). While natural language is an extremely desirable form of user-system interaction, successful implementation of it is ultimately determined by the advancement of research on natural language processing, a topic explored in Chapter 12.

Closely related to the natural language mode of interaction is voice activation in IR systems. The user in this circumstance interacts with the system via spoken rather than written language. This mode of interaction relies heavily on voice recognition technology, which is still in the development stage.

Organic user interface (OUI) began appearing in the literature (e.g., Vertegaal & Poupyrev, 2008) as an envisioned form of user-system interaction. The name was chosen because: 1) The underpinning technologies for some of the most important OUI developments are organic electronics, and 2) the millions of organic shapes observed in nature are of amazing variety, flexibility, transformability, natural adaptability, and evolutionary potential, while extremely resilient and reliable at the same time. Vertegaal and Poupyrev (2008) enumerated three themes that define OUI. First, input equals output: The display is also the input device. The touch screen serves as an example in this case, and Rekimoto (2008) further illustrates this theme of OUI with elaborate examples such as HoloWall and SmartSkin. Second, function equals form: The display can take on any shape. The OUI replaces the rigid, rectangular matrix with more fluid notions that feature thin, flexible, and tactile surfaces customized to form and space (Co & Pashenkov, 2008). An ebook reader that can be folded might become a reality using the emerging OUI display technology. The third theme of OUI is that form follows flow (i.e., the flow of user interaction): Displays can change their shape to perform functionalities needed during user-system interaction. What is involved in this theme is the so-called kinetic design, through which physical transformability can be embedded in the interface (Parkes, Poupyrev, & Ishii, 2008). Because OUI is still a vision to be accomplished, it is too early to stipulate its pros and cons as a mode of user-system interaction.

10.3.1.5 The Hybrid Mode of Interaction

Recent years have witnessed the emergence of a hybrid mode of interaction, particularly in internet retrieval systems. Any combination of the interaction modes described earlier could form a hybrid interface, although command language is often not incorporated due to its shortcomings. For example, Exalead, a France-based internet retrieval system, supports menu selection, hyperlinks, command language (for Boolean operators, proximity operators, and the like), and graphical interface. The hybrid mode of interaction can eliminate the limitations of a single mode and enhance its efficiency and user-friendliness. In fact, unimode user-system interaction is rarely seen in newly developed IR systems because every single-interaction mode has limitations.

10.3.2 Other Dimensions of User-System Interaction

In addition to interaction mode, there are other aspects that a user should consider when interacting with an IR system. These dimensions include display features, output options, and help facilities.

10.3.2.1 Display Features

The user and the IR system interact via a certain kind of display, but physical devices for interaction (e.g., keyboard or mouse) are beyond the scope of this book. The interaction is further defined by such display features as color, font, density, and screen layout.

Screen layout marks out how information for interaction purpose is displayed on an interface (usually a computer screen). Does it support overlaying, frames, or multiple windows? Does the user need to scroll up and down to view all the information presented? Excessive use of the overlaying feature or too many frames or windows in one display can affect the user's ability to interact with the system efficiently. Likewise, most users (novices in particular) are not adept at scrolling techniques. It is always better to display all the information on one screen, if possible, rather than on multiple screens.

Font type, style, and size determine the display quality of textual information. The minimum standard for displaying texts is clarity and readability. Galitz (1997) suggests that no more than two font types (e.g., Times New Roman or Courier), two styles (e.g., regular and italic), and three sizes be used for one display. Illegible font type or font size that is too small should be avoided. Font style, if appropriately used, can facilitate the interaction process.

Color, contrast, and brightness decide another display dimension, namely, the comfort level of the user when interacting with the system. The number of colors and the combination of colors affect whether the final display looks pleasant to the user. The right degrees of contrast and brightness should also be tested because extremes in either measure can cause discomfort to users' eyes. Background color and background image fall into this category of display features. Experience shows that black on white is generally a good combination for display. Caution should be exercised when images are used as background because images may overshadow other important information that needs to be displayed. It may also take a longer time to load such a display. For these reasons, some internet retrieval systems that utilized an image background in earlier days soon discontinued the practice.

Density of display is another factor that can influence the friendliness of user-system interaction. For example, how much information should be displayed on one screen? While a detailed specification about density seems unlikely because parameters such as fonts also have an impact on density, an optimal degree of density should be sought in a given setting. Generally, neither a crowded screen nor too much blank space will appear welcoming to the user.

Special effects such as highlighting, blinking, and inverse video can all help achieve particular results in user-system interaction if used properly. Inconsistent use or overuse of any special effect can cause confusion or even discomfort to the user. Among all the major types of IR systems, internet retrieval systems seem most prone to busy screens, a consequence of overusing special effects and other display features.

10.3.2.2 Output Options

Retrieval results can be presented differently depending on such parameters as formats and quantities. Output formats in online systems are most versatile. The user can choose from predefined formats (e.g., bibliographic information only or bibliographic information plus abstract) or specify particular fields (e.g., author and title) for output. OPAC systems usually support three output formats: short, long, and MARC records. As for internet retrieval systems, they have limited choices of output formats because of their indexing mechanism. Retrieval results from the internet usually consist of titles and an extract (i.e., first few lines of a site). Incomplete sentences are the norm rather than an exception in such extracts.

IR systems commonly provide the user with different means for obtaining results: download, print, email, or screen display. Output quantity refers to the number of results to be presented each time the user makes a request. Online retrieval systems generally allow the user to specify any number of the results retrieved for outputs. OPAC systems, in comparison, require users to indicate their choices by first marking or selecting individual records. It is well known that internet retrieval systems can easily generate thousands, if not millions, of search results. But the user normally can only get 10, 20, or 30 results each time a request for outputs is made. There is no mechanism that allows the user to have all the outputs at once. However, the limitation in obtaining internet search results is not a major concern to the user because outputs from internet retrieval systems are usually ranked in decreasing order of relevance, and few users really want to go through all the search results.

Output options are not a crucial factor in user-system interaction. However, flexibility in presenting retrieval results can enhance user-friendliness. Visualization of search results is increasingly offered by some IR systems to help the user obtain a graphical view of what has been retrieved. In general, OPACs (e.g., aqua.queenslibrary.org) and internet retrieval systems (e.g., www.quintura.com) seem to be moving faster than online systems in visualizing search results. A number of IR systems also provide thumbnail images of book covers (e.g., books.google.com) or webpages (e.g., www.ask.com) along with text search results so that the user has more information for judging the relevance of retrieved results.

10.3.2.3 Help Facilities

Help facilities (e.g., manual, tutorial, or cue cards) determine to a great extent the user-friendliness of IR systems. Help facilities should truly help users find answers to the questions they may have when interacting with IR systems. Trenner (1989) identified six such questions in a study comparing the online help facilities in 16 IR systems:

1. What have I done wrong or why have I received this error message?

2. Am I doing the right thing?

3. Where am I and what can I do next?

4. How do I do something?

5. How do I get some information?

6. Why has the system failed?

The first question deals with the situation in which the user did something wrong or received an error message. Ideally, the help facility will not only indicate what was done wrong but also specify what can be done to correct the mistake. However, most help facilities of IR systems are able to do the former but fail to carry out the latter. As a result, the user is left in the dark, bewildered and baffled. As for the rest of the questions Trenner (1989) listed, most help facilities can answer the fourth and fifth questions reasonably well but are weak in handling second, third, and sixth questions. At present, help facilities are generally good at listing procedural information for retrieval activities. When it comes to questions that require an explanation, most help facilities in IR systems show their incompetence.

Researchers (e.g., Shneiderman & Plaisant, 2005; Trenner, 1989) have proposed guidelines for designing help facilities for computerized systems, including IR systems. From the user's viewpoint, a good help facility should be able to provide answers to users' questions rather than simply present some data the system has pre-prepared. The answers should also be free of jargon and threatening language (e.g., "an illegal operation has been performed") and be available all the time and for users at different levels. Users seek help from IR systems when they need to. If the help facility cannot satisfy users' needs, even the function of IR systems may not be fulfilled, let alone the issue of user-friendliness.

10.3.3 Evaluation of User-System Interaction

User-friendliness is a broad criterion for evaluating user-system interaction. More specific measures have been developed (e.g., Shneiderman & Plaisant, 2005) for the same purpose.

10.3.3.1 Time Needed for the User to Learn Specific Information Retrieval Functions

Learning takes place when the user interacts with an IR system. That is, users need to learn how to use an IR system before actually conducting searches. The ease of learning is reflected in the time needed for the user to acquire a particular retrieval skill (e.g., Boolean searching). The shorter the learning time, the better the IR system becomes with regard to its user-friendliness. A hostile system does not present a relaxing environment in which the user can learn.

10.3.3.2 Speed of Interaction

How long will it take for the user to receive feedback from the IR system during the interaction? The longer the process takes, the less user-friendly the system becomes. According to Shneiderman and Plaisant (2005), response time for common tasks should be between 2 and 4 seconds, and a waiting time longer than 15 seconds will be disruptive. Although these response time guidelines are for interaction in general, they are certainly applicable to the IR environment. This criterion is decided basically by the IR system's processing capability. Powerful processors usually provide fast speed of interaction.

10.3.3.3 Rate of Errors by the User

If an IR system is intuitive and self-explanatory, users commit few errors in interacting with it. Otherwise, errors are inevitable (e.g., making a wrong choice). The number of errors the user makes during the retrieval process becomes another measurement for judging the user-friendliness of an IR system. The help facility discussed previously can play an important role in reducing error rate. Users naturally make fewer mistakes if help is available to them when it is needed and if the interaction process is transparent to them.

10.3.3.4 Retention Over Time

Interaction techniques, especially in the command mode, need to be learned and practiced in order to be mastered. Retaining these skills over a period of time is an assessment of the user-friendliness of IR systems from a different perspective. For example, a command language can be easy to remember if the commands are mnemonic and consistent, just as a print command should use the word *print* instead of *prt*, *type*, or anything else. A friendly interface will, because of positive reinforcement, enable users to retain what they know about the system longer than a hostile one will.

10.3.3.5 The User's Satisfaction

This measurement of user-friendliness is subjective because it is difficult to evaluate satisfaction objectively even though satisfaction can be quantified in some ways (e.g., number of results retrieved). Nevertheless, this criterion should be considered in the evaluation of the qualitative part in user-system interaction. For instance, how does the user feel about the interaction? Some researchers (e.g., Hildreth, 2001) categorize user satisfaction as either material satisfaction (i.e., results obtained from the IR interaction) or emotional satisfaction (i.e., a sense of achievement as a result of the interaction). In general, the friendlier a user-system interaction is, the more satisfied the user becomes.

There are, however, forced trade-offs among the five criteria just described (Shneiderman & Plaisant, 2005). It is hard for any user-system interaction to achieve top performance in all the aspects. Consideration should always be given to the user because all the IR activities are centered on the user rather than the system.

Despite the fact that there is still much to be desired in user-system interaction, the situation has definitely improved as more experience has been gained in meeting user requirements (Large, et al., 1999). From command language mode to hybrid mode of interaction, from monochrome display to artistic application of various features, from help messages loaded with technical terms to cue cards free of jargon, user-system interaction is friendlier today than in the past.

10.4 The User and Information Retrieval in the Digital Age

Digital technology indeed improves the efficiency of IR activities. It also brings about some concerns and issues to the user, especially the neophyte. For instance, IR in the digital age depends on digital technology that might cause anxiety and alienation to the user. Not everyone is comfortable conducting searches in a computerized system. Due to the imperfection of current IR systems, the user may feel disoriented when trying to retrieve information in the digital environment. In addition, specialized equipment is needed to retrieve information digitally. The pencil-and-paper approach to searching for information manually in the print world no longer works effectively in the digital age.

Furthermore, IR systems in the digital age are constantly upgraded, or new ones are introduced. A user may have to learn or be trained on a regular basis to keep up with the changes, which adds extra work to the user's already demanding schedule. In other words, IR in the digital age can have side effects for the user because of the technology factor.

In addition to the technology factor, users of different IR systems should be treated differently because they tend to have different IR experiences. For instance, online system users are either information professionals serving as intermediaries or end users who have received proper training. In contrast, users of internet retrieval systems are less likely to have training in IR. The user dimension thus becomes increasingly diversified for IR in the digital age.

Although information representation in the digital age does not have as direct an impact on the user as does IR, the influence of digital technology in this area is by no means negligible. What makes the influence less visible is the fact that people who do information representation are usually information professionals who have adapted to the rhythm and tempo of the digital age through their training and work.

References

Allen, Thomas. (1970). Communication networks in R & D laboratories. *R & D Management*, 1. Reprinted in Belver C. Griffith (Ed.), *Key papers in information science* (pp. 66–73). White Plains, NY: Knowledge Industry Publications.

Bates, Marcia J. (1989). The design of browsing and berrypicking techniques for the online searching interface. *Online Review*, 13(5), 407–424.

Belkin, Nicholas J., et al. (1995). Cases, scripts and information seeking strategies: On the design of interactive information retrieval systems. *Expert Systems With Applications*, 9(3), 379–395.

Belkin, Nicholas J., Oddy, Robert N., and Brooks, Helen M. (1982). ASK for information retrieval. Part I. Background and theory. *Journal of Documentation*, 38(2), 61–71.

Borgman, Christine L. (1989). All users of information retrieval systems are not created equal: An exploration into individual differences. *Information Processing & Management*, 25(3), 237–251.

Buente, Wayne, and Robbin, Alice. (2008). Trends in internet information behavior 2000–2004. *Journal of the American Society for Information Science and Technology*, 59(11), 1743–1760.

Byström, Katriina, and Järvelin, Kalervo. (1995). Task complexity affects information seeking and use. *Information Processing & Management*, 31(2), 191–213.

Case, Donald O. (2006). Information behavior. *Annual Review of Information Science and Technology*, 40, 293–327.

Case, Donald O. (2007). *Looking for information: A survey of research on information seeking, needs, and behavior.* 2nd ed. Boston: Academic Press.

Chowdhury, Gobinda G. (1999). *Introduction to modern information retrieval.* London: Library Association Publishing.

Co, Elise, and Pashenkov, Nikita. (2008). Emerging display technologies for organic user interfaces. *Communications of the ACM*, 51(6), 45–47.

Crane, Diane. (1972). *Invisible colleges: Diffusion of knowledge in scientific communities.* Chicago: University of Chicago Press.

Dervin, Brenda (1992). From the mind's eye of the user: The sense-making qualitative-quantitative methodology. In Jack D. Glazier and Ronald R. Powell (Eds.), *Qualitative Research in Information Management* (pp. 61–84). Englewood, CO: Libraries Unlimited.

Ellis, David. (1989). A behavioural approach to information retrieval design. *Journal of Documentation*, 45(3), 171–212.

Farooq, Umer, et al. (2007). Evaluating tagging behavior in social bookmarking systems: Metrics and design heuristics. *Proceedings of the ACM Conference on Supporting Group Work* (pp. 351–360). New York: Association of Computing Machinery.

Fenichel, Carol H. (1981). Online searching: Measures that discriminate among users with different types of experiences. *Journal of the American Society for Information Science*, 32, 23–32.

Frants, Valery I., and Brush, Craig B. (1988). The need for information and some aspects of information retrieval systems construction. *Journal of the American Society for Information Science*, 39(2), 86–91.

Galitz, Wilbert O. (1997). *Essential guide to user interface design: An introduction to GUI design: Principles and techniques*. New York: John Wiley & Sons.

Gorman, Paul, et al. (2002). Following experts at work in their own information spaces: Using observational methods to develop tools for the digital library. *Journal of the American Society for Information Science and Technology*, 53(14), 1245–1250.

Hildreth, Charles. (2001). Accounting for users' inflated assessments of online catalog search performance and usefulness: An experimental study. *Information Research*, 6(2). Retrieved January 21, 2009, from informationr.net/ir/6-2/paper101.html

Huotari, Maija-Leena, and Chatman, Elfreda. (2001). Using everyday life information seeking to explain organizational behavior. *Library & Information Science Research*, 23(4), 351–366.

Ingwersen, Peter. (1982). Search procedures in the library analyzed from the cognitive point of view. *Journal of Documentation*, 38, 165–191.

Ingwersen, Peter. (1992). *Information retrieval interaction*. London: Taylor Graham.

Ingwersen, Peter. (1996). Cognitive perspectives of information retrieval interaction: Elements of a cognitive IR theory. *Journal of Documentation*, 52(1), 3–50.

Ingwersen, Peter, and Järvelin, Kalervo. (2005). *The turn: Integrating of information seeking and retrieval in context*. Dordrecht, The Netherlands: Springer.

Jarvelin, Kalervo, and Wilson, Tom D. (2003). On conceptual models for information seeking and retrieval research. *Information Research*, 9(1), paper 163. Retrieved December 20, 2008, from informationr.net/ir/9-1/paper163.html

Julien, Heidi, and Duggan, Lawrence J. (2000). A longitudinal analysis of the information needs and uses literature. *Library & Information Science Research*, 22(3), 291–309.

Kipp, Margaret E. I., and Campbell, D. Grant. (2006). Patterns and inconsistencies in collaborative tagging systems: An examination of tagging practices. *Proceedings of the Annual Meeting of the American Society for Information Science and Technology*, 43. [CD-ROM]. Retrieved January 5, 2009, from dlist.sir.arizona.edu/1704/01/KippCampbellASIST.pdf

Komlodi, Anita, Soergel, Dagobert, and Marchionini, Gary. (2006). Search histories for user support in user interfaces. *Journal of the American Society for Information Science and Technology*, 57(6), 803–807.

Kuhlthau, Carol C. (1993). *Seeking information: A process approach to library and information services.* Norwood, NJ: Alblex.

Lancaster, F. W., and Warner, Amy J. (1993). *Information retrieval today.* Arlington, VA: Information Resources Press.

Large, Andrew, Tedd, Lucy A., and Hartley, R. J. (1999). *Information seeking in the online age: Principles and practice.* London: Bowker-Saur.

Marchionini, Gary, et al. (1993). Information seeking in full-text end-user-oriented search systems: The roles of domain and search expertise. *Library & Information Science Research*, 15, 35–69.

Miller, George A. (1956). The magical number seven plus or minus two: Some limits on our capacity for processing information. *Psychological Review*, 63, 81–97.

Paisley, William J. (1968). Information needs and uses. *Annual Review of Information Science and Technology*, 3, 1–30.

Parkes, Amanda, Poupyrev, Ivan, and Ishii, Hiroshi. (2008). Designing kinetic interactions for organic user interfaces. *Communications of the ACM*, 51(6), 58–65.

Pettigrew, Karen E., Fidel, Raya, and Bruce, Harry. (2001). Conceptual frameworks in information behavior. *Annual Review of Information Science and Technology*, 35, 43–78.

Pirolli, Peter, and Card, Stuart K. (1999). Information foraging. *Psychological Review*, 106(4), 643–675.

Price, Derek J. de Solla. (1963). *Little science, big science.* New York: Columbia University Press.

Rekimoto, Jun. (2008). Organic interaction technologies: From stone to skin. *Communications of the ACM*, 51(6), 38–44.

Resnick, Marc L., and Vaughan, Misha W. (2006). Best interface and future visions for search user interfaces. *Journal of the American Society for Information Science and Technology*, 57(6), 781–887.

Rogers, Yvonne. (2004). New theoretical approaches for human-computer interaction. *Annual Review of Information Science and Technology*, 38, 87–143.

Rose, Daniel E. (2006). Reconciling information-seeking behavior with search user interfaces for the web. *Journal of the American Society for Information Science and Technology*, 57(6), 797–799.

Rowlands, Ian, et al. (2008). The Google generation: The information behaviour of the researcher of the future. *ASLIB Proceedings*, 60(4), 290–310.

Shaw, Debora. (1991). The human-computer interface for information retrieval. *Annual Review of Information Science and Technology*, 26, 155–195.

Shneiderman, Ben, and Plaisant, Catherine. (2005). *Designing the user interface: Strategies for effective human-computer interaction.* 4th ed. Boston: Addison-Wesley.

Soukhanov, Anne H., et al. (Eds.). (1984). *Webster's II new Riverside university dictionary.* Boston: Riverside Publishing Co.

Spink, Amanda, and Cole, Charles. (2006). Human information behavior: Integrating diverse approaches and information use. *Journal of the American Society for Information Science and Technology*, 57(1), 25–35.

Trenner, L. (1989). A comparative survey of the friendliness of online "help" in interactive information retrieval systems. *Information Processing & Management*, 25(2), 119–136.

Vertegaal, Roel, and Poupyrev, Ivan. (2008). Organic user interfaces. *Communications of the ACM*, 51(6), 26–30.

Wilson, Tom D. (1999). Models of information behaviour research. *Journal of Documentation*, 55(3), 249–270.

Wilson, Tom D. (2008). The information user: Past, present and future. *Journal of Information Science*, 34(4), 457–464.

Zhang, Xiangmin, and Chignell, Mark. (2001). Assessment of the effects of user characteristics on mental models of information retrieval systems. *Journal of the American Society for Information Science and Technology*, 52(6), 445–459.

CHAPTER 11

Evaluation of Information Representation and Retrieval

Now that the various aspects and components of information representation and retrieval (IRR) have been discussed, it is time to evaluate these interrelated activities. Many researchers (e.g., Keen, 1971; Large, Tedd, & Hartley, 1999; Swanson, R. W., 1978) have elaborated on the need for evaluating IRR. It is hoped that IRR will be improved when the weaknesses of IRR systems are identified and eventually eliminated as a result of the evaluation process.

Evaluation of IRR is a subject that has been of interest to many great minds in the field for more than 50 years. Nevertheless, there exists much controversy over evaluation measures and methodologies. In this chapter, three major topics will be discussed: 1) evaluation measures (e.g., precision and recall) for representation and retrieval performance, 2) evaluation criteria for different types of IR systems, including a note on usability, and 3) two major IRR evaluation projects: the Cranfield tests and the Text REtrieval Conference (TREC) series. The issue of evaluation methodology is examined, along with the major experiments in the field.

11.1 Evaluation Measures for Information Representation and Retrieval

Many measures have been developed for evaluating IRR. For clarity, evaluation measures will be discussed separately for information representation and information retrieval (IR).

11.1.1 Evaluation Measures for Information Representation

As depicted in Chapters 2 and 3, information can be represented in a variety of ways. Indexing, categorization, and summarization are some major forms of information representation. Although each form of information representation has its unique features, collectively they are intended to bring out the essence in information and make the information retrievable at a later time. Therefore, a common set of evaluation criteria (e.g., accuracy, brevity, consistency, and objectivity) is applicable to all kinds of information representation.

11.1.1.1 Accuracy

Accuracy is the most important measure in evaluating the quality of information representation because a distorted representation of original documents would lose the entire point of representing them. Accuracy means that the representation accurately represents the content of original documents. Reduction in representation would happen in terms of magnitude but not in terms of content. Consideration should also be given to accuracy in, for example, citation and spelling.

Specificity is a concept closely related to accuracy and commonly used to measure indexing quality. By definition, specificity means the extent to which a concept or topic in a document is identified by a precise term in the hierarchy of its genus-species relations (Wellisch, 1995). For example, in the hierarchy of *information retrieval—multimedia retrieval—video retrieval,* the term *video retrieval* will be assigned to a document dealing with the topic to ensure the highest indexing specificity. The other two terms in the hierarchy have lower specificity. Specificity is determined by the indexing language (i.e., controlled vocabulary or natural language) used. Natural language generally enables one to achieve high indexing specificity.

11.1.1.2 Brevity

One of the objectives of representing information is to help users save time and effort in getting the information they need. Information explosion is one phrase coined to describe the enormous amount of information that users have to deal with. On the other hand, it is an acknowledged fact that it takes a user much less time to go over a representation (e.g., abstracts, summaries, and indexing terms) than to read an original document. Brevity thus becomes a principal measure for judging whether the objective of saving time and effort is achieved.

Specific criteria have been set up for different formats of information representation (e.g., Lancaster, 1998) with regard to brevity. Take journal articles as an example: usually five to 10 indexing terms are assigned and an abstract of 250 words or fewer is prepared. If a representation takes a lengthy format, it offers little help to users in reducing their time in information retrieval. Exhaustivity in indexing can be treated as a term related to brevity. Wellisch (1995) defined exhaustivity as the extent to which concepts and topics are made retrievable by means of index terms. Exhaustivity is decided by the indexing policy adopted in the practice.

11.1.1.3 Consistency

The same document may be represented in multiple formats (e.g., indexing and abstract) and by different people. It is also common to see one publication (e.g., a journal) indexed by different indexing services. For example, the *Journal of the American Society for Information Science and Technology* is indexed in *Chemical Abstracts, Computer Literature Index,* and 10 other abstracting and indexing service products. While this practice implements the poly-representation of information that Ingwersen (1996) suggested, the end products may be inconsistent in coverage and style. Studies in indexing have found that a high level of consistency is very difficult to obtain, and indexing consistency ranges from 10 percent to 80 percent (e.g., Hooper, 1965). Cleverdon (1984) reported that when two experienced indexers indexed the same document, using the same controlled vocabulary, they assigned only 30 percent of the terms in common. Information representation in the digital age, thanks to automated and automatic techniques, can theoretically attain better consistency, but empirical research in this area has yet to be conducted.

Consistency does not imply just word-by-word matches. Rather, it refers to a uniform representation (e.g., vocabulary, depth of coverage) of the essence of original documents, regardless of format or the person who does the representation. Inconsistency can affect the quality of representation and eventually retrieval performance as well.

11.1.1.4 Objectivity

Objectivity constitutes another evaluation criterion for information representation because subjectivity and personal interpretations are likely to be brought in during the representation process. Information representation should be an authentic description of the original document, without any alteration of its content. It is also important not to project one's personal preferences onto the representation. More specifically, any reinforcement of the opinions of the author, deliberate interpolation of the attitudes of the indexer, selection of terminology implying attitudes, or suppression of ideas from the document in the index impairs the objectivity of information representation (Bell, 1991). A subjective representation does not reflect the true image of the original document.

11.1.1.5 Clarity, Readability, and Usability

In addition to the measures just described, other criteria have been put forward for evaluating information representation. Clarity, readability, and usability are among them. These measures all attempt to show user-friendliness and make users more at ease when they deal with information representation.

Evaluation measures for information representation are fewer than those for IR, and this kind of evaluation also does not distinguish the representation process from representation performance. Strictly speaking, the quality of representation cannot be truly evaluated unless it is used in information retrieval. At the same time, the quality of IR depends on the quality of information representation. Good information representation plays an essential role in ensuring good retrieval performance. It is only through IR that the quality of information representation can ultimately be judged.

11.1.2 Evaluation Measures for Information Retrieval

Compared with information representation, information retrieval has received much more attention from researchers in terms of evaluation measures, partly because the former is merely a prerequisite for the latter. As previously mentioned, the quality of representation cannot be truly assessed until the representation is used in retrieval. Information retrieval is both performance-oriented and process-oriented, although people, especially end users, are typically more interested in what has been retrieved than in what has been done during the process. A better understanding of the retrieval process would, however, help improve retrieval performance. For this reason, evaluation measures developed for IR can be approximately categorized into two kinds, one concentrating on performance and the other on process. The former kind of measure is discussed in §11.1.2 whereas measures for evaluating retrieval process or the entire IR system are covered in §11.2. Among the measures for evaluating retrieval performance, recall and precision are the two most well-known and widely adopted criteria (Salton, 1992).

11.1.2.1 Recall and Precision

Table 11.1 presents all the possible outcomes for a retrieval task, using the notation and terminology commonly seen in IR publications. For instance, "hits" mean retrieved documents that are relevant. "Misses" are defined as documents that are relevant but not retrieved. Based on these possible retrieval outcomes, a variety of evaluation measures are derived. Recall and precision, initially proposed by Kent and his colleagues (1955) as *pertinency factor* and *recall factor*, are two such measures.

Table 11.1 Possible Retrieval Outcomes

Judgment / Result	Relevant	Not Relevant	Total
Retrieved	a (hits)	b (noise)	a + b (all retrieved)
Not retrieved	c (misses)	d (rejects)	c + d (all nonretrieved)
Total	a + c (all relevant)	b + d (all nonrelevant)	a + b + c + d (total in the system)

As discussed in §5.2.2, recall (R in the formulas that follow) is defined as the ratio between the number of relevant documents retrieved and the total number of relevant documents in a system. Using the notation given in Table 11.1, the following formula an be written:

$$R = a/(a + c)$$

Accordingly, precision (P) is the ratio between the number of relevant documents retrieved and the total number of documents retrieved from a system:

$$P = a/(a + b)$$

The relationship between recall and precision tends to be inverse (e.g., Lancaster & Warner, 1993) although Fugmann (1993) challenged that statement with several examples. Fugmann found that an increase in precision is not always accompanied by a corresponding decrease in recall, and an increase in recall is by no means observed to always leave a decrease in precision in its wake. A partial explanation of Fugmann's finding is that retrieval of relevant documents affects both recall and precision while retrieval of nonrelevant documents affects only precision (Korfhage, 1997).

Recall is supposed to measure the retrievability of an IR system, whereas precision should assess the ability of an IR system to separate the nonrelevant from the relevant. But there are two major stumbling blocks in the calculation of these two measures. First, how can relevance be defined and measured? Second, how can the total number of relevant documents in a system be known?

11.1.2.1.1 The Notion of Relevance

The discussion or, more precisely, the debate on the meaning of relevance has been long and heated. Mizzaro (1997) presented a history of relevance by reviewing about 160 papers written on the topic from before the 1950s through the mid-1990s. Even though so much attention has been given to the matter, no agreement has been reached on how relevance should be defined and how it can be measured simply, because relevance is essentially a subjective judgment dictated by many interrelated factors. Relevance, like love, is, in a sense, in the eye of the beholder. It is not a concept that can be explicitly described and easily quantified.

Nevertheless, a great number of definitions have been suggested for relevance. Saracevic (1975) traced, analyzed, and summarized many existing definitions of relevance. He concluded that our understanding of relevance is much better, clearer, deeper, and broader than it was shortly after World War II. But there is still a long way to go. Schamber, Eisenberg, and Nilan (1990) reexamined the issue of defining relevance and indicated that people still had not reached a consensus with regard to a definition. These researchers believed that relevance is a multidimensional concept, dependent on both internal and external factors. It is also based on a dynamic human judgment process. Specifically, 80 factors affecting relevance judgment can be identified and grouped into six categories: judges, requests, documents, information systems, judgment conditions, and choice of scale (Schamber, 1994). Furthermore, the learning factor and the sequence of presentation also affect relevance judgment (Froehlich, 1994). A judge will be able to learn during the process of relevance judgment. The same document will likely be judged more relevant if presented earlier rather than later in the evaluation process. Adding to the already mounting complexity, difficulty, and frustration in relevance judgment is that someone other than the end user (e.g., an information professional) often makes the judgment, particularly in assisted searching environments such as online systems.

Relevance is indeed a complicated notion, but it is a systematic and measurable phenomenon (Schamber, Eisenberg, & Nilan, 1990). Simply put, relevance is a property that reflects the relationship between a document and the user's query. While an accurate and objective judgment of relevance appears hard to get, an estimation of its value is possible to obtain. Meanwhile, assessors should keep in mind the issues discussed in this subsection, when judging the relevance of retrieval results.

More than 30 years after the publication of his review on relevance (Saracevic, 1975), Saracevic prepared a two-part review with the same title, but labeled them as Part II (Saracevic, 2007a) and Part III (Saracevic, 2007b) to show that they are both subsequent to his seminal 1975 writing even though it was not labeled as Part I then. After further reviewing the relevance concept in terms of its nature, manifestations, and implications, Saracevic concluded that relevance, as the fundamental notion in IR, is timeless. Therefore, research and discussion about relevance will always be timely.

11.1.2.1.2 Determination of All the Relevant Documents in a System

How to define and measure relevance is only one problem in computing recall and precision. The other predicament involves the determination of all the relevant documents in an IR system. Unless a system is created for experimental purposes, there seems no way of knowing exactly the total number of documents in a system that are relevant to a given query. Yet that number, the denominator in the formula $R = a/(a + c)$, is required for calculating recall.

Several methods have been proposed over the years to get around the problem (Large, Tedd, & Hartley, 1999). Pooling is one such method. Basically, different users conduct the same search on the assumption that if the search is tried enough times, eventually most, if not all, relevant documents will be found at least once. Results from all the searches will then be aggregated and duplicates removed. To calculate recall, then, any individual search results can be compared with this aggregated set of relevant documents in the system. This pooling method has been implemented in the TREC series for recall computation (Harman, 1995), in addition to other projects (e.g., Clarke & Willett, 1997). Consequently, the question arises as to how many repetitive searches need to be done before people using the pooling method can feel confident that enough relevant documents have been collected.

Another approach to estimating the total number of documents in a system is to ask one or more experts with both searching experience and subject knowledge to conduct the searches and to assume that these experts will find all the relevant documents in the system. Results obtained by other searchers, such as novices, can then be checked against these expert searches to measure recall. This approach can be called the expert method.

In addition to the pooling method and the expert method, Large, Tedd, & Hartley, (1999), described a subset method. In this method, documents in a small subset of the system database are examined one by one to locate relevant ones. The underlying assumption is that the subset is representative of the entire system, suggesting that a random sampling procedure must be applied for choosing the subset. The estimation based on the subset then becomes the denominator for calculating recall.

As can be seen, getting the recall measure for evaluating retrieval performance is similar to counting the number of fish in a lake. The task is close to impossible because the system database is dynamic and constantly changing. All the methods discussed here are thus at best good estimates and at worst plain guesses (Large, Tedd, & Hartley, 1999).

11.1.2.1.3 Other Criticisms of Recall and Precision

Apparently no satisfactory answers have been found to the two previous questions regarding relevance and the total number of relevant documents in a system. Nevertheless, more criticisms have been made about recall and precision as evaluation measures. For example, it has been pointed out that recall and precision are incomplete measures for evaluation because factors such as interactivity, cost, and speed of retrieval should also be taken into consideration (e.g., Large, Tedd, & Hartley, 1999). Miller and Tegler (1986) further argued that:

> The traditional methods of evaluating information searches— recall and precision—have completely overlooked this generative, creative aspect of a search. By evaluating the product and not the

process, recall and precision limit our understanding of information searches and fail to measure them effectively. (p. 371)

In other words, measures other than recall and precision should be applied in IR evaluation. As Salton (1992) noted, the main assumption behind the use of measures such as recall and precision is that the average user is interested in retrieving large amounts of relevant materials (producing high recall) while at the same time rejecting a large proportion of the extraneous items (producing high precision). These assumptions may not always be satisfied. For example, except in cases such as patent retrieval, users may not be interested in an exhaustive search, which questions the validity of recall as an evaluation measure.

Furthermore, there is no mechanism for expressing different degrees of relevance in calculating recall. All relevant documents are usually assumed to have equal value, no matter whether they are marginally or fully relevant (Chowdhury, 1999). This assumption cannot be changed, particularly when the total number of relevant documents in a system needs to be estimated by means of the methods discussed in §11.1.2.1.2.

Recall and precision, as evaluation measures, appear far from perfect, and recall seems the more controversial of the two. Despite all the criticism and debate, however, recall and precision measures have formed the basis for the better-known evaluations of both operational and laboratory-type retrieval systems (Salton, 1992). Meanwhile, variations of recall and precision measures have been developed with the intention to eliminate the limitations associated with these two evaluation criteria.

11.1.2.1.4 Variations of Recall and Precision Measures

Average recall or precision has been proposed to challenge the assumption of the equal relevance value of retrieved documents. In this method, relevance is no longer a binary property (i.e., relevant or not relevant) in computing average recall or precision. Rather, it is measured on an X-point scale (X = 3, 4, ... 11) to show different degrees of relevance. For example, if a 3-point scale is used, each retrieved document would be assigned a value of 0, 0.5, or 1.0. The assigned values would then be averaged across all the documents retrieved on a topic so that the variance of relevance in each retrieved document can be taken into account. The number of points on the scale is not necessarily limited to 11 or fewer, but a finer division can complicate computation. As discussed earlier, it is harder to compute average recall than average precision due to the difficulty in determining the total number of relevant documents in a system.

In an extension of the this method, average recall or precision is often calculated for the top N (N = 10, 15, 20, 30, ...) documents retrieved on a topic if the results are ranked in the order of perceived relevance. The TREC series has widely applied this measure, that is, average recall or precision at output cutoffs (Harman, 1995). Chu and Rosenthal (1996) calculated average precision for the top 10 results retrieved when they evaluated the internet retrieval systems AltaVista, Excite, and Lycos. Average recall or precision at output cutoffs provides a practicable alternative to regular recall and precision measures, especially when retrieval outputs are ranked and large in number.

Normalized recall or precision, another variation of recall and precision, takes into consideration the sequence in which documents are presented to the user. Ideally, an IR system would present all relevant documents before displaying any of the nonrelevant ones. If a value of 1 is given to an ideal system and 0 is assigned to the worst possible system, in which all the nonrelevant documents would be presented to the user before any relevant ones were presented, that value becomes the coefficient in calculating normalized recall or precision. Korfhage (1997) and Foskett (1996) described respectively two different methods for computing normalized recall. Normalized precision can be obtained similarly. The other assumption of this measure is that one has knowledge about all the relevant documents within a system—a similar predicament for computing recall. The potential of this measure thus again suffers from that improbable assumption. In addition, normalized recall or precision in essence requires that retrieval outputs be ranked in the order of perceived relevance.

Relative recall is the ratio of the retrieved relevant documents examined by the user and the number of relevant documents the user knows are in the system (Harter & Hert, 1997) or would have liked to examine (Korfhage, 1997). For instance, suppose the user believes that there are 20 relevant documents about a given query in the system. After conducting the search, the user retrieves 10 documents that are judged relevant. The relative recall for this search is 50 percent. Obviously, relative recall is proposed with the intention to tackle the problems associated with recall, but, once again, how can the user know, for example, the number of relevant documents in a system? The answer is what has been suggested in §11.1.2.1.2 for determining the total number of relevant documents in the system (e.g., pooling method). The same old problem resurfaces after a detour to the so-called relative recall.

E-measure, proposed by Swets (1969), is a weighted combination of precision and recall for measuring retrieval effectiveness. It can be calculated using the following formula:

$$E = 1 - 1 / [\beta P^{-1} + (1 - \beta) R^{-1}]$$

The parameter β in the formula is used to reflect the emphasis on either precision or recall. For example, $\beta = 1$ corresponds to attaching equal importance to precision and recall. $\beta = 0.5$ and 2 correspond to attaching half or twice as much importance to recall as to precision, respectively. The lower the E-measure, the better the effectiveness of the retrieval system. E-measure was, for example, applied by Griffiths, Luckhurst, and Willett (1986) in their study. Two comments can be made about E-measure. First, it can put different degrees of emphasis on either recall or precision. Second, it includes both recall and precision in a single measure of effectiveness. As will be discussed later, a single evaluation measure is very much favored in the IR community.

The variations of recall and precision provide different views and alternatives of the two evaluation measures. Nevertheless, none of the variations can even substantially, let alone entirely, circumvent the problems recall and precision confront. Consequently, additional evaluation measures (e.g., fallout) have been introduced over the years.

11.1.2.2 Fallout

Fallout, initially put forward by Swets (1963), is defined as the ratio between non-relevant documents retrieved and all nonrelevant document in a system database. Fallout (F) is defined as follows with the notation in Table 11.1:

$$F = b/(b + d)$$

Fallout measures the inability of an IR system to exclude nonrelevant documents from retrieval results, which Robertson (1969) called the noise factor. The value for fallout ranges from 0 to 1, the same as for recall and precision. But the smaller the fallout value, the better the IR system is from the evaluation viewpoint.

As in the case of recall computation, the total number of nonrelevant documents in a system is not known. That number, therefore, has to be estimated using the methods discussed earlier for generating recall. Overall, fallout does not appear to be an extensively used evaluation measure, although Robertson (1969) stated that a recall-precision graph (a graph plotting the values of these two measures) is not as easy to interpret as a recall-fallout graph and claimed that precision is not as useful a measure of performance as is fallout in conjunction with recall.

11.1.2.3 Generality

Generality is defined as the proportion of documents in a system database that are relevant to a particular topic. According to the notation given in Table 11.1, G (for generality) can be calculated as follows:

$$G = (a + c)/(a + b + c + d)$$

The higher the generality number (or the greater the density of relevant items in the database), the easier the search tends to be (Lancaster & Warner, 1993). But generality is, strictly speaking, a measure of database quality from the perspective of relevance rather than of retrieval performance directly. In addition, it is always difficult to determine the number of relevant documents not retrieved from the system, that is, the value of c in Table 11.1.

11.1.2.4 Single Measures for Information Retrieval Evaluation

One of the criticisms of recall and precision is their incompleteness as evaluation measures (see §11.1.2.1.3). That is why recall and precision are normally used in combination and possibly along with other criteria for evaluation purposes. It would be ideal if a single evaluation measure could be used by including related factors in the computation. E-measure comes close to being an example of a single measure for evaluating IR. Cooper (1973a, 1973b) suggested a utility measure, based on a user's subjective judgment of an IR system in terms of its usefulness. The utility of a system can be measured differently as long as it is in accordance with Cooper's utility theory. For instance, Su (1991) asked users to rate the usefulness of search results according to a 7-point Likert-type scale by treating the value of the search results as a whole. She found that this utility measure was the best single measure of interactive IR performance among the 20 measures she had selected for her study.

Utility measures can also be defined differently, such as worth of retrieved documents as a whole versus time spent, worth assigned in dollars, and contribution to problem resolution (Saracevic, et al., 1988; Saracevic & Kantor, 1988). But no matter how utility is defined in evaluation, the measure always relies on the user's subjective judgment. The subjectivity of this measure leads to the same concern people have when making relevance judgments for the calculation of recall and precision.

11.1.2.5 Other Evaluation Measures for Information Retrieval

Griffith (1986) once commented that only three numbers should be used in evaluating an IR system: number of relevant items retrieved, number of nonrelevant items retrieved, and total number of items in a system database. All three numbers can be obtained without any estimation or guess. The ratio of the number of relevant items retrieved to the total number of items in a system database would illustrate the system's ability in locating relevant documents. Similarly, the ratio of the number of nonrelevant items retrieved to the total number of items in a system database would demonstrate the system's discriminating power, that is, the ability to reject nonrelevant items. However, few evaluation projects have implemented Griffith's idea.

Evaluation measures for IR have gone through a long journey that is still continuing. Among all the measures discussed here, recall and precision have received the most attention, as well as the most criticism. Nevertheless, they are the de facto measures for the majority of evaluation efforts because they are easy to interpret in terms of the retrieval of wanted items and the rejection of extraneous ones (Salton, 1992). Recall and precision will remain the key evaluation measures for information retrieval unless better alternatives are developed and proven.

11.2 Evaluation Criteria for Information Retrieval Systems

Recall, precision, and other measures discussed previously are basically for evaluating retrieval performance. Retrieval performance apparently only represents one aspect of information retrieval, even though, as indicated earlier, the end user pays the most attention to it. However, to get a complete view of how well an IR system works, measures other than those for evaluating IR performance should be considered. Different measures should be used for different types of IR systems. The following sections examine evaluation criteria for each of the four types of IR systems: online systems, online public access catalogs (OPACs), internet retrieval systems, and multimedia retrieval systems (although multimedia IR systems are not treated as a distinct type in previous chapters).

11.2.1 Evaluation Criteria for Online Systems

Online systems have had the longest history among the four major types of IR systems (see Chapter 8), and consequently, they have been the subject of many evaluation studies. The criteria for evaluating online systems are designed in different ways.

According to Lancaster and Warner (1993), evaluations of online systems can possibly be done at three levels: 1) evaluations of effectiveness, 2) evaluations of cost-effectiveness, and 3) cost-benefit evaluations. The first level, evaluations of effectiveness, considers cost, time, and quality of a system. Such evaluations try to find out whether a system functions effectively with regard to the user's need. The second level, evaluations of cost-effectiveness, associates the cost factor to system effectiveness so that two different IR systems can be easily contrasted at this level. For example, how much does it cost to retrieve one relevant document from an IR system? The same kind of comparison would be hard to do at the first level because those measures are not normalized. The third level, cost-benefit evaluation, goes even further than the previous two levels by assessing the cost of running an IR system against the benefits received as a result of having the system. As the level of evaluation goes up, so does the sophistication of the evaluation criteria. Level 1 criteria (e.g., response time or database coverage) tend to be straightforward. Level 2 measures need some computation. In comparison, Level 3 criteria require judgment and reasoning, far beyond a simple appraisal. Evaluation criteria at all three levels can possibly be applied in a single evaluation project. In practice, however, measures for Levels 1 and 2, particularly those of Level 1, are used most of the time in evaluating online systems because of their feasibility and practicability.

Although various criteria have been established for evaluating online systems, a consensus seems to have been reached about what aspects should be inspected. Lancaster and Fayen (1973) recapitulated them in the form of six criteria: 1) coverage, 2) recall, 3) precision, 4) response time, 5) user effort, and 6) form of output. It is surprising to see that searching capability is not included in this set of evaluation criteria.

Coverage is a typical measure for evaluating the system database. Specific facets of database coverage include types of documents (e.g., patents, journal articles, and technical reports), number of documents, update frequency, and retrospectiveness. The coverage of a system database determines what can be retrieved later from the system.

Recall and precision are part of the evaluation criteria for measuring retrieval performance. These two measures, as pointed out in §11.1.2, become the regular components in most evaluation efforts. But no standard has been set for satisfactory recall and precision ratios, for two reasons. One is that different users would have different expectations of recall and precision in different circumstances. For example, if a user intends to do a state-of-the-art review of a subject, high recall will be anticipated. If the user is interested only in the newest development in a field, high precision would be expected. The other reason for not having a standard for acceptable recall and precision ratio is the inverse relationship presumably existing between the two measures. An increase in one measure would likely lead to a decrease in the other. It is then difficult to find an optimal point for both recall and precision. Besides, the size of the system database affects the determination of satisfactory recall and precision. Low precision ratios may be less tolerable in a larger database than in a smaller one. For instance, a user may be willing to look at 60 retrieved records to identify that 20 are useful, but much less willing to examine 600 to find 200, although in both cases the precision ratio (33 percent) is the same (Lancaster & Warner, 1993).

Response time refers to the time needed between the submission of a query and return of results. The criterion appears indispensable, particularly in the online systems of the early days, when information technology (e.g., telecommunication and computing power) was in its infant stage and information retrieval using online systems was expensive. If an IR system can process queries rapidly, the cost of using it will be minimized, which explains the importance of having this criterion in the evaluation.

User effort as an evaluation criterion implies several elements, all of which measure how much effort a user must make to conduct searches in the online retrieval environment. For example, how long does it take for the user to learn about or become familiar with one system? How friendly is the user-system interaction? What kinds of support (e.g., printed manual or online help) are provided for the user? The less effort the user needs to make, the better the online system is. One unique feature of online systems is that information professionals as intermediaries often conduct searches on behalf of end users and are better trained than end users. This difference should be remembered when one is considering the factor of user effort in evaluation.

Form of output constitutes the last criterion devised for evaluating online systems. Output of online searches can be presented in a variety of ways (e.g., bibliographic information only or bibliographic information plus abstract). Online systems usually offer many output options but do not automatically rank search results because the use of the ranking facility (e.g., the RANK command in DIALOG) turns out to be quite expensive. Retrieval results from online systems are typically presented in reverse chronological order, that is, items most recently added to a system are presented first. As depicted in §10.3.2.2, flexibility is the keyword for getting a top rating in this regard.

In sum, coverage, recall, precision, response time, user effort, and form of output have served as evaluation criteria for online systems even though variations are seen occasionally. These criteria may also provide a baseline for evaluating other types of IR systems.

11.2.2 Evaluation Criteria for OPACs

OPACs, designed for finding bibliographic information about a library collection, stand for a unique type of IR system. Evaluation criteria for OPACs have been developed mainly through comparative studies; the report by Hildreth (1982) appears to be the most influential. Jones (in Hildreth, 1982, p. xii) even predicted that no subsequent effort in this field could escape being affected by Hildreth's report. Indeed, the framework presented in the report has shaped subsequent efforts in evaluating OPACs (e.g., O'Rourke, 1987; Salmon, 1983) although the research was not intended as an evaluation of the 10 OPACs studied (Hildreth, 1985). After consulting relevant research on the topic (e.g., Hildreth, 1982), O'Rourke (1987) created for evaluation purposes a checklist of 95 questions, divided among five categories:

1) operational features, 2) access points, 3) search features, 4) display features, and 5) user assistance features. These five categories could reasonably serve as evaluation criteria for OPACs.

The criterion of operational features relates to how the user actually interacts with an OPAC. For example, how does the user access the system? Does the system allow the user to select a target (e.g., a local library collection or a collection of a library consortium) for doing searches in addition to the default option? Can the user modify a search or change system default settings (e.g., display short records)? Is it easy for the user to move from one display level to another, from one record to the next or the previous? Interface (i.e., command language versus menu selection) was a major consideration when those evaluation criteria were established but is less relevant to today's OPACs as few of them still apply command language. The switching from card catalogs to OPACs has had a great impact on user-system interaction, which seems to be the chief justification for choosing this criterion for evaluating OPACs.

Access points decide how OPAC information can be searched and make up another criterion for OPAC evaluation. In the early years of OPAC development (i.e., the 1980s), author, title, call number, International Standard Book Number (ISBN), and International Standard Serial Number (ISSN) were the common access points. Keyword and subject headings have been added since. Theoretically speaking, the more access points an OPAC provides, the easier it is for the user to locate the information in the system. However, some of the access points (e.g., ISBN and subject headings) are not used frequently because users, particularly novices, know little about their implications. By contrast, access points per se did not become an evaluation criterion for online systems partly because there are so many of them in this retrieval environment. Field searching in search facilities can be chosen instead to cover the dimension of access points.

Search features of OPACs vary from system to system. When OPACs are evaluated from the perspective of search features, several elements are observed. First, what kinds of searching capabilities are supported? Are all three Boolean operators available? How about truncation and proximity searching? Second, does the system offer any search-related features such as a list of subject headings online, cross-references, and suggestions for improving searches? Third, can users limit their searches by publication year, document type, or the like? The more options a system can support, the better the system.

Display features, a broader concept than output options, are chosen as a measure for the evaluation of OPACs. This criterion can be broken down to record length (e.g., brief or full display), number of records per listing, and other display-related features. Full records may also be displayed in MARC format, a feature used mostly by information professionals. O'Rourke (1987) posed more specific questions for checking OPAC display quality. For example, will a system automatically display the record when it is the sole response to a search term? Are tags (e.g., TI for title) self-explanatory in tagged record displays? Are record displays free of abbreviations, codes, and jargon? In addition, questions can be asked about font type, style, size, or cases used in OPAC displays. All uppercase type and a small font size (e.g., 10 point), for instance, are not recommended for displaying information on OPACs.

User assistance comprises another criterion for evaluating OPACs. The more assistance a system can provide to the user, the less likely the user is to feel helpless when interacting with the OPAC. Many facilities may be designed for helping OPAC users. Examples include an introductory message describing the OPAC in general, a list of accessible files or searchable fields, explanations for error messages, online tutorials, and operation-specific online help. The OPAC should also be checked to see, for example, whether it can show search history and whether it gives procedural or guiding comments routinely. No assumptions should be made about users' familiarity with the system when discussing user assistance. Help messages ought to be clear, simple, and precise.

These five evaluation criteria were created in the 1980s, when OPACs were first adopted in libraries. Improvements and new features have been introduced and should be considered in evaluating later versions of OPACs, especially the emerging generation. For example, the majority of OPACs are now networked, allowing remote access from home, office, and locations other than the library. Is the remote access convenient? Are adequate supports provided for helping the user gain remote access? On the other hand, as discussed in §8.3, a large number of OPACs today serve as a gateway to other information sources and IR systems. What facilities are available for users to take advantage of this feature? Attention should be given to these new features and developments of OPACs for evaluation purposes in addition to the five criteria discussed here.

Indeed, the so-called next generation of OPACs has acquired new features that earlier versions of OPACs do not possess. Examples of such features include relevance feedback, ranking of search results, improved environment for browsing, and spell-checking of search queries (Antelman, Lynema, & Pace, 2006; Markey, 2007). Evaluation of next-generation OPACs at present is mostly carried out when a newly installed OPAC is assessed (e.g., Antelman, Lynema, & Pace, 2006; Lombardo & Condic, 2000), but a new framework for that purpose has yet to be established. However, this situation will undoubtedly change as more next-generation OPACs are implemented and, particularly, when many (e.g., Marcum, 2006; Markey, 2007) already expressed serious concerns over the fate of OPACs at the mighty presence of Google.

11.2.3 Evaluation Criteria for Internet Retrieval Systems

Relatively few evaluation projects have addressed internet retrieval systems, the newest member in the family of IR systems, although some researchers (e.g., Chu & Rosenthal, 1996; Ding & Marchionini, 1996; Leighton, 1995; Leighton & Srivastava, 1999) have attempted to examine their retrieval performance. As retrieval performance represents only one aspect of IR systems, other dimensions of internet retrieval systems should also be considered in an evaluation.

Chu and Rosenthal (1996) proposed an evaluation framework for web search engines, the dominant type of internet retrieval system as of this writing. The framework is derived from the 1970s evaluation criteria that Lancaster and Fayen (1973) established for online systems, with additions and revisions tailored for internet retrieval systems. Because of the changes brought to internet retrieval systems as a whole, some aspects specified in the five broad evaluation criteria (i.e., composition of web indexes, search capability, retrieval performance, output, and user effort) at the time of the study are outdated today. However, the conceptual framework remains pertinent for evaluating internet retrieval systems.

The composition of indexes in an IR system is an important component for evaluation because the content of indexes determines how information in the system can be retrieved. For example, whenever a web search request is issued, it is the web index rather than the webpages themselves that has been checked for retrieving information. Coverage, update frequency, and the portions of internet documents indexed (e.g., the title plus the first several lines, or the entire document) are the three elements examined. While the extent of all three components depends largely on the power and sophistication of the hardware and software that manage the index or database, larger coverage, frequent updates, and full-text indexing do not necessarily result in better internet retrieval systems in other measurements. There are other factors (e.g., the interface and search capability) that play a role in the quality of internet retrieval systems.

Search capability constitutes another criterion for evaluating internet retrieval systems because variance is the norm rather than the exception in this case. Search facilities that are basic and common may not be found in major internet retrieval systems. On the other hand, retrieval features (e.g., fuzzy searching) that could be seen only in laboratories in the past are now implemented in some internet retrieval systems. A competent internet retrieval system must include the fundamental search facilities that users are familiar with, which include Boolean logic, phrase searching, and limiting facility (e.g., limiting by field). Because the searching capabilities of an internet retrieval system ultimately determine its performance, absence of these basic functions will severely handicap the system.

Retrieval performance is traditionally evaluated with three parameters: precision, recall, and response time. While the three variables can all be quantitatively measured, extra caution should be exercised when one judges the relevance of retrieved items and estimates the total number of documents relevant to a specific topic in a network-based system. Because representations of internet documents (e.g., summaries or extracts) are done mostly by automatic means, relevance judgment based on such representations could cause more concern about reliability. Furthermore, the dynamic and fluctuating nature of the internet makes it virtually impossible to determine the total number of relevant documents in an internet retrieval system. Recall, therefore, is even harder to calculate in the internet environment than for other kinds of IR systems. Oppenheim, et al. (2000), nevertheless suggested that relative recall can be computed using the method proposed by Clarke and Willett (1997) when evaluating the performance of internet retrieval systems. As for response time as a performance parameter, it is becoming less and less important as internet retrieval systems are increasingly improved in terms of processing power.

Output as an evaluation criterion for internet retrieval systems should be examined from three perspectives: accessibility, content, and format. Thanks to the hyperlink feature, the user can access full documents of retrieved outcome if the links function properly. But there exist dysfunctional links such as broken links (e.g., links to sites that have changed URLs) or dead links (e.g., links to sites that are no longer available). An ideal internet retrieval system should keep the number of dysfunctional links to a minimum, thus allowing maximum accessibility to final results. The output content, to a certain degree, is decided by the way an internet retrieval system is constructed. That is, does the system purely extract or actually index what it includes when building its database? The answer should be apparent. Extracts are not of much help to the user in determining the "aboutness" of retrieved results. Another facet relating to output content is the amount of duplication in the results. Currently, only some of the meta-internet retrieval systems are capable of removing duplicates. The concern about output formats of internet retrieval systems, however, is less of an issue because systems tend to predefine all possible output formats, and source documents represented by the output can be viewed easily if the user so desires. Therefore, accessibility and content are the two output features unique and important to the evaluation of internet retrieval systems.

User effort in the current context refers to documentation and interface because these two factors critically affect users' efforts in learning and using internet retrieval systems. Well-prepared documentation and a user-friendly interface play a notable role in users' selections of internet retrieval systems. Unlike other types of IR systems, internet retrieval systems are generally free, and the distinctions among them do not appear obvious. The attractiveness of each internet retrieval system is therefore expressed to its users mainly via its interface and documentation. In other words, users will not choose an internet retrieval system unless they are comfortable with its interface and able to read and comprehend its documentation when they consult it. Internet retrieval systems, as a group, have tried to minimize users' efforts by implementing form fill-in and graphical modes of interaction and by providing online help facilities. When internet retrieval systems are evaluated from the viewpoint of user effort, one needs to examine particularly whether the screen is too busy or whether the help message is too technical and terse, as such concerns seem common for some of the systems. On the other hand, users of internet retrieval systems are different from those of other IR systems. They are the most heterogeneous group in terms of IR skills and experiences. They may not have received any form of training before actually using an internet retrieval system. Yet there is usually no intermediary, as in the case of online systems, to perform the search task for the user. The absence of an intermediary and the inexperience of most internet retrieval system users set a stricter requirement for minimizing user effort than pertains in any other IR environment.

In addition to the five aforementioned evaluation criteria, passage retrieval, multilingual retrieval, and cross-language searching should also be considered in the evaluation of internet retrieval systems. The concept of passage retrieval is explained in §1.2.1 before internet retrieval systems are specifically discussed. Since the web has become one of the major internet applications and web documents take the hyperlink structure, it seems increasingly necessary to have passage retrieval on the internet. The traditional approach of retrieving the entire document offers little help to the user of internet retrieval systems in pinpointing the needed information, in part due to the hyperstructure of web documents. The desired piece or passage of information could possibly be buried deep in the structure, and the sheer size of some web documents poses a problem in itself. For this reason, passage retrieval is a desirable feature for internet retrieval systems to support. In 1997, the famous TREC series started a research task on passage retrieval called the Question Answering track (Voorhees, 2000).

Multilingual retrieval or cross-language searching, discussed in §9.1, deals with the language dimension of IR systems. As described in Chapter 9, information in languages other than English is increasingly being posted on the internet, suggesting that the language factor is becoming increasingly important for evaluating internet retrieval systems. Other types of IR systems carry multilingual information but not approaching a level comparable to that of internet retrieval systems. Non-English-speaking users accounted for more than 70 percent of the total on the internet in June 2008 (Miniwatts

Marketing Group, 2009), and the number is rising. It seems only reasonable, then, to include the language dimension in the evaluation of internet retrieval systems. Both multilingual retrieval and cross-language searching are studied in TREC (Voorhees & Harman, 2000). Clough (2007) summarized the efforts at ImageCLEF, a track of the Cross-Language Evaluation Forum (CLEF) created for large-scale evaluation of cross-language image retrieval systems. A description of CLEF is provided in §9.1.3.

Passage retrieval, multilingual retrieval, and cross-language searching in fact all belong to the evaluation criterion of searching capability. They are discussed separately in this case, however, to emphasize their significance and to reflect the changes in the evaluation framework Chu and Rosenthal (1996) proposed for internet retrieval systems.

At the peak of evaluation activities for internet retrieval systems, Oppenheim, et al. (2000), pointed out that little consistency is found among related studies in terms of evaluation criteria or methods applied. They recommended consequently that a standardized set of tools be developed for future evaluations and also made some preliminary suggestions as to what this standardized set of tools should contain. As internet retrieval systems remain the most rapidly evolving species in the family of IR systems, it is time to renew our research efforts in evaluating them to further facilitate their advancement and development.

11.2.4 Evaluation Criteria for Multimedia Retrieval Systems

Multimedia IR is discussed in §9.2 under the subheadings "Still-Image Retrieval," "Sound Retrieval," and "Moving-Image Retrieval." Research and development endeavors in this area are expanding rapidly as related technologies mature. As a result, a good number of operational IR systems for multimedia information have become available to users. The need for assessing such multimedia IR systems is thus observed by researchers in the field. In the report Trant (2004) prepared, TREC tracks SDR (Spoken Document Retrieval) and Video (succeeded in 2003 by TRECVid; www-nlpir.nist.gov/projects/trecvid), as well as projects such as ImageCLEF (imageclef.org), all indicate the necessity of conducting evaluation of multimedia IR.

Unlike text IR evaluation, which has accumulated in the course of 50 years of work and experience (e.g., the groundbreaking Cranfield tests), few researchers appeared eager to undertake the evaluation of multimedia IR. This reluctance partially explains why the Council on Library and Information Resources, as well as the Coalition for Networked Information, both located in the U.S., initiated a project with the intention to develop a benchmark database service for image retrieval (Trant, 2004). Individual tests of specific multimedia IR systems are common (e.g., Chang, 2002; Deselaers, Keysers, & Ney, 2008) while other studies are often designed to compare content-based methods of multimedia IR against the description-based approach (e.g., Petrelli & Auld, 2008). What is lacking in this domain of evaluation research is a framework or a set of criteria that can be applied to judge the quality of multimedia IR systems. For example, only retrieval performance is measured, with traditional criteria such as precision and recall, even in the carefully planned TREC Video track (Smeaton & Over, 2003) and its successor TRECVid (Smeaton, 2007). Other aspects of multimedia IR systems are still unexamined in the evaluation effort.

Researchers in music IR (MIR), a distinct division in multimedia IR, set up their own platform for evaluation, modeled after the TREC paradigm (Downie, 2003). According to documents collected by Downie (2004), MIR evaluation appears to be only at the beginning stage as most authors merely did some conceptual discussion of the theme without carrying out any actual assessment. In other words, much needs to be done to fill the void of MIR evaluation in particular and multimedia IR evaluation in general.

11.2.5 Usability as Evaluation Criteria

Usability is a term coined not long ago, to some extent, for replacing the phrase *user-friendliness*, which used to be a keyword commonly seen in the context of human-computer interaction (Rowley & Hartley, 2008) although its roots can be traced back to Mooers' law for IR systems, proposed in 1960 (see §1.1.2.3 of this book). According to the International Organization for Standardization (ISO; 1998), usability is defined as "the extent to which a product can be used by specified users to achieve specified goals with effectiveness, efficiency and satisfaction in a specified context of use." This ISO standard explains how to identify the information necessary to be taken into account when specifying or evaluating usability in terms of product performance and user satisfaction (Bevan, 2001). On the other hand, Jakob Nielsen, who has made significant contributions to popularizing usability as an alternative method for evaluating websites, offers a plain definition of usability: "Usability ... basically is a question of whether the system is good enough to satisfy all the needs and requirements of the users and other potential stakeholders, such as the users' clients and managers" (1993, p. 24).

It is obvious that both the ISO definition and the one by Nielsen imply broader connotations, while, in the field of IRR, usability essentially refers to an assessment of IR system performance and user satisfaction. In that sense, usability is not a single measure for evaluating IR systems. Rather, it encompasses a set of criteria for assessment purposes. Nielsen (1993, 2003) suggests the following five attributes of quality usability:

- Learnability: How easy is it for users to accomplish basic tasks the first time they encounter the design?

- Efficiency: Once users have learned the design, how quickly can they perform tasks?

- Memorability: When users return to the design after a period of not using it, how easily can they reestablish proficiency?

- Errors: How many errors do users make, how severe are these errors, and how easily can users recover from the errors?

- Satisfaction: How pleasant is it to use the design?

These five components clearly echo the five points discussed in §10.3.3 of this book. Shneiderman and Plaisant (2005), on the other hand, tend to treat the term *usability* as a synonym for *good interface design* in the fourth edition of the classic *Designing the User Interface: Strategies for Effective Human-Computer Interaction*. Usability, regardless of how its connotation is interpreted, has been widely adopted as a method for assessing the quality of various IR systems. For example, usability testing was performed on newly implemented OPACs (e.g., Antelman, Lynema, & Pace, 2006; Guha & Saraf, 2007) and other types of IR systems. In addition, a search interface "Flamenco" was examined by Hearst, et al. (2002), and Haga and Kaneda (2005) examined a video retrieval system from the viewpoint of usability. Numerous usability labs have been established since the late 1990s, with specially configured equipment and software placed in a physical space designed particularly for that purpose, even though what they test generally goes beyond the usability of IR systems.

11.3 Major Evaluation Projects for Information Representation and Retrieval

More than half a century has passed since the first evaluation study in IR was conducted in 1953 (Lancaster, 1979). Numerous projects have been carried out to evaluate IRR since that time. The Cranfield tests (e.g., Cleverdon, 1962), the MEDLARS (MEDical Literature Analysis and Retrieval System) project (e.g., Lancaster, 1968), the SMART (System for the Manipulation and Retrieval of Texts) experiment (e.g., Salton, 1981), the STAIRS (STorage and Information Retrieval System) study (e.g., Blair & Maron, 1985), and the TREC series (e.g., Harman, 1993; Harman & Voorhees, 2006) are some of the major projects in this category. Of all the major evaluation studies, the Cranfield test and the TREC series will be examined in detail, as they are the most influential in the history of IRR evaluation. Problems and issues surrounding IRR evaluation projects will also be discussed.

11.3.1 The Cranfield Tests

The Cranfield tests were carried out in two phases, named *Cranfield I* and *Cranfield II*, between 1957 and 1967. They are the first extensive evaluation projects undertaken with the leadership of C. W. Cleverdon, then a librarian at the College of Aeronautics in Cranfield, England. Although the Cranfield tests were about the evaluation of manual IRR systems, the methodology devised in the project has subsequently been used for evaluating many digital IRR systems. Studies similar to the Cranfield tests are often referred to as *Cranfield-like* projects.

11.3.1.1 Cranfield I

Cranfield I was designed to test the comparative efficiency of four indexing systems on retrieval performance in an environment involving many other variables, such as indexer, document, and search question. Recall and precision were used to measure retrieval performance in this project, the first such practice in large-scale IRR evaluation experiments. Moreover, it is possible to calculate recall in Cranfield because the test collections, created specifically for the project, are closed and known. The four indexing systems chosen for Cranfield I are:

- Universal Decimal Classification (UDC)

- An alphabetical subject catalog

- A faceted classification scheme

- A uniterm system of coordinate indexing

11.3.1.1.1 Test Design

Three indexers were chosen for the test, and they had various types of experience and familiarity with the systems being tested: One had subject knowledge, one had indexing experience, and one came straight from a public library and had neither subject knowledge nor indexing experience. A total of 100 documents were obtained in equal numbers from the general field of aeronautics and the specialized field of high-speed aerodynamics. Each indexer was asked to index each of the 100 documents five times, spending 2, 4, 8, 12, and 16 minutes per document. The average number of indexing terms assigned to each document was 2 to 10 (Cleverdon, 1962). Search questions for the test were "manufactured" as members outside the project examined each document and then formulated the questions to which a given document would be relevant. In all, 400 search questions were created, and they were used in three rounds of searches in the form of 1,200 (400 x 3 rounds) queries.

The searching was done mainly by project staff. The first search round was conducted on the first set of 400 queries as a pretest. The second search round was designed to tackle the two problems encountered in the pretest, using a second set of 400 queries derived from the 400 questions. First, how long was a searcher justified in continuing a search when the one relevant document was known to be in the file somewhere? Second, how could the searcher decide exactly what constituted a different search strategy when using terms particularly from the four index languages? A stopping point for the search was then prescribed in the second round, and changes of search strategies for the same query were required to be both in general and in terms of each indexing system in as fair a manner as possible. Failure analysis of the results for the second round revealed cases in which a search on one indexing system had succeeded but the same query on another system had failed due to search formulation. So a third round of search using another set of 400 queries was constructed to eliminate searcher and search strategy variations by adopting a standardized and fixed strategy for all four systems.

11.3.1.1.2 Test Findings

The most important finding in Cranfield I is that the uniterm system gave the best recall among the four different indexing systems included in the test (see Table 11.2) although all systems achieved a similar level of performance efficiency (Cleverdon, 1962).

Table 11.2 Recall Ratio of Four Indexing Systems

Indexing System	Recall (%)
Uniterm	82.0
Alphabetical subject	81.5
UDC	75.6
Faceted classification	73.8

Cranfield I also revealed that increased time in indexing increased recall up to a certain level, after which the positive correlation between indexing time and recall might reverse, as shown in Table 11.3 (Cleverdon, 1962).

Table 11.3   Indexing Time Versus Recall Ratio

Indexing Time (minute)	Recall (%)
2	72.9
4	80.2
8	76.2
12	82.7
16	84.3

While the three indexers were different in terms of indexing experience and subject knowledge, no significant difference was observed among them in their retrieving documents indexed by them or in their indexing performance. In addition, success rates in retrieving documents on the general area of aeronautics were noted to be 4 percent to 5 percent better than those on the specialized field of high-speed aerodynamics. Other findings of Cranfield I include the following:

- There is an inverse relationship between recall and precision.

- A 1 percent increase in precision could be achieved at a cost of 3 percent loss in recall.

- Systems operated at recall of 70 to 90 percent and precision of 8 to 20 percent.

Among all the results summarized here, three of them are beyond expectation or even contradictory to some general beliefs held in the IRR community. First, in terms of recall, the uniterm system outperformed three controlled vocabulary systems included in the project in spite of the theory that controlled vocabulary yields better retrieval performance. This finding has indirectly promoted research on automatic indexing, which relies heavily on uniterms or keywords. Second, the finding was that the performance of an indexing system on retrieval does not depend on the indexer's experience or subject knowledge, while the traditional thinking was the opposite—that the indexer's experience and knowledge would help improve performance. Third, Cranfield I found that increased time in indexing would not necessarily increase recall. To the contrary, there was even a decrease in recall when the indexing time was increased from 4 minutes to 8 minutes (see Table 11.3). While the recall ratio increased again as a result of longer indexing time, the gain in retrieval performance does not appear to be in proportion to the indexing time spent. For example, the recall ratio increased only by 4 percent (i.e., from 80.2 percent to 84.3 percent) whereas the indexing time was quadrupled (i.e., from 4 minutes to 16 minutes).

11.3.1.2 Cranfield II

Cranfield II was designed to assess the effects of different indexing devices on retrieval performance. Indexing devices are measures employed by the indexer to improve either recall or precision. Examples of indexing devices include synonyms, generic relations, coordination, links, and roles. The explanation about the test was given in Cleverdon's project report (Cleverdon, 1962):

> We started from the belief that all index languages are amalgams of different kinds of devices. Such devices fall into two groups of those which are intended to improve the recall ratio and those which are intended to improve the precision ratio. ... The purpose of the test was to investigate the effect which each of these devices, alone or in any possible combination, would have on recall and precision. (p. 17)

11.3.1.2.1 Test Design

About 200 research papers were gathered, each generally having five to 10 references. Then, each author was asked to state, in the form of a search question, the basic problem that was the reason for his or her investigation on the assumption that a research paper is written as the result of an investigation undertaken to provide the answer to a question or questions in the author's mind. Each author was also requested to write up to three additional questions describing any subsidiary questions that arose in the course of the research. After that, abstracts of these references (i.e., cited documents) were obtained, along with some noncited papers identified by graduate students at the college on titles or via bibliographical coupling (i.e., two documents are bibliographically coupled when their reference lists have one or more documents in common). The author was asked to indicate the relevance of the references and noncited papers to each question on the scale of 1 to 5, with 1 being the most relevant, on the assumption that the references were made because they must have something to do with the subject of the paper (Cleverdon & Mills, 1963). The authors identified a total of 1,961 cited documents fully or partially relevant to the 279 questions they posed, from which 1,400 documents and 221 questions were finally selected for Cranfield II.

The test collection of 1,400 documents is mainly in the field of high-speed aerodynamics and aircraft structures. Each document was "indexed" in three ways. First, the most important concepts were selected and recorded in the natural language of the document. Second, the single words in each of the chosen concepts were listed. Third, the concepts were combined in different ways to form the main themes of the documents. Each term was also given a weight (i.e., 1, 2, or 3, with 1 being the most important) at the time of index-ing to indicate its relative importance. Various indexing devices were applied as well during the indexing process in order to probe their effects on retrieval performance.

Searching was done by making use of the various indexing devices imple-mented in three major types of indexing languages: single term, simple con-cept, and controlled term index languages. Specifications about these indexing languages were detailed in Figure 3 to Figure 5 of Cleverdon (1967). Indexing languages formed by keywords in the titles and abstracts were also tested in the project. Queries were decomposed into individual words, and a search was first made for a match for all the words. The matching was then done at different levels by dropping one query term at a time and for all pos-sible coordination with remaining terms. For a query with five individual words, for instance, the first search was done with all the five terms. The sec-ond search would be done with any four out of the five terms by dropping off one from the query. Then a search was made with any three terms, then any two, until only one term was left for matching. Synonyms, broader terms, narrower terms, and other facilities could be used to replace the original words. The searches were carried out in such a way that all the factors were kept constant except one. In the previous example, the number of terms in a query was the only factor allowed to vary while all other parameters were kept constant. Both hits and false drops were recorded for every search so that recall and precision ratios could be calculated.

The entire design was noted for its volume, variety, and complexity. The test was by no means trivial, especially given that it was done manually.

11.3.1.2.2 Test Findings

Recall and precision ratios of all the searches in each language were averaged and used to measure the effects of indexing devices on retrieval performance in Cranfield II. The test reported the following findings:

- Single term indexing languages were superior to any other type in terms of performance.

- When single terms were used for indexing, the inclusion of collateral classes and, in particular, quasi-synonyms wors-ened the performance.

- When concepts were used for indexing, the performance worsened with the inclusion of superordinate, subordinate, and collateral classes along with the original concepts.

- When controlled terms were used for indexing, the inclusion of narrower and broader terms worsened the performance.

- Indexing languages formed out of titles performed better than those formed out of abstracts.

It was quite astonishing and seemingly inexplicable that, as shown in Cranfield II, the best performing index languages were composed of uncontrolled single words derived from documents. No explanations about the surprise could be found by the research participants (Cleverdon, Mills, & Keen, 1966). This finding also conforms to one of the Cranfield I findings, that is, that the uniterm system outperformed three other controlled vocabulary systems included in the project in terms of recall. According to Cranfield II, it seems that the original terms always performed better alone, without any additional variations (e.g., broader or narrower terms). Title-based indexing languages offered better performance than abstract-based ones because titles are in general more indicative and precise than abstracts. The inverse relationship between recall and precision was further confirmed in Cranfield II when indexing devices became part of the experiment environment.

11.3.1.3 Problems With the Cranfield Tests

A large number of reviews and criticisms (e.g., Harter, 1971; Swanson, D. R., 1965, 1971; Vickery, 1966, 1967) have been published since the conduct of the Cranfield tests, pointing out various problems with them. Harter and Hert (1997) categorized these problems into four types: validity and reliability, generalizability, usefulness, and conceptual issues. In consideration of the fact that the conceptual issues (e.g., how to define and measure concepts such as relevance and satisfaction) exist in all IRR evaluation projects, the following discussion will only center around three types of problems relating specifically to the Cranfield tests, namely, validity and reliability, generalizability, and applicability.

The validity and reliability of the tests were questioned because of several arguments. For example, the documents actually submitted to authors who posed the questions for relevance assessments with respect to the corresponding questions might favor the simple term matching techniques at the expense of the more complex matching systems. Large numbers of potentially relevant but not retrieved items were never included in the evaluation. Yet the system was not penalized for not retrieving these items. There were also unwarranted or untested assumptions in the tests. For instance, one must assume that relevance judgments made on a number of documents for a given question are independent of each other. Furthermore, the connection of the source document and question in Cranfield II is much less narrow than that in Cranfield I. All these affect the validity and reliability of the Cranfield tests, that is, whether the tests actually measured what they were intended to measure and whether the tests are repeatable if the same procedure is followed.

The Cranfield results are not generalizable because no random sampling was applied in the tests. In addition, the test collections were small (i.e., 100 and 1,400 documents respectively) compared with the actual number of documents in an IRR system. Some of the findings, as discussed earlier, appear contradictory to common beliefs and experience of the IRR community. All these facts caused concerns about the generalizability of the tests.

The applicability of the tests in operational systems becomes questionable as artificiality is reflected in several aspects of the Cranfield tests. First, there was no real user involvement throughout the tests. Second, search questions were manufactured rather than asked by real users. Third, the testing system is not an operational one. Rather, it is designed merely for the experiments. Obviously, it is impossible to control test variables (e.g., number of terms in a query, time spent on document retrieval) involved in an operational system. Therefore, what was found in the artificial Cranfield test environment may not be applicable to operational IRR systems.

11.3.1.4 Significance of the Cranfield Tests

In spite of all the criticisms, the Cranfield tests have exerted a great impact on many other evaluation projects in the following ways. First, the Cranfield tests identified the major factors that affect the performance of retrieval systems. Indexing languages and indexing devices are some examples of such factors. Second, the Cranfield tests developed for the first time a methodology that is still with us in TREC despite its many defects. Third, the Cranfield tests have manifestly influenced our view of IR systems and how we should study them, almost entirely for the good (Spärck Jones, 1981). Fourth, the Cranfield tests also pointed the way forward to effective and attainable automatic indexing methods because they demonstrated that uniterm and natural language systems tend to perform the same as, if not better than, controlled vocabulary systems.

The significance of the Cranfield tests cannot be overstated even though their problems appear serious. As far as the evaluation of IRR systems is concerned, all major projects, including the TREC series, are influenced by the Cranfield tests in one way or another. Not a single large-scale evaluation project becomes an exception in the field of IRR. That is the very reason the term "Cranfield-like projects" was coined.

11.3.2 The TREC Series

The TREC series constitutes a succession of conferences that have been held in the U.S. annually since 1992 (i.e., TREC-1) with the intention to meet the following goals (TREC, 2000):

- To encourage research in text retrieval based on large text data collections

- To increase communication among industry, academia, and government by creating an open forum for the exchange of research ideas

- To speed the transfer of technology from research labs into commercial products by demonstrating substantial improvements in retrieval methodologies on real-world problems

- To increase the availability of the appropriate evaluation techniques for use by industry and academia, including development of new evaluation techniques more applicable to current systems

The conferences have been sponsored jointly by the National Institute of Standards and Technology (NIST), the Defense Advanced Research Projects Agency (DARPA), and other related agencies and institutions (e.g., the Advanced Research and Development Activity [ARDA] office of the Department of Defense) in the U.S.

By the end of 2008, 17 TREC conferences had been held. Although specifics about the TREC series have changed over the years, such as participants and tracks (i.e., subproblems in IR), the goals for the largest evaluation endeavor in the history of IRR remain the same.

11.3.2.1 The Design of the TREC Series

The TREC series, unlike the Cranfield tests, is an ongoing evaluation undertaking that involves various participating teams. Some of them develop their own retrieval systems. Every time, teams that decide to take part in a particular TREC obtain the test collection and related information provided by the conference sponsors and track coordinators. The actual retrieving is completed at the home base of the participating teams. Top-ranked retrieval results are submitted to the sponsors for evaluation. The participating teams of each TREC also meet at a preset time to exchange their viewpoints and experience and make plans for the next TREC.

11.3.2.1.1 Participant Teams

Participating teams of TREC (e.g., Bellcore, Carnegie Mellon University) come from industry, academia, and government in the U.S. as well as from other countries (e.g., China, France). Participation in TREC was only by invitation in the beginning but is now open to all who are able to take part in the project. Table 11.4 gives the number of participating teams in the first nine TRECs.

Table 11.4 Number of Participating Teams in TREC

TREC	Year	Number of Teams
TREC-1	1992	25
TREC-2	1993	31
TREC-3	1994	33
TREC-4	1995	36
TREC-5	1996	38
TREC-6	1997	51
TREC-7	1998	56
TREC-8	1999	66
TREC-9	2000	69

The participating teams are able to choose from three levels of participation: full participation, full participation using one-quarter of the full document set, and participation in evaluation only, to allow commercial systems to protect proprietary algorithms (Harman, 1995).

11.3.2.1.2 Test Documents

The test documents were collected mainly from newspapers (e.g., the *Wall Street Journal*), newswires (e.g., Associated Press Newswire), and other kinds of sources (e.g., the *Federal Register*). They were uniformly formatted into Standard Generalized Markup Language (SGML) and distributed as CD-ROMs with about 1 gigabyte (GB) of data each. TREC-1 started with two disks of test data; the number of disks used in the experiments eventually increased to five. Disks 4 and 5 contain data for the ad hoc task described below. The document lengths range from 300–400 terms to several hundred pages. The test set consists of more than 1 million documents.

The expansion of TREC into multiple tracks led to the design and building of many specialized text collections. In addition to those listed in Table 4.1 in Harman and Voorhees (2006), other test documents are assembled for tracks such as Genome and Legal. In other words, test collections used in current tracks are no longer the same as those created for earlier ones in terms of content, format, and scope.

11.3.2.1.3 Topics and Queries

Topics for retrieval are written by people who are actually users of a retrieval system and devised to mimic real users' needs. The topics are constructed by doing trial retrievals against a sample of the document set, and then those topics that have roughly 25 to 100 hits in that sample are selected. Each topic is formatted in the same standard method (i.e., in SGML with a sequential number, a short title, one-sentence description, and the like) to allow easier automatic construction of queries. The same 50 topics are created for the routing task in every TREC, and 50 new topics are generated for each TREC for the ad hoc task. The ad hoc and routing retrieval tasks of TREC will be explained shortly. Training topics are also prepared to allow participants to get to know the test data set. The quality of topics for TREC-1 and TREC-2 was so high that it was possible to reach a very good level of performance without the use of unduly demanding indexing and searching strategies. Therefore, the topics have been prepared from TREC-3 onward with an eye to great realism while recognizing diagnostic interests in laboratory evaluation (Spärck Jones, 2000).

Topics are provided as need statements rather than as traditional requests, based on three considerations (Voorhees & Harman, 2005, pp. 28–29). First, topics in the form of need statements would allow a wider range of query construction methods. Second, topics in such a format would supply more information for both the searcher and the assessor to use to make relevance judgments. Third, topics of this kind would facilitate the reuse of the same test collection in the future for different experiments because detailed information contained in topics is part of the collection. Retrieval queries are subsequently constructed based on the topics, either automatically or manually. The manual method could possibly be used with some machine assistance. Some ad hoc queries were formulated using relevance feedback.

11.3.2.1.4 Retrieval Tasks

Two types of retrieval tasks, ad hoc and routing, are examined in TREC. Ad hoc tasks correspond to retrospective retrieval, that is, finding all the information on a certain topic, while routing retrieval matches with selective dissemination of information by locating newly produced information about a query.

Starting with TREC-4, a set of additional retrieval tasks, called tracks, was introduced, each focusing on a particular retrieval subproblem. Spärck Jones (2000) explained about tracks by making the following apt analogy:

> Informally, TREC as a whole can be seen as a wheel, with a central hub (the ad hoc task) and radiating spokes (tracks) linked both to the hub and round the rim to one another. New spokes can be inserted, existing ones strengthened, or worn-out ones removed. We can thus look for a continuously improved TREC IR wheel, and indeed not just with more and better spokes, but with hub and rim redesign and reinforcement as well. (pp. 43–44)

Table 11.5 lists the tracks covered from TREC-4 to TREC-10, which is also known as TREC 2001. In fact, TRECs since then have consistently been labeled by year (e.g., TREC 2002, TREC 2009) instead of the previous numbering scheme. Table 11.6 records the tracks experimented with from TREC 2002 to TREC 2009. In recognition that sufficient infrastructure exists to support researchers interested in retrospective retrieval tasks, the ad hoc task was discontinued in TREC-9 so that more TREC resources could be allocated to building evaluation infrastructure for tracks (Voorhees, 2000).

Given the fact that the routing task has been merged with the filtering track since TREC-7, all the retrieval tasks probed in TRECs as of TREC-7 are in the form of tracks.

Table 11.5   An Overview of TREC Tracks: TREC-4 through TREC-10

TRACKS	TREC-4	TREC-5	TREC-6	TREC-7	TREC-8	TREC-9	TREC-10
Interactive	X	X	X	X	X	X	X
Database Merging	X	X					
Multilingual	Spanish	Spanish Chinese	Chinese				
Confusion	X	X					
SDR			X	X	X	X	
Filtering	X	X	X	X	X	X	X
NLP		X	X				
VLC		X	X	X			
CLIR			X	X	X	X	X
High Precision			X	X			
Query			X	X	X		
QA				X	X	X	X
Web				X	X	X	X
Video							X

Table 11.6   An Overview of TREC Tracks: TREC 2002 through TREC 2009

TRACKS	TREC 2002	TREC 2003	TREC 2004	TREC 2005	TREC 2006	TREC 2007	TREC 2008	TREC 2009
Interactive	X							
Filtering	X							
CLIR	X	X						
QA	X	X	X	X	X	X		
Web	X	X	X					X
Video/TRECVid	X	TRECVid	X	X	X	X	X	X
Novelty	X	X	X					
Genomics		X	X	X	X	X		
HARD		X	X	X				
Robust Retrieval		X	X	X				
Terabyte			X	X	X			
Enterprise				X	X	X	X	
Spam				X	X	X		
Blog					X	X	X	X
Legal					X	X	X	X
Million Query						X	X	X
Relevance Feedback							X	X
Chemical IR								X
Entity								X

More than two dozen tracks had been created by 2009, reflecting the research focuses of the IR community during that time. While some tracks have been discontinued, new ones have been established to investigate emerging problems in IR. Based on the overviews and reflections prepared for all the TRECs held so far (e.g., Harman, 1995; Harman & Voorhees, 2006; Spärck Jones, 1995, 2000; Voorhees & Harman, 2005), a brief description is provided for each track, listed alphabetically:

- The *Blog track* is a track commenced in TREC 2006 to explore information seeking behavior in the blogosphere. It was still running as of TREC 2009.

- The *Chemical IR track*, one of the two new tracks added in TREC 2009 (along with the Entity track), seeks to develop and evaluate technology for large-scale search in chemical documents, including academic papers and patents. The target users of this track are professional searchers, specifically patent searchers and chemists.

- The *Confusion track* represented efforts in dealing with corrupted data that would come from, for example, optical character recognition (OCR) or speech input. Data of that nature is also called *noisy* or *confused data*. This track was run in TREC-4 and TREC-5 and is related to fuzzy searching, discussed in §5.1.2.1 of this book.

- The *Cross-Language Information Retrieval (CLIR) track* is a task in which documents cover several languages (e.g., English, German, French, or Italian) and topics are in each language. The focus of this track is to retrieve documents in one target language using topics written in a different language. Participants also performed monolingual runs in the target language to act as a baseline. In TREC-10, the focus of this track was on retrieving Arabic documents using English or French topics. This track last ran in TREC 2003, but further research on this topic is continued at CLEF (Cross-Language Evaluation Forum) and the National Institute of Informatics' Test Collection for IR Systems (NTCIR); both venues are described in §9.1.3.

- The *Database Merging track* was run only in TREC-4 and TREC-5. It investigated methods for the handling of heterogeneous collections, such as the production of a single document ranking for queries when the underlying data sets were diverse.

- The *Enterprise track* began in TREC 2005, aiming to study enterprise searching (when the user looks for data of an organization or in a corporate environment), and ended in TREC 2008.

- The *Entity track*, one of the two new tracks started in TREC 2009, has as its overall aim to perform entity-related searches on web data. These search tasks (e.g., finding entities and properties of entities) address common information needs that are not yet well-modeled as ad hoc document searches.

- The *Filtering track* is regarded as the "real" form of the routing task, which has been merged with this track since TREC-7. The Filtering track deals with tasks in which the topics are stable and some relevant documents are known, but there is a stream of new documents being added into the system. For each document, the system must make a binary decision between retrieving the document or forming a ranked list. This track was discontinued in TREC 2003 after eight runs.

- The *Genomics track* was designed to explore retrieval tasks in a domain with its interest on genomics data. It ran from TREC 2003 through TREC 2007. Genomics data in this track was broadly construed to include not just gene sequences but also support documentation such as research papers and lab reports, covering a wide range of information in the field.

- The *High Accuracy Retrieval from Documents (HARD) track* was created to achieve high accuracy retrieval by leveraging additional information about the searcher or the search context. Techniques applied in this track include passage retrieval and targeted interaction with the searcher. It ran from TREC 2003 through TREC 2005.

- The *High Precision track* tested the effectiveness, efficiency, and user interface of participating systems in TREC-6 and TREC-7. Using the same set of 50 topics and documents as used in the ad hoc task, a user was asked to find, within five minutes, 10 documents that answered the topic. Users could not collaborate on a single topic, nor could the system or user have prior knowledge about the topic. Otherwise, the user was free to consult any available sources as long as the retrieval time did not exceed five minutes.

- The *Interactive track* is a task for studying user interaction with text retrieval systems and for developing methodologies for interactive evaluation. The task in TREC-10 involved observing subjects using the live web to accomplish a specific task (Voorhees & Harman, 2002). It last ran in TREC 2002 after being a track in eight consecutive TRECs.

- The *Legal track*, introduced in TREC 2006, attempts to develop search technology that meets the needs of lawyers and helps them locate information effectively in digital document collections. It was still running in TREC 2009.

- The *Million Query track*, started in 2007, is similar to standard ad hoc retrieval but with a different focus. Namely, this track is intended to evaluate large numbers of queries (thus the name *million query*) incompletely rather than a small number of queries more completely, as was done in previous ad hoc tasks. It remained a track in TREC 2009.

- The *Multilingual track* considered issues of retrieval in languages other than English. A preliminary Spanish test was carried out in TREC-4, with a formal track in TREC-5. Chinese retrieval was examined in TREC-5 and TREC-6. Further research on multilingual IR is continued at CLEF and NTCIR, which are described in §9.1.3.

- The *Natural Language Processing (NLP) track* in TREC-5 and TREC-6 explored whether the NLP techniques (syntactic and semantic) available were mature enough to have an impact on IR, and whether they could offer an advantage over purely quantitative (e.g., statistical) retrieval methods.

- The *Novelty track*, from TREC 2002 through TREC 2004, investigated systems' abilities to locate new (i.e., nonredundant) and relevant information. It worked with 50 of the older TREC topics, using a fixed, ranked list of known relevant documents.

- The *Query track* was introduced in TREC-7 to foster research on the effects of query variability and analysis on retrieval performance. Participants each constructed several different versions of existing TREC topics, mostly concentrating on different natural language versions of the topics. All groups then ran the various versions. The track evolved into a "station" after TREC-9, and the TREC website (trec.nist.gov) now serves as a repository for both query statements and the retrieval results produced from those queries.

- The *Question Answering (QA) track* started in TREC-8 to take a step closer to information retrieval (i.e., passage retrieval) rather than document retrieval. For test questions, systems produced a text extract that answered the question. Different runs had different limits on the maximum length of the extract, ranging from a short phrase (two or three words) to an entire document (1,000 words). TREC-10 conducted a pilot study with questions that required information from multiple documents to be combined to form a correct answer (Voorhees & Harman, 2002). This track ended after TREC 2007.

- The *Relevance Feedback track* plans to devise a framework for exploring the effects of different factors on the success of relevance feedback, a technique increasingly applied in IR. This track first ran in TREC 2008 and continued in TREC 2009.

- The *Robust Retrieval track*, continued from the Web track, was launched in TREC 2003. It resembled a traditional ad hoc retrieval task but concentrated more on individual topic effectiveness and less on average effectiveness. Although this track was discontinued after TREC 2005, some data that resulted from the track is used in other ad hoc tasks.

- The *SPAM track* was initiated in TREC 2005 to conduct a standard evaluation of existing and proposed spam filtering methods. It was also expected to subsequently lay the foundation for the evaluation of more general email filtering and retrieval tasks. This track ended after TREC 2007.

- The *Spoken Document Retrieval (SDR) track* was the successor to the Confusion track and investigated a retrieval system's ability to retrieve spoken documents (i.e., recordings of speech). This track was offered with the support of the speech group at NIST. Participants compared the effectiveness of their retrieval system on human-produced transcripts of broadcast news, on transcripts produced by a baseline speech recognition system, and, optionally, on transcripts produced by their own recognizer. This track was discontinued in TREC-10.

- The *Terabyte track* first ran in TREC 2004. Its purpose was to investigate whether and how the IR community can scale traditional IR test-collection-based evaluation to significantly larger databases than those used in TREC then. It last ran in TREC 2006.

- The *Very Large Corpus (VLC) track* had a trial run in TREC-5 and was discontinued after TREC-7. It performed ad hoc searches on approximately 20 GB of text, exploring the effectiveness and efficiency of retrieval. Participants were evaluated on the precision of the top 20 documents retrieved, query response time, data structure building time, and some cost measures.

- The *Video track*, new in TREC-10, focused on content-based access to digital video to continue TREC's interest in multimedia retrieval (Voorhees & Harman, 2002). Interest in this track has been high although there is overlap in techniques for video and text retrieval. As a result, the track was spun off in 2003 as a separate evaluation effort called TRECVid (www-nlpir.nist.gov/projects/trecvid).

- The *Web track* features ad hoc tasks whose document set is a snapshot of the World Wide Web. The main task involves approximately 10GB of web data. Participants are encouraged to investigate a variety of web retrieval strategies, such as whether links can be used to enhance retrieval. The track started in TREC-8 and was discontinued after TREC 2004. The Web track, however, was reintroduced in TREC 2009 for exploring web-specific retrieval tasks, including diversity and efficiency tasks, and collections of up to 1 billion webpages. Compared with its ancestor between TREC-8 and TREC 2004, the current track would be using a larger and more recent web crawl as the document set.

This description of all the tracks illustrates the magnitude and extent of retrieval tasks investigated in TREC. Some of the tracks actually go beyond the goals TREC initially set. For example, TREC is essentially an evaluation project for text retrieval, yet a track on video retrieval was run in TREC-10. Such tracks, as Spärck Jones (2000) put it, are extensions of TREC. In addition, Harman and Voorhees (2006) summarize in Figure 4.3 of their paper that most of the tracks run from TREC-1 through TREC 2003 fall into the following categories (with tracks introduced after TREC 2003 added where appropriate):

- Static text: Ad hoc, Robust, Relevance Feedback

- Streamed text: Routing, Filtering

- Human: Interactive, HARD

- Beyond just English: Multilingual, CLIR

- Beyond text: Confusion, Spoken Document Retrieval, Video, TRECVid

- Web searching: Very Large Corpus, Web, Terabyte, Entity

- Answers, not documents: Question Answering, Novelty

- Domain: Genomics, Enterprise, Legal, Chemical IR

11.3.2.1.5 Evaluation and Relevance Judgments

Evaluation in TREC has used traditional recall and precision measures, so relevance judgment is a must. People who created the topics are sometimes also assessors for making evaluation. The pooling method described in §11.1.2.1.2 was used to form the data pool for assessment in all TRECs. Each participating team submits to the sponsors the top 100 documents retrieved in each run for a given topic, as a ranking algorithm is implemented in all the test systems to output retrieval results in the order of perceived relevance.

An assessor on average judges approximately 2,000 documents per topic. The completeness and consistency of TREC judgments were checked in separate studies, and the outcomes appear positive (Voorhees & Harman, 2000). A standard evaluation package is used to record each of the submitted runs. The evaluation measure used most frequently in TREC is the average precision discussed in §11.1.2.1.4. Other kinds of recall- and precision-based evaluation measures are also computed in TREC. Spärck Jones (2000) summarized track performance measures applied from TREC-4 to TREC-6. Buckley and Voorhees (2005) also provided a comprehensive description of the evaluation measures used in TRECs. All the evaluation measures, however, assess only retrieval performance because they all are variations of precision and recall, leaving other dimensions of IR systems untouched. The TREC series therefore treats the measure of high precision and recall as its final goal rather than a sub-goal (Robertson, 2008).

11.3.2.2 Findings of TREC

The findings in TREC are too many and diversified to be enumerated here. Therefore, only the general ones are recapitulated as follows:

Many very different approaches give similar performance, indicating that "All roads lead to Rome" and different methods can be sought to achieve the same objective.

Automatic processing (i.e., query construction or retrieval) is as good as manual processing but may not be quite so convincing for poor queries.

Statistically based indexing and searching techniques are cheap and competitive, particularly for large collections or databases. They can do much better than simple term baselines although they need to subsume some collection training.

Simple phrases along with single terms contribute something, implying additional promise for automatic methods in the field.

Relevance feedback is valuable, and moderate query expansion seems helpful. However, there is not much progress in TREC toward the goal of designing effective individual query, as opposed to query class, strategies for the ad hoc task. In other words, a system still cannot automatically analyze a request for the implications of its term makeup and choose one particular query formation strategy that is likely to give the best results.

11.3.2.3 Problems With TREC

The main criticism of TREC is that it basically follows in the footsteps of the Cranfield tests by using an artificial test environment and by choosing recall and precision as retrieval performance measures.

The artificiality of the TREC series is threefold. First, the test documents used in early TRECs, consisting of mainly newspapers, were gathered for the project rather than being a collection built naturally over the years. While newspapers can be a valuable source for many other purposes, they are not heavily consulted for most research endeavors. Second, TREC does not have genuine and hands-on users. The topics or search requests, as in Cranfield, are manufactured specifically for the project. The retrieval is done by system developers, and retrieval performance is judged by assessors who perhaps also created the topics. Third, the tests are done in a traditional laboratory environment, with a certain degree of control and manipulation. It is hard to relate such an environment to the real, operational system.

In addition, there are problems associated with the evaluation methodology adopted in TREC. On one hand, the limitations of using recall and precision as evaluation criteria for retrieval performance are all present in TREC because recall and precision are the major selected measures for assessment in the project. On the other hand, only the top-ranked results retrieved from each system are pooled for evaluation. The TREC assessments would consequently appear better than the cases if all the results were included in the evaluation. According to the research reported by Zobel (1998), the recall in TREC was overestimated. Moreover, the need for more statistical evaluation seems obvious as the recall-precision curves provided by each participating team are often close, and there is a need to check whether there are truly any statistically significant differences between two systems' results or two sets of results from the same system. It also seems necessary to get beyond the averages to better understand systems performance. In addition, it is very difficult to perform failure analysis on the results because of the huge number of test documents involved and the threshold set for retrieval outputs (Harman, 1995). The lack of failure analysis in TREC has also been pointed out by Robertson (2008).

Overall, TREC uses the black box approach for evaluation, with systems compared as wholes for performance through their team run results (Spärck Jones, 2000). Little knowledge has been gained about how a particular strategy or device makes the system performance change even though TREC has been held since 1992. The glass box approach is apparently needed for the evaluation task. Spärck Jones (2006) restated this need by calling for TREC's attention to addressing particularization in IR evaluation.

11.3.2.4 Significance of TREC

With many of its unique features (e.g., test document size and the increasing number of participating teams), TREC holds a significant place in the history of IRR evaluation. Its significance has been reflected in the following aspects.

First, it provides an open and stimulating forum for evaluating IRR. By being an open forum, it has encouraged participation by many institutions and organizations from home and abroad. By being a stimulating forum, it has motivated participants to further improve their systems. Indeed, for instance, significant improvement in retrieval performance was observed in TREC-2 over that in TREC-1 (Spärck Jones, 1995).

Second, many different approaches have been tried in TREC, including passage retrieval, data fusion, statistical and probabilistic indexing, and term weighting strategies. The Boolean retrieval mechanism, although important, is no longer dominant in the project. In addition, the test collection size now reaches the magnitude of gigabytes instead of megabytes, as in earlier evaluation efforts, thus getting closer to the real-life situation in terms of volume. TREC has been evolving to approximate a real-world operational environment that allows transition of the test results to the inclusion in commercial products with known benefits (Kowalski & Maybury, 2000). Internet retrieval systems are prime examples of the fruits of TREC research. Their ability to point users to the information they seek has been fundamental to the success of the web (Harman & Voorhees, 2006).

Third, TREC is more generalizable than many other projects, in part because it is a continuing research effort. It attempts to answer many questions, which can be put into such broad categories as indexing and retrieval models, indexing vocabulary, document descriptions, indexing sources, queries and query sources, search strategy, scoring criteria, and learning ability of IR systems (Spärck Jones, 2000).

In all, TREC is of great importance to the field. New research possibilities have also been suggested for the future, including:

- Hold TREC less frequently so that time can be spent digesting the results already obtained.

- Concentrate effort on fewer tasks or tracks in order to pursue them in more depth.

- Get real users involved in the project to improve the applicability of the research findings.

- Place the application of IR test findings up front, and move TREC more firmly toward studies of retrieval in operational contexts.

- Adopt the glass box evaluation approach by engaging individual teams at the particular strategy, device, or even parameter level rather than using the black box approach by comparing systems as wholes for performance through their team run results.

- Embark on multiple-task studies by applying the TREC experience in them. Retrieval will be examined as only one component of a system that might also offer automatic summarization of retrieved texts, for example.

11.4 A Final Word on Evaluation of Information Representation and Retrieval

The Cranfield tests and the TREC series symbolize the problems and issues in IRR evaluation. Generally speaking, most evaluation projects are carried out in laboratories rather than real-life situations with artificial collections and manufactured requests. The size of test collection is usually small—although the TREC series is an exception. Recall, precision, and fallout are used as predominant evaluation measures. Yet they are unreliable because, among other concerns, they are based on subjective judgments of relevance. In addition, most evaluation projects focus on these individual criteria (e.g., recall and precision) without a framework for evaluating the entire system. After all the efforts, we have learned what happens in such systems, but it is not quite clear as to why it happens and how it happens because of the black box evaluation approach.

Proposals and suggestions have been made to advance research in evaluating information representation and retrieval by going beyond the existing models and implementing methodology pluralism. For example, Harter and Hert (1997) described an emerging framework for IRR evaluation, emphasizing the use of multiple dimensions and methods, and evaluation from the perspective of several IRR system stakeholders. They also believe strongly that user-system interaction must be considered during the evaluation process in the digital age. On the other hand, future evaluation projects should be done in a real-life environment and use measures other than recall, precision, and fallout to overcome the two most notorious limitations of previous assessments in the field, namely, subjectivity in judging relevance and inability to determine the total number of relevant documents in a system.

References

Antelman, Kristin, Lynema, Emily, and Pace, Andrew K. (2006). Toward a twenty-first century library catalog. *Information Technology & Libraries*, 25(3), 128–139.

Bell, Hazel K. (1991). Bias in indexing and loaded language. *The Indexer*, 17(3), 173–177.

Bevan, Nigel. (2001). International standards for HCI and usability. *International Journal of Human Computer Studies*, 55(4), 533–552.

Blair, D. C., and Maron, M. E. (1985). An evaluation of retrieval effectiveness for a full-text document retrieval system. *Communications of the ACM*, 28(3), 289–299.

Buckley, Chris, and Voorhees, Ellen M. (2005). Retrieval system evaluation. In Ellen M. Voorhees and Donna K. Harman (Eds.), *TREC: Experiment and evaluation in information retrieval* (pp. 53–75). Cambridge, MA: MIT Press.

Chang, Shih-Fu. (2002). The holy grail of content-based media analysis. *IEEE Multimedia Magazine*, 9(2), 6–10.

Chowdhury, Gobinda G. (1999). *Introduction to modern information retrieval*. London: Library Association Publishing.

Chu, Heting, and Rosenthal, Marilyn. (1996). Search engines for the World Wide Web: A comparative study and evaluation methodology. *Proceedings of the 59th Annual Meeting of the American Society for Information Science*, 33, 127–135. Retrieved January 21, 2009, from www.asis.org/annual-96/Electronic Proceedings/chu.html

Clarke, Sarah J., and Willett, Peter. (1997). Estimating the recall performance of web search engines. *Aslib Proceedings*, 49(7), 184–189.

Cleverdon, C. W. (1962). *Report on the testing and analysis of an investigation into the comparative efficiency of indexing systems*. Cranfield, England: College of Aeronautics.

Cleverdon, C. W. (1967). The Cranfield tests on indexing language devices. *Aslib Proceedings*, 19, 173–192.

Cleverdon, C. W. (1984). Optimizing convenient online access to bibliographic databases. *Information Services and Use*, 4(1–2), 37–47.

Cleverdon, C. W., and Mills, J. (1963). The testing of indexing language devices. *Aslib Proceedings*, 15(4), 106–130.

Cleverdon, C. W., Mills, J., and Keen, E. M. (1966). *Factors determining the performance of indexing systems, Vol. 1—Design.* Cranfield, England: Aslib Cranfield Research Project.

Clough, Paul. (2007). Large-scale evaluation of cross-language image retrieval systems. *Bulletin of the American Society for Information Science and Technology*, 33(3). Retrieved December 19, 2008, from www.asis.org/Bulletin/Feb-07/clough.html

Cooper, William S. (1973a). On selecting a measure of retrieval effectiveness. Part I. *Journal of the American Society for Information Science*, 24, 87–100.

Cooper, William S. (1973b). On selecting a measure of retrieval effectiveness. Part II. *Journal of the American Society for Information Science*, 24, 413–424.

Deselaers, Thomas, Keysers, Daniel, and Ney, Hermann. (2008). Features for image retrieval: An experimental comparison. *Information Retrieval*, 11(2), 77–107.

Ding, Wei, and Marchionini, Gary. (1996). A comparative study of web search service performance. *Proceedings of the 59th Annual Meeting of the American Society for Information Science*, 33, 136–142.

Downie, J. Stephen. (2003). The TREC-like evaluation of music retrieval systems. *Proceedings of the 26th annual international ACM SIGIR conference* (pp. 453–454). New York: Association for Computing Machinery.

Downie, J. Stephen. (Ed.). (2004). The MIR/MDL Evaluation Project white paper collection. 3rd ed. Retrieved January 7, 2009, from www.music-ir.org/evaluation/wp.html

Foskett, A. C. (1996). *Subject approach to information.* 5th ed. London: Library Association Publishing.

Froehlich, Thomas J. (1994). Relevance revisited—Towards an agenda for the 21st century: Introduction to special topic issue on relevance research. *Journal of the American Society for Information Science*, 45(3), 123–134.

Fugmann, Robert. (1993). *Subject analysis and indexing: Theoretical foundation and practical advice.* Frankfurt/Main: Indeks Verlag.

Griffith, Belver C. (1986). *Evaluation of information systems: Class notes.* Philadelphia: Drexel University, College of Information Studies.

Griffiths, Alan, Luckhurst, H. Claire, and Willett, Peter. (1986). Using inter-document similarity information in document retrieval systems. *Journal of the American Society for Information Science,* 37(1), 3–11.

Guha, Tamal Kumar, and Saraf, Veena. (2007). OPAC usability: Assessment through verbal protocol. *Electronic Library,* 23(4), 463–473.

Haga, Hirohide, and Kaneda, Shigeo. (2005). A usability survey of a contents-based video retrieval system by combining digital video and an electronic bulletin board. *Internet & Higher Education,* 8(3), 251–262.

Harman, Donna. (1993). A special conference report: The first Text Retrieval Conference (TREC-1) Rockville, MD, U.S.A., 4–6 Nov. 1992. *Information Processing & Management, 29*(4), 411–414.

Harman, Donna. (1995). Overview of the second Text Retrieval Conference (TREC-2). *Information Processing & Management,* 31(3), 271–290.

Harman, Donna K., and Voorhees, Ellen M. (2006). TREC: An overview. *Annual Review of Information Science and Technology,* 40, 113–155.

Harter, Stephen P. (1971). The Cranfield II relevance assessments: A critical evaluation. *Library Quarterly,* 41, 229–243.

Harter, Stephen P., and Hert, Carol A. (1997). Evaluation of information retrieval systems: Approaches, issues, and methods. *Annual Review of Information Science and Technology,* 32, 3–94.

Hearst, Marti, et al. (2002). Finding the flow in Web site search. *Communications of the ACM,* 45(9), 42–49.

Hildreth, Charles R. (1982). *Online public access catalogues: The user inter-face.* Dublin, OH: OCLC.

Hildreth, Charles R. (1985). Online public access catalogs. *Annual Review of Information Science and Technology,* 20, 233–285.

Hooper, R. S. (1965). *Indexer consistency tests—Origin, measurements, results and utilization.* Bethesda, MD: IBM.

Ingwersen, Peter. (1996). Cognitive perspectives of information retrieval interaction: Elements of a cognitive IR theory. *Journal of Documentation,* 52(1), 3–50.

International Organization for Standardization (ISO). (1998). *Guidance on usability* (ISO 9241–11). Geneva, Switzerland: ISO.

Keen, E.M. (1971). Evaluation parameters. In Gerard Salton (Ed.), *The SMART retrieval system: Experiments in automatic document processing* (pp. 74–111). Englewood Cliffs, NJ: Prentice Hall.

Kent, Allen, et al. (1955). Machine literature searching. VIII. Operational criteria for designing information retrieval systems. *American Documentation,* 6(2), 93–101.

Korfhage, Robert R. (1997). *Information storage and retrieval.* New York: John Wiley & Sons.

Kowalski, Gerald, and Maybury, Mark T. (2000). *Information storage and retrieval systems: Theory and implementation.* 2nd ed. Boston: Kluwer Academic Publishers.

Lancaster, F. W. (1968). *Evaluation of the MEDLARS demand search service.* Bethesda, MD: National Library of Medicine.

Lancaster, F. W. (1979). *Information retrieval systems: Characteristics, testing and evaluation.* 2nd ed. New York: Wiley.

Lancaster, F. W. (1998). *Indexing and abstracting in theory and practice.* 2nd ed. Champaign-Urbana, IL: University of Illinois, Graduate School of Library and Information Science.

Lancaster, F. W., and Fayen, E. G. (1973). *Information retrieval online.* Los Angeles: Melville.

Lancaster, F. W., and Warner, Amy J. (1993). *Information retrieval today.* Arlington, VA: Information Resources Press.

Large, Andrew, Tedd, Lucy A., and Hartley, Richard J. (1999). *Information seeking in the online age: Principles and practice.* London: Bowker-Saur.

Leighton, H. Vernon. (1995). Performance of four World Wide Web (WWW) index services: Infoseek, Lycos, WebCrawler, and WWWWorm. Retrieved October 11, 2009, from www.winona.edu/library/staff/vL/WEBIND.HTM

Leighton, H. Vernon, and Srivastava, Jaideep. (1999). First 20 precision among World Wide Web search services (search engines). *Journal of the American Society for Information Science,* 50(10), 870–881.

Lombardo, Shawn V., and Condic, Kristine S. (2000). Empowering users with a new online catalog. *Library Hi Tech,* 18(2), 130–141.

Marcum, Deanna B. (2006). The future of cataloging. *Library Resources & Technical Services,* 50(1), 5–9.

Markey, Karen. (2007). The online library catalog: Paradise lost or paradise gained. *D-Lib Magazine*, 13(1/2). Retrieved December 6, 2008, from dlib.org/dlib/january07/markey/01markey.html

Miller, C., and Tegler, P. (1986). Online searching and the research process. *College and Research Libraries*, 47(4), 370–373.

Miniwatts Marketing Group. (2009). Internet world users by language. Retrieved October 8, 2009, from www.internetworldstats.com/stats7.htm

Mizzaro, Stefno. (1997). Relevance: The whole history. *Journal of the American Society for Information Science*, 48(9), 801–832.

Nielsen, Jakob. (1993). *Usability engineering*. New York: Morgan Kaufmann.

Nielsen, Jakob. (2003). Usability 101: Introduction to usability. Retrieved January 8, 2009, from www.useit.com/alertbox/20030825.html

Oppenheim, Charles, et al. (2000). The evaluation of WWW search engines. *Journal of Documentation*, 56(2), 190–211.

O'Rourke, Victoria. (1987). Selection of an online public access catalog: A checklist approach. *Information Technology and Libraries*, 6(4), 278–287.

Petrelli, Daniela, and Auld, Daniel. (2008). An examination of automatic video retrieval technology on access to the contents of an historical video archive. *Program: Electronic Library & Information Systems*, 42(2), 115–136.

Robertson, Stephen E. (1969). The parametric description of retrieval tests. Part I: The basic parameters. *Journal of Documentation*, 25(12), 1–27.

Robertson, Stephen E. (2008). On the history of evaluation in IR. *Journal of Information Science*, 34(4), 439–456.

Rowley, Jennifer E., and Hartley, Richard J. (2008). *Organizing knowledge: An introduction to managing access to information*. Burlington, VT: Ashgate.

Salmon, Stephen R. (1983). Characteristics of online public catalogs. *Library Resources & Technical Services*, 27(1), 36–67.

Salton, Gerard. (1981). The SMART environment for retrieval system evaluation: Advantages and problem areas. In Karen Spärck Jones (Ed.), *Information retrieval experiment* (pp. 316–329). London: Butterworth.

Salton, Gerard. (1992). The state of retrieval system evaluation. *Information Processing & Management*, 28(4), 441–449.

Saracevic, Tefko. (1975). Relevance: A review of the literature and a framework for thinking on the notion in information science. *Journal of the American Society for Information Science*, 26(6), 321–343.

Saracevic, Tefko. (2007a). Relevance: A review of the literature and a framework for thinking on the notion in information science. Part II: Nature and manifestations of relevance. *Journal of the American Society for Information Science and Technology*, 58(13), 1915–1933.

Saracevic, Tefko. (2007b). Relevance: A review of the literature and a framework for thinking on the notion in information science. Part III: Behavior and effects of relevance. *Journal of the American Society for Information Science and Technology*, 58(13), 2126–2144.

Saracevic, Tefko, et al. (1988). A study of information seeking and retrieving. Part I: Background and methodology. *Journal of the American Society for Information Science*, 39(3), 161–176.

Saracevic, Tefko, and Kantor, Paul. (1988). A study of information seeking and retrieving. Part II: Users, questions, and effectiveness. *Journal of the American Society for Information Science*, 39(3), 177–196.

Schamber, Linda. (1994). Relevance and information behavior. *Annual Review of Information Science and Technology*, 29, 3–48.

Schamber, Linda, Eisenberg, Michael B., and Nilan, Michael S. (1990). A reexamination of relevance: Toward a dynamic, situational definition. *Information Processing & Management*, 26(6), 755–776.

Shneiderman, Ben, and Plaisant, Catherine. (2005). *Designing the user interface: Strategies for effective human-computer interaction.* 4th ed. Boston: Addison-Wesley.

Smeaton, Alan F. (2007). TRECVid: Video evaluation. *Bulletin of the American Society for Information Science and Technology*, 33(3). Retrieved December 19, 2008, from www.asis.org/Bulletin/Feb-07/smeaton.html

Smeaton, Alan F., and Over, Paul. (2003). The TREC-2002 video track report. *Proceedings of the Eleventh Text REtrieval Conference (TREC2002)*. Retrieved January 7, 2008, from trec.nist.gov//pubs/trec11/papers/VIDEO.OVER.pdf

Spärck Jones, Karen. (1981). The Cranfield tests. In Karen Spärck Jones (Ed.), *Information retrieval experiment* (pp. 256–284). London: Butterworths.

Spärck Jones, Karen. (1995). Reflections on TREC. *Information Processing & Management*, 31(3), 191–314.

Spärck Jones, Karen. (2000). Further reflections on TREC. *Information Processing & Management*, 36(1), 37–85.

Spärck Jones, Karen. (2006). What's the value of TREC? Is there a gap to jump or a chasm to bridge? *ACM SIGIR Forum*, 40(1), 10–20.

Su, Louise T. (1991). *An investigation to find appropriate measures for evaluating interactive information retrieval*. Unpublished Ph.D. Dissertation. New Brunswick, NJ: Rutgers, the State University of New Jersey.

Swanson, Don R. (1965). The evidence underlying the Cranfield results. *Library Quarterly*, 35(1), 1–20.

Swanson, Don R. (1971). Some unexplained aspects of the Cranfield tests of indexing performance factors. *Library Quarterly*, 41(3), 223–228.

Swanson, Rowena Weiss. (1978). Performing evaluation studies in information science. In D. W. King (Ed.), *Key papers in design and evaluation of retrieval systems* (pp. 58–74). New York: Knowledge Industry.

Swets, John A. (1963). Information retrieval systems. *Science*, 141, 245–250.

Swets, John A. (1969). Effectiveness of information retrieval methods. *American Documentation*, 20(1), 72–89.

Trant, Jennifer. (2004). Image retrieval benchmark database service: A needs assessment and preliminary development plan. *A Report Prepared for the Council on Library and Information Resources and the Coalition for Networked Information*. Retrieved December 18, 2008, from www.clir.org/pubs/reports/trant04/tranttext.htm

TREC. (2000). Overview [of TREC]. Retrieved June 17, 2001, from trec.nist.gov/overview.html

Vickery, B. C. (1966). Review of Cleverdon, Mills, and Keen. *Journal of Documentation*, 22, 247–249.

Vickery, B. C. (1967). Review of Cleverdon and Keen. *Journal of Documentation*, 23, 338–340.

Voorhees, Ellen M. (2000). Report on TREC-9. *SIGIR Forum*, 34(2), 1–8.

Voorhees, Ellen M., and Harman, Donna. (2000). Overview of the sixth Text REtrieval Conference (TREC-6). *Information Processing & Management*, 36(1), 3–35.

Voorhees, Ellen M., and Harman, Donna K. (2002). Overview of TREC 2001. *Proceedings of the Tenth Text REtrieval Conference (TREC 2001)* (pp. 1–15).

NIST Special Publication 500–250. Retrieved September 2, 2002, from trec.nist.gov/pubs/trec10/papers/overview_10.pdf

Voorhees, Ellen M., and Harman, Donna K. (Eds.). (2005). *TREC: Experiment and evaluation in information retrieval.* Cambridge, MA: MIT Press.

Wellisch, Hans H. (1995). *Indexing from A to Z.* 2nd ed. New York: H.W. Wilson.

Zobel, J. (1998). How reliable are the results of large-scale information retrieval experiments? In *Proceedings of the 21 Annual International Conference on Research and Development in Information Retrieval— SIGIR-98* (pp. 307–314). New York: Association for Computing Machinery.

CHAPTER 12

Artificial Intelligence in Information Representation and Retrieval

Artificial intelligence (AI) is a field aiming to make machines do things that would require intelligence if done by people. The information representation and retrieval (IRR) community has shown great interest in AI research, hoping to bring AI applications to IRR. Although AI researchers have experienced excitement as well as disappointment in pursuing their goals, their enthusiasm has not waned. To the contrary, an increasing number of attempts have been made to develop AI applications for representing and retrieving information, particularly since the web became the major platform for IRR. This chapter provides an overview of AI research in the context of IRR. Two active AI research areas for IRR, natural language processing (NLP) and the semantic web, are discussed, in addition to the limitations and potential of AI research for IRR.

12.1 Overview of Artificial Intelligence Research

AI has been established as a research field at least since 1956, when the Dartmouth Conference was held (Spärck Jones, 1991). The goal of AI is to develop systems that behave intelligently, using computers to carry out tasks that require reasoning on world knowledge. Knowledge in AI should be interpreted as a combination of information, facts, rules of thumb, or even the intuition and common sense necessary for intellectual activities such as solving problems and making decisions. More important, AI is supposed to have a component that is able to reason, as human beings can, in situations in which only partial knowledge or indirect connectivity is available. For example, an AI system for information representation should be able to generate broader, narrower, and related terms according to the content of a document. In other words, the system needs to be able to identify and establish relationships among the terms contained in the document. The system must have AI, mimicking human intelligence, to complete the task.

Knowledge in AI is obtained via the knowledge engineering process, in which the knowledge engineer acquires knowledge from the domain expert, a person extremely knowledgeable about a specific area or domain, by such methods as interview, observation, and thinking-aloud protocols. The acquired knowledge is then represented using, for instance, production rules, semantic networks, or frames to form a knowledge base. The knowledge base, along with other provisions (e.g., inference engine and self-learning facility), makes up an AI application.

Different methods have been tried in AI research in the past decades. Mullins (2005) referred to the following knowledge-based approaches to AI when revisiting the topic of machines that think: symbolic reasoning, artificial neural networks, Bayesian inference, and functional magnetic resonance imaging (fMRI).

Symbolic reasoning is a mathematical approach in which ideas and concepts are represented by symbols such as production rules or concept hierarchies. These symbols are then processed according to the rules of logic. Given enough information, the hope is that these symbolic reasoning systems can eventually become intelligent. In explaining symbolic machine learning techniques, an indispensable component in symbolic reasoning, Chen (1995) indicated that learning from examples, a special case of inductive learning, appears to be the most promising symbolic machine learning technique for knowledge discovery or data analysis. For instance, a user retrieves an initial set of articles and marks them as relevant or irrelevant to his or her interest. These positive and negative examples are then used to train the system to capture the features common to relevant articles (Jennings & Higuchi, 1992).

Artificial neural networks, at a rudimentary level, imitate the way neurons in the brain work. They are made up of interconnecting artificial neurons, namely, programming constructs that mimic the properties of biological neurons. Genetic algorithms, one type of neural network development, imitate genetic inheritance and fitness to evolve better solutions to a problem with every generation, while connectionist algorithms enable knowledge learning by a network of interconnected neurons (nodes), weighted synapses (links), and threshold logic units. Learning algorithms can be applied to adjust connection weights so that the system can predict or classify unknown examples correctly (Chen, 1995). Using neural network-based concept classification, for example, Chen, et al. (1994), generated a tentative list of the important ideas and topics represented in meeting comments.

Systems using the mathematical technique known as Bayesian inference have improved the performance of many AI programs to the point that they can be used in the real world. The Microsoft Office paper clip assistant is an implementation based on Bayesian inference systems, although it was not well received. Lau and Coiera (2006), on the other hand, adopted the

Bayesian model for predicting the impact of web searching on selected clinicians' decision making.

Functional magnetic resonance imaging (fMRI) is a technique used to see which parts of the brain become active when a person thinks about a specific object. When people are asked to imagine a tool (e.g., a hammer) or a building (e.g., a house), the same areas of the brain are activated as when they are shown a picture of these objects. AI researchers can presumably train a program to look at the brain images and determine with 90 percent accuracy whether that person is thinking about a tool or a building (Mullins, 2005). Such a program could eventually read the user's mind, making it possible that people's information needs can be understood better and more explicitly.

These four methods of AI research certainly do not exhaust all available options. The linguistic approach widely applied to process natural language in AI is only one example. While it is beyond the scope of this book to offer a complete survey of AI methods, it is apparent that AI researchers, regardless of what particular techniques they may study, all aspire to develop applications for many areas (e.g., robotics and pattern recognition), and IRR is one of them. Efforts have been made in IRR to apply AI to, among other things, information extraction, automatic summarization, question answering, natural language searching, and intelligent agents. NLP and the semantic web appear to be the two AI research areas that may contribute the most to the field of IRR.

12.2 Natural Language Processing

NLP is an area of research and application that explores how the natural language text, entered into a computer system, can be manipulated and transformed into a form more suitable for further manipulation (Chowdhury, 1999). According to Liddy (1998), NLP is a range of computational techniques for analyzing and representing naturally occurring texts at one or more levels of linguistic analysis for the purpose of achieving humanlike language processing for a range of particular tasks or applications. These tasks or applications mainly include automatic summarization and question answering (Carbonell, et al., 2000). Both applications will be discussed here individually after a description of the role of NLP in IRR.

12.2.1 The Role of Natural Language Processing in Information Representation and Retrieval

Language, spoken or written, is an essential component in both information representation and information retrieval (IR) because information has to be expressed in a language when being processed, transferred, or communicated. Natural language in IRR, as opposed to any other artificial language, is the language people would naturally use to represent information or form a query. Natural language can be processed in AI at phonological, morphological, lexical, syntactic, semantic, discourse, and pragmatic levels (Doszkocs, 1986; Liddy, 1998), and each holds implications for IRR.

The phonological level of analysis involves treatment of speech sounds. This type of processing could be important in sound retrieval (see §9.2.2), which includes, for example, voice input or spoken information. The "sound like" feature in IR (e.g., find documents containing terms that sound like "music") can be implemented only at the phonological level of NLP.

The morphological level of processing deals with constituencies used to make up individual words, such as word stems or bases, prefixes, infixes, suffixes, and compound words. For example, the word *uniterm* consists of the prefix *uni* and word base *term*. Truncation is a retrieval technique that derives from this level of processing. Information representation such as automatic indexing can also be done, to a certain degree, with documents processed at the morphological level.

Lexical-level processing typically refers to the signification and application of words, such as determining whether *book* is meant as in a published volume or as in making a reservation. Implications for IRR with this level of language analysis include 1) stop-word removal, 2) automatic search term substitution and augmentation (e.g., thesaurus lookups), 3) spelling error detection and correction, and 4) the handling of acronyms and abbreviations through lookups in word lists.

The syntactic level of analysis parses sentences to make the grammatical relationships between words in sentences clear. For example, is the structural unit a sentence, a phrase, or a clause? This process also involves the need for a grammar that describes the possible word order and different rules of agreement. Noun phrases, for instance, identified in the syntactic level analysis, can be candidates for indexing terms. Phrase searching and proximity searching are all applications of language processed at the syntactic level.

Semantic-level processing tries to assign meaning to the various syntactic constituents in a sentence. Various semantic aids (e.g., thesauri) might be needed to conduct language analysis at this level. Sample applications in this regard for IRR consist of automatic display of cross-references, synonyms, and related terms. However, semantic-level processing cannot be completed successfully without language analysis at the pragmatic level.

The discourse level of language processing (not mentioned in Doszkocs, 1986) interprets the structure and meaning conveyed by texts larger than a sentence. In other words, such processing would enable the communication of meaning above and beyond that conveyed in individual words or sentences.

Natural language processed at the discourse level can be used to understand what the specific role of a piece of information is in a document. For example, is this a conclusion, an opinion, a prediction, or simply a fact? This structure obviously has specific implications for passage retrieval because a passage in this context could be longer than a sentence.

The pragmatic level, the highest level of language processing, attempts to decide the meaning of the language by considering the surrounding context, the author, the user, and knowledge of the real world. This level of processing presents the greatest challenge to AI researchers in NLP. Indeed, human beings depend on context and other knowledge to understand language and eliminate ambiguity. Yet the complexity and difficulty involved in this process are still not fully comprehended, and systems have not yet been developed that can imitate how human beings process language at this level. The application of this process to IRR would be extraordinary and of fundamental significance if a breakthrough in NLP at this level can be achieved. Many applications that have been dreamed of in IRR, such as automatic summarization and natural language query, could then be a reality. Vocabulary switching, briefly described at the end of Chapter 4 as a mechanism for automatically changing from one IRR language to another across different subject domains, would also benefit from this line of AI research.

If language processing can be done successfully at the semantic, discourse, and pragmatic levels, the semantic web envisioned by Tim Berners-Lee and his associates would have become a reality already. The topic of the semantic web is explored in §12.3. On the other hand, the seven different levels involved in NLP define what NLP can do for IRR. The larger the unit of analysis becomes (i.e., from morpheme to word to sentence to paragraph to full document), the less precise the language phenomena and the greater the free choice and variability. While the first four levels of processing can be done reasonably well today, further research into performing language analysis at the semantic level, the discourse level, and especially the pragmatic level is called for. Research efforts in computational linguistics, linguistics in general, philosophy of language, and sociolinguistics would facilitate AI research in NLP (Cercone & McCalla, 1984).

Given the importance of language in IRR, implications of NLP for IRR are far-reaching. Automatic summarization and question answering (QA) constitute the two major applications in this category (Carbonell, et al., 2000) while others (e.g., information extraction, natural language searching) can be viewed as either an extension or a derivation of what is involved in the two major applications. In subsequent sections, automatic summarization and QA are discussed, followed by other AI applications in the field of IRR.

12.2.2 Automatic Summarization

Automatic summarization (or summarizing), simply put, is the creation of a shortened version of a text by a computer program. Research efforts in this respect date back to the 1950s, when Hans Peter Luhn experimented with automatic abstract creation (1958). As information in the digital age grows exponentially and reaches the peta level (i.e., 10^{15}) in a very short time (Campbell, 2008), different methods such as automatic summarization have been used to cope with the data torrents. In fact, automatic summarization is evolving into a domain by itself in the field of IR with the exclusive intention of producing summaries through the use of NLP technologies.

Summarization in the current context carries two meanings: One is extraction and the other is abstraction, although it has to be pointed out that the latter is not the same as the conventional abstract discussed in §2.3.1.1. According to Mani (2001), an extract is a summary consisting entirely of material copied from the input source, while an abstract is a summary containing at least some material that is not present in the original input. Other parameters for automatic summarization include compression rate (i.e., the ratio between summary length and source length), audience (i.e., generic or focused), source size (i.e., single document or multiple documents), genre (e.g., news, email messages, blog messages, webpages), language (i.e., monolingual, multilingual, or cross-lingual), and media (e.g., text, sound, images, videos). Summaries are typically labeled according to these parameters. For instance, summaries generated for the public are called generic summaries.

12.2.2.1 The Process of Automatic Summarization

As can be seen from the list of parameters previously mentioned, some types of automatic summaries (e.g., for single documents) are easier to obtain than others (e.g., for multiple documents). The process of automatic summarization, in general, comprises the following basic steps: sentence identification and selection, sentence extraction, and summary smoothing operations. While the first two steps are required for any automatic summarization, summary smoothing operations may not be performed because the majority of automatic summarization does only sentence ordering instead of summary smoothing in this step. Genuine summary smoothing operations, namely, making the summary more readable, are performed only when the end product is an abstract (Mani, 2001). Current systems of automatic summarization commonly are able to generate extracts rather than abstracts (Over, Dang, & Harman, 2007; Spärck Jones, 2007). Among the three steps identified in the automatic summarization process, sentence identification and selection is the most essential and most difficult whereas sentence extraction is chiefly mechanical and summary smoothing is done only for abstracts. The schematic text summary processing model Spärck Jones (2007) presented as Figure 1 in her report appears therefore more suitable for producing abstracts. The same is true for the high-level summarizer architecture Mani (2001) portrayed.

12.2.2.2 Major Approaches to Automatic Summarization

As with other IRR activities, there are different approaches to automatic summarization. Spärck Jones (2007) categorized them as extractive versus nonextractive based on whether the end product is an extract. She further identified three subcategories of the extractive approach: basic statistical, enriched statistical, and machine learning. Basic statistical methods for automatic summarization refer to the use of the tf.idf (see §5.1.2.2) or similar weighting algorithms for ranking source sentences. Sentences are selected from the ranked list of top scores until the summary length threshold (e.g., 10 percent of the source length) is reached. The selected sentences are usually delivered in the same order as they occurred in the original source. Limitations of such summaries include sentences ordered as they are in the source and ranked only by frequency-based algorithms.

The enriched statistical approaches are designed, to some extent, for overcoming the weaknesses of basic statistical methods. These kinds of strategies are enriched via either lexical units and features or source structure. In the former method of enrichment, a more sophisticated treatment is made of the lexical elements for which statistics are computed. This treatment encompasses both the types of units chosen (e.g., co-words or word groups) and differential weighting for unit types. Specific lexical items with importance-signaling properties (e.g., conclusions) and unique entities of web sources (e.g., links and URLs) are also investigated in the summarization process. By comparison, the other method of enrichment makes a more comprehensive use of source structure by going beyond sentences and taking into consideration such information as discourse structures.

Machine learning represents the third subcategory of extractive approaches to automatic summarization. Summarization, if done correctly, is supposed to be a representation of what characterizes the source. It is then natural to seek if summarization via machine learning can choose appropriate source features, including feature weights and feature combination, out of the range of possible choices. Machine learning, a technique frequently applied in AI research, can be divided into supervised and unsupervised learning. The learning is supervised if some intervention (e.g., providing training examples) is required from the user for the learning process (Turmo, Ageno, & Gatala, 2006). Researchers in the past have used machine learning in extractive summarization to guide extraction, identify discourse relations, arrange extracted sentences, and more (Spärck Jones, 2007).

In contrast with the extractive strategies discussed earlier, nonextractive methods have been developed to create abstracts in automatic summarization. Such abstracts, presumably representing the source text beyond individual lexical items, should be a better manifestation of the source. However, there has been relatively little nonextractive summarizing in the past decade (Spärck Jones, 2007), which in turn partly reflects the paucity of feasible and successful techniques for producing nonextractive summaries. In addition, what has been generated in this category of summaries typically contains some degree of paraphrase of the source content (Mani, 2001) rather than a concise representation.

From the perspective of linguistic representation, Mani (2001) categorized summarization approaches differently from Spärck Jones (2007), although there are again three types of strategies: shallow, deeper, and hybrid. Shallow methods in summarization do not venture beyond the syntactic level of NLP whereas deeper strategies generally assume at least the sentential semantic level of representation. Deeper strategies in automatic summarization are more difficult than shallow ones in application due to the state of the art of NLP technologies. The third summarization approach Mani (2001) defined is labeled as hybrid and involves considerable rearrangement of text, including alteration of discourse-dependent references as part of the summary-smoothing operations. As previously discussed, summary smoothing operations are not carried out regularly during summarization, in part because technologies for such operations are still under development.

12.2.2.3 Evaluation of Automatic Summarization

Because evaluation is crucial in improving IRR efforts, the Document Understanding Conference (DUC; duc.nist.gov)—a program similar to the TREC series in many aspects, except that DUC's focus is on text summarization—has been held since 2001. Over, Dang, & Harman (2007), examined closely the evaluations done at DUC 2001–2006, along with similar activities at SUMMAC (Summarization Evaluation Conference) and NTCIR (NII Test Collection for IR Systems). Two major types of evaluation have been used at these venues for testing summaries: intrinsic and extrinsic. Specifically, intrinsic evaluation places emphases on measuring the quality of created summaries directly while extrinsic evaluation focuses on measuring how well the summary aids performance on a given task. The theme of DUC is text summarization, which encompasses automatic summarization but also includes manual approaches in the practice. Besides indicating that automatic summaries generated at DUC 2001–2006 are largely extracts, Over, Dang, & Harman (2007) reported the following results:

- Most manual summaries are clearly better than most automatic summaries.

- Most automatic summaries do not differ significantly.

- Automatic summaries at the extremes usually differ significantly.

- Automatic summaries seldom performed better than simple baselines (i.e., taking the lead sentence/paragraph) based on the structure of news articles.

In addition, Over, Dang, & Harman (2007) suggested that future DUCs need to move not only beyond the news genre but into new summarization tasks that are inspired by real uses of summaries (e.g., summaries in specific domains such as medicine and law).

Text Analysis Conference (TAC; www.nist.gov/tac), initiated in 2008, grows out of DUC and the question answering (QA) track of the TREC. TAC aims to support research within the NLP community by providing the infrastructure necessary for large-scale evaluation of NLP methodologies. Sponsored by NIST and other U.S. government agencies, TAC basically supersedes DUC while assuming other roles (e.g., QA evaluation) in the domain of NLP.

Automatic summarization is anything but a simple topic due to its multidimensionality (Carbonell, et al., 2000). The parameters Mani (2001) described (e.g., compression rate, audience, source size, genre, and summary type) all contribute to this multidimensionality that subsequently defines the complexity and difficulty in automatic summarization. On the other hand, research in summarization is expanding, and progress is being made (e.g., McDonald & Chen, 2006). Future achievements in automatic summarization should greatly facilitate many activities in IRR.

12.2.3 Question Answering

Anyone who conducts a search using a retrieval system (i.e., an online system, OPAC, or web search engine) would receive some results in return. Such results may or may not contain the answer one seeks, and the user has to browse the results. In other words, the IR system is only capable of obtaining and presenting some results to the user, while the user has to examine the results to physically locate the answer, if it is there. The user's task of finding an answer from retrieved results is not trivial for numerous reasons (e.g., time, relevance judgment, inaccessible sources, and collections). The QA mechanism is thus proposed to relieve the user of the burden of sifting the answer from search results, which in the digital age often number in the millions.

QA, in brief, implies that the IR system is able to present the very answer in results to the user in a search process without any extra irrelevant information mixed in. Maybury (2004) provided a more comprehensive definition of QA:

> Question answering (QA) is an interactive human computer process that encompasses understanding a user information need, typically expressed in a natural language query; retrieving relevant documents, data, or knowledge from selected sources; extracting, qualifying and prioritizing available answers from these sources; and presenting and explaining responses in an effective manner. (p. 3)

12.2.3.1 The Process of Question Answering

While the concept of QA sounds extremely attractive, achieving this objective involves challenges in each step of the process. Researchers in the area normally describe how QA is done from the perspective of their own knowledge and experience (e.g., Kwok, Etzioni, & Weld, 2001; Lin & Katz, 2006). A typical QA mechanism in general includes query parsing, question classification, query formulation, answer extraction, and answer selection and presentation.

The first step in the QA process is query parsing, or analyzing the query to understand what question was asked. If an IR system supports natural language searching (see §12.2.4), this step will be handled by a built-in mechanism. Otherwise, the query inputted into the search box of an IR system has to be parsed before it can move to the next step of QA.

The next step would be to classify the question according to some framework. Various frameworks for classifying questions of this nature have been constructed over the years. Carbonell, et al. (2000), grouped all such questions into four levels (i.e., the casual questioner, the template questioner, the cub reporter, and the professional information analyst), while Pomerantz (2005) surveyed five major question taxonomies (i.e., frameworks for classifying questions) in QA:

1. The six Ws (i.e., Who, What, When, Where, Why, and How): Many questions of this framework belong to the factual or factoid category. Classifying them by and large appears straightforward. Example questions of the kind include, When was George Washington's birthday? and What building is the tallest in the world?

2. Subjects of questions: Questions in this framework are classified using certain controlled vocabularies (e.g., Library of

Congress Classification, Art & Architecture Thesaurus). These questions are categorized according to their subject content. A sample question would be: What is the most effective teaching method in college education?

3. Functions of expected answers: Questions in this framework are categorized by considering the functions of expected answers. For example, will an answer to the question be used for comparison or interpretation purposes? Pomerantz (2005, Table 1) developed a taxonomy of functions of expected answers.

4. Forms of expected answers: This classification approach seems similar to the way in which traditional reference questions are categorized (e.g., directional, ready reference). Pomerantz (2005, Table 2) also compiled common forms of expected answers.

5. Types of sources: Questions in this classification framework are grouped by types (or genres) of sources from which answers may be drawn. However, this taxonomy has not been adopted for classifying questions in the QA process (Pomerantz, 2005). Sample sources include abstracts, indexes, dictionaries, encyclopedias, and yearbooks.

Similar to the third kind of taxonomy Pomerantz (2005) summarized, Carbonell, et al. (2000), presented a scheme in which questions are classified based on how the questioner (i.e., the user) would make use of the answer retrieved by the QA mechanism. Typically, the casual questioner asks simple and factual questions. The template questioner, however, poses questions that can be handled with standard templates from which certain types of information will be found. Examples of such questions include: What do we know about Company ABC? and What is the biography of actor X? Answers to template questions might be harder for the QA mechanism to locate than for the casual questioner because they frequently need to be retrieved from multiple sources. The third type of questioner in this framework is labeled cub reporter. The name was chosen simply as an analogy (Carbonell, et al., 2000). The cub reporter focuses on locating factual data but needs to pull together information from a variety of sources. Besides, no standard template is available in this case because some information the user is looking for would be central to his or her need while the rest is peripheral at best. The QA system has to decide what should be retrieved using appropriate techniques. The last category in this taxonomy for classifying questions is called the professional information analyst and represents different kinds of users at the high end of the QA spectrum. These users, as a group, are in need of answers to sophisticated questions even though they work in different professions (e.g., senior news reporters, scientists working on cutting-edge problems, officers analyzing national-level intelligence). It often is a daunting task to develop QA systems for this group of users.

Regardless of which framework is used for classifying questions, this action has to be taken before the next step in QA—query formulation—to ensure that subsequent operations will be carried out accordingly. For example, operations for obtaining an answer to a factual question would be different from those for answering a question about a subject topic. At this step of query formulation, the question, or query, submitted by the user is actually transformed using the syntax and other specifics the QA system supports so that it can be processed by the system's search engine properly. Techniques such as verb conversion, relevance feedback, and noun phrase formation may also be applied in reformulating the query for QA (e.g., Kwok, Etzioni, & Weld, 2001).

The fourth step in the QA process is answer extraction, which actually pulls out certain information from sources according to some rules. Behind this step is information extraction (IE). The sources used in the IE process could be either specially built collections (e.g., Lin & Katz, 2006) or merely what is available on the web (e.g., Neumann & Xu, 2004). Rules that guide the extraction are defined as wrappers usually tailored to a particular information source (Gregg & Walczak, 2006). The wrappers are generated via a combination of NLP technology, machine learning, statistical modeling, and domain knowledge (e.g., Flesca, et al., 2004). With the help of such wrappers, key contents in the source (e.g., proper names, dates, and locations) are identified for extraction (El Hadi, 2003). The major difficulty in IE, however, lies in its intrinsic domain dependence, because linguistic knowledge for each domain varies widely. Manual tuning of domain-dependent linguistic knowledge, such as terminological dictionaries, domain-specific lexico-semantics, and extraction patterns, has typically been tried (Turmo, Ageno, & Gatala, 2006), but performing IE across domains remains a serious challenge.

IE can be performed at several level of granularity (Godby & Reighart, 2001). For example, Mojsillovic, Gomes, and Rogowitz (2004) attempted to extract semantic cues such as skin, sky, grass, snow, and man-made objects from image collections. In addition, extraction for QA purposes can also be done with flexibility in terms of length. Some extracted contents are as short as one word or number while others might be several hundred words long.

IE is also a crucial component in passage retrieval, which means that it is mandatory for passage retrieval to have the extraction mechanism. Passage retrieval can be regarded to a certain degree as a derivation in the development of QA systems. The relation between QA and passage retrieval is that the former presents to the user exact answers as results while the latter promises only that answers are contained in the passage retrieved (Cater, 2005). The length of results in passage retrieval is significantly reduced compared, of course, with that of document retrieval.

The last step in QA is answer selection after key contents in the source are extracted. This step resembles relevance judgment in a regular IR process except that human beings, rather than the system, make the judgment in searching activities without the QA mechanism. Apparently, it is exceedingly hard to have a QA system perform relevance judgment because, as discussed in §11.1.2.1, relevance is such a complex concept that even human beings seem unable to deal with it satisfactorily. However, a QA system has no other option but selecting answers from the extracted contents by itself. Lin and Katz (2006) suggested the following for answer selection: Extracted contents are first judged supportive, unsupportive, or irrelevant before the selection decision is made. Supportive contents not only contain the answer string, but the answer must be identified confidently, when done by a person, as correct from the source. Unsupportive content contains the answer string that appears in the right context but does not actually answer the question. Irrelevant content either does not mention the correct answer string at all or mentions it coincidentally. The latter happens in keyword searching most, if not all, of the time. Of the three kinds of judgment outcomes, only supportive contents can be selected as answers and presented to the user, although it should be noted that human judges are involved in determining supportive contents. Answer granularity, nonetheless, is another area to be considered in answer selection (Lin & Katz, 2006). For example, how specific must the date be in a question of this nature? Is year alone sufficient, or should month and day also be given?

At the completion of the answer selection step, the entire QA process reaches a conclusion, although answer presentation is sometimes listed as one more or the last step (Maybury, 2004). As researchers did in automatic summarization, assorted methods (e.g., statistical, linguistic, knowledge-based, interactive) are chosen in developing QA systems. These methods form a long array and are often used in various combinations. The QA track, which ran from TREC-8 through TREC 2007 and was thus one of the longest-running ad hoc tasks, provided a valuable platform for QA researchers to communicate with each other. Moreover, this track fostered a resurgence in QA research, which in turn has produced new QA technology (Voorhees, 2005). The establishment of TAC, briefly mentioned in §12.2.2.3, would certainly provide further impetus to research in QA.

12.2.3.2 Implementations of Question Answering

There are currently two types of QA applications, one with human involvement in the QA process and the other without. IR operations in the former case depend chiefly on a question database, along with a corresponding answer database. The IR system first builds a database of questions that are gathered from a variety of sources (e.g., queries in search logs). Then answers to each question in the database are developed using resources that are available to target users (e.g., websites) and stored in the answer database. When a request is entered into the search box, the IR system checks its question database to see whether there is a match. If a match is found between the search request and the question database, the IR system retrieves an answer from the answer database by following the linkage between the two databases. Otherwise, no search result is presented. The initial version of Ask.com (previously known as Ask Jeeves), an internet retrieval system, used this method of question-answer databases, which explains why it provides perfect answers to some questions but no answer except noise on most occasions.

The other category of QA systems (i.e., implemented with AI-complete technology and by taking the steps discussed previously) is nonexistent because such systems remain well beyond the current state of the art (Voorhees, 2005). Researchers in this area, consequently, adopt a divide-and-conquer approach to QA by dealing with more manageable tasks (e.g., factoid QA, IE from web sources) first. On the other hand, a road map has been drawn to plan systematically and specifically for future research in QA (Maybury, 2002).

Finally, it is pertinent to examine the particularly useful complementarity existing between automatic summarization and QA systems as the development of other applications (e.g., natural language searching) depends on both of them. From the viewpoint of summarization, QA is one way to provide the focus for summarization oriented toward queries. From the viewpoint of QA, summarization is a way of extracting and fusing just the relevant information from a heap of text in answer to a specific nonfactoid question (Carbonell, et al., 2000). In addition, automatic summarization and QA face similar and substantial challenges on their paths to fruition as two major applications of AI in information representation and retrieval.

12.2.4 Natural Language Searching

Natural language searching (or querying) means that users can enter specific searches (e.g., a phrase or a question) without going through the query representation process. Query representation, discussed in §5.3, refers to the process of translating one's search requests into queries that the IR system can process. For example, *Why is the sky blue?* is a natural language search question that a traditional IR system cannot adequately handle. But the same IR system should be able to deal with a search query such as *sky* AND *blue* without any problem.

This example illustrates the major difference between IR systems that support natural language searching and those that do not. In the former case, the IR system accomplishes the task of query representation for the user, while in the latter, the user is expected to complete the query representation process so that the IR system can process it. In other words, with the question *Why is the sky blue?* as an example, IR systems with the capability of processing natural language queries should at least be able to do the following:

- The word *why* indicates that what is to be searched for is about cause, reason, or other similar answers to the question.

- The words *is* and *the* contained in the question are the so-called function words and should not be included in the search query.

- The words *sky* and *blue* are significant words and should be linked by the Boolean operator AND to form a query for this question.

- The question mark is ignored in processing the natural language query, as punctuations normally are not part of a query unless particularly specified otherwise.

These steps may sound easy to a human being but pose enormous challenges for an IR system. Those challenges are essentially what researchers in the NLP area attempt to meet. Although natural language searching indeed seems very appealing, its implementation relies heavily on research and development in automatic summarization and QA, discussed in §12.2.2 and §12.2.3, respectively.

The two main approaches for developing QA systems (see §12.2.3.2) are also applied to implement natural language searching. The method of question-answer databases, as explained earlier, is limited in that its underlying mechanism is actually manual. In addition, a request can be searched only if it is already included in the question database of an IR system. Yet it is impossible for a single database, no matter how large it may be, to contain all the questions users might ask. The IR system then becomes pointless when a particular question is not in the database even if the system supports so-called natural language searching. The other approach to natural language searching, as illustrated in §12.2.3.2, remains a vision rather than a reality because the NLP technology for creating operational QA systems is still under development. As a result, few IR systems that support natural language searching have materialized thus far.

Natural language search is sometimes referred to as natural language interface because the interface is what the user interacts with in an IR system during the search process. In addition, the first two steps in the QA process (i.e., query parsing and question classification) in essence lay the foundation for natural language searching. Therefore, natural language searching, like passage retrieval, is a derivation of QA mechanism development. Finally, it should be pointed out that natural language searching is not searching without any use of controlled vocabularies (e.g., thesauri). The latter is called keyword searching.

12.3 The Semantic Web

The semantic web is the most ambitious project that the W3C (World Wide Web Consortium) and many researchers have undertaken thus far. It has been part of Tim Berners-Lee's vision since he created the first version of the web in the early 1990s, although a formal statement and description of the envisioned semantic web was made around a decade later in Berners-Lee, Hendler, and Lassila (2001). In that influential paper, the authors define the semantic web as an extension of the current web in which information is given well-defined meaning, better enabling people and computers to work in collaboration. When rationalizing why a new discipline—web science—should be instituted in higher education, Berners-Lee, Hall, and Hendler (2006) further specified that, in the web of human-readable documents, NLP techniques can extract some meaning from the human-readable text of the pages. A web of relational data, logical assertions, and heuristic methods together can recapitulate the intended meanings used in human communication. Moreover, the semantic web, once implemented, would allow independently developed data systems to be connected together without requiring global agreement as to terms and concepts.

Because the semantic web is still a vision despite exciting, imaginary descriptions presented in numerous writings, further conceptual elaboration would not provide any substantiation but only more speculation about it. On the other hand, active research has been conducted in multiple areas such as semantic web architecture to facilitate the development of the semantic web.

12.3.1 Semantic Web Architecture

Even before the phrase semantic web became widely known, Berners-Lee (2000) illustrated its architecture in a seven-layer diagram (Figure 12.1). Interpretations of this diagram have been offered ever since by different

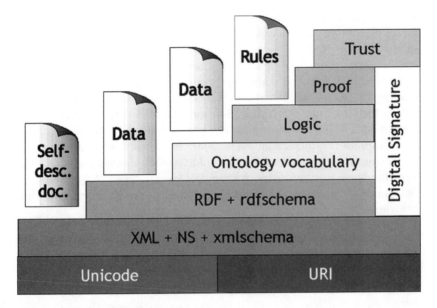

Figure 12.1 Semantic Web Architecture

authors in different contexts and from different perspectives (e.g., Greenberg, 2003; Legg, 2007). It seems unnecessary to explain once more each of the seven layers in this architecture. Instead, a closer examination will be given to, from bottom to top, the second (XML + NS + xmlschema), third (RDF + rdfschema), and fourth (Ontology vocabulary) layers in the diagram for their immediate importance to IRR. The other four layers, namely, the first (Unicode and URI), fifth (Logic), sixth (Proof), and seventh (Trust) are not discussed in this book because Unicode and URI represent the pre-semantic web while the last three layers have an indirect relationship with IRR in this context, although all play crucial roles in the creation of the semantic web.

As seen from Figure 12.1, the semantics to be gathered, organized, and diffused via the semantic web are derived as well as defined by the three layers of its architecture explored here. The second layer consists of three elements: XML (eXtensible Markup Language) enables the creation of metadata for web resources beyond the syntax level, whereas both Namespace (NS) and xmlschema (i.e., a framework for XML coding) facilitate the use and interoperability of metadata in XML. Unlike HTML (HyperText Markup Language), which only formats what is on the web (e.g., font and size), XML can code web information in the same way as database indexing by field (e.g., author and title). Suppose we have an author John Doe who published Article B.

Using HTML, all we can do is format *John Doe* and *Article B* with available formatting options such as italics, Times New Roman font, and 12-point type. In the case of XML, however, the same information can be coded as <author>John Doe</author> and <publication>Article B</publication>, respectively. Because XML coding functions very similarly to field indexing—one step in creating traditional databases—some control mechanism should be provided to ensure that XML codes created by different systems in different domains would be exchangeable or interoperable later on. For example, <publication> ... </publication> is the XML code for all kinds of writings, and no variations, such as <document> ... </document>, should be used. NS and xmlschema are two control mechanisms for such purposes. NS represents a domain (e.g., domestic ecommerce), and xmlschema provides rules and guidelines for generating XML codes for the target domain.

Resource Description Framework (RDF; see also §3.1.3.2) and rdfschema, as the third layer of the semantic web architecture, are employed to express relations among metadata (i.e., XML codes) created for web information in the form of RDF graphs (Figure 12.2). In "an author John Doe who published Article B," for example, the relation in this statement (i.e., John Doe is "author of" Article B) is illustrated in the lower right-hand corner of Figure 12.2. The function of rdfschema, like that of xmlschema, is to ensure that all RDF graphs are created by following a similar schema so that these graphs are interoperable universally on the semantic web.

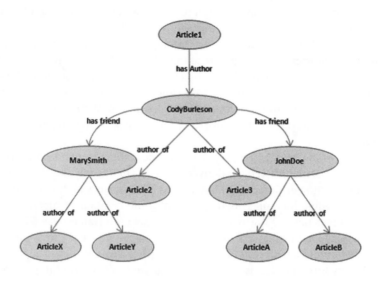

Figure 12.2 Example of RDF Graph

As discussed in §4.4.3, ontology is a quintessential component of the semantic web because the success of a worldwide semantic web ultimately depends on it to integrate web resources coded in XML and charted in RDF graphs from all corners of the world, along with corresponding logic rules for reasoning. Ontology, to a certain degree, can be regarded as a universal controlled vocabulary (e.g., classification schemes or thesauri) for representing web resources. The major difference between an ontology and a traditional controlled vocabulary is that the former is intended for the entire web, with automatic means, while the latter is in general manual and never applied to a sphere covering all domains in the world. In other words, ontology vocabulary, the fourth layer of the semantic web architecture, would help the computer understand the meaning of web resources processed at the two previous layers, when implemented on a universal scale.

Two points become evident from this description of the second, third, and fourth layers of the semantic web architecture. First, what the semantic web might do in terms of bringing out the semantics of information on the web sounds exciting as well as ambitious. Second, what the three layers could do is nothing other than information representation on the web platform, ranging from field indexing (i.e., XML coding) to overall vocabulary control for the process (e.g., ontology vocabulary).

12.3.2 The Semantic Web and Information Representation and Retrieval

According to the semantic web architecture described in §12.3.1, the semantic web has great implications for IRR. Semantic IRR on the web and intelligent agents are two examples of such implications.

12.3.2.1 Semantic Information Representation and Retrieval on the Web

Web IR is notorious for its low precision and high noise. While there are many factors (e.g., no control on input) that cause the dilemma, keyword indexing of web information remains the major reason. Various efforts (e.g., using subject headings for indexing) have been made to provide non-keyword, or more precisely, concept representation of web information. They have been made, nevertheless, only on a limited scale and have had little impact on improving IRR performance on the web given the enormous amount of information in this environment in addition to other features of web information.

The issue of low precision and high noise in web retrieval relates basically to semantics or "the intended meanings used in human communication," as Berners-Lee, Hall, & Hendler (2006, p. 770) put it. If the semantic web can bring out the semantics from web information as anticipated, the problem of low precision plaguing IR on the web would be solved or at least alleviated. For example, the implementation of XML in coding web information would allow the user to bid farewell to fieldless web retrieval and welcome the use of field searching. In addition, vocabulary control in web IRR via ontology would enable the user to differentiate, for instance, whether the word *bank* means a financial institution or the rising ground bordering a river. In a nutshell, semantic IRR on the web would be a reality once the semantic web is developed.

12.3.2.2 Intelligent Agents

Intelligent agents, employing assorted AI techniques and in the form of software programs, are able to perform certain tasks without human intervention. Expert systems, on the other hand, are defined as software programs that inform, make recommendations, or solve problems in a manner and at a level of performance comparable to that displayed by a human expert in the field. In essence, expert systems are intelligent agents on a larger scale or the predecessor of intelligent agents. The word *bots* (an abbreviation of *robots*) is increasingly used as a synonym for intelligent agents.

The concept of intelligent agents, to some extent, was popularized by Berners-Lee, Hendler, & Lassila (2001), when they formally introduced the semantic web to the public. In that article, the authors vividly described an agent that is capable of scheduling medical appointments. Dent (2007) reviewed many aspects of intelligent agents, such as their features and functions, from the perspective of modern libraries. According to Hendler (1999), an ideal intelligent agent should have four characteristics:

1. Communicative: the ability to understand the user's goals, preferences, and constraints

2. Capable: the ability to take options rather than simply provide advice

3. Autonomous: the ability to act without the user's being in control the whole time

4. Adaptive: the ability to learn from experience about its tasks and its users' preferences

The applications of intelligent agents are many and varied, both inside and outside the IRR field. No matter for what purpose an intelligent agent is created, it should possess the four characteristics Hendler specified. Intelligent agents can be used in many different settings, ranging from our everyday lives to complex research and development projects. A great number of agents, mostly in the public domain, can be found at BotSpot (www.botspot.com).

Intelligent agents for IRR target specific subdivisions of the field. In general, IRR tasks that are well understood, can be explicitly specified, and have a clearly defined boundary would be feasible at present for intelligent agents to accomplish. Selective dissemination of information (SDI) is one such example. Intelligent agents monitor one or more IR systems and notify the user when new information appears in the system on a given topic. Categorization of retrieval results, common in internet retrieval systems because of their huge amounts of output, represents another example. The best-known examples of intelligent agents in IRR are the data collection programs for internet retrieval systems, referred to variously as crawlers, robots, or spiders. These agents periodically visit target sites, copy certain information, and send it to the system database.

Integrating information retrieved from different sources should, likewise, not be an insurmountable task for intelligent agents. Intelligent agents for more challenging IRR tasks such as query formulation and information representation are being researched. For example, the question-answer mechanism implemented in some IR systems is intended to find out by asking questions what a user really wants when making a request for information. Attempts to develop intelligent agents that can compile automatic summaries and abstracts are also on the rise, especially for news and business information (see §12.2.2). The success of these efforts ultimately depends on research in AI.

Personalized search, roughly speaking, can be regarded as an extension of intelligent agents in that the IR system is designed in such a way that the user's profile, search history, and other related information would be put together to form an agent-like mechanism. This mechanism will be activated in the retrieval process to help the IR system learn what the user truly wants in the current situation. For example, the user enters *Java* as a query into the search box. The mechanism for personalized searching will immediately do a series of activities (e.g., checking the user's profile and search history) to find out what *Java* is intended to mean in this case. If the user has a background in programming, *Java* would very likely be a programming language the user wants to locate. If the user's profile contains no information about programming but his or her search history shows that sites for travel agents have recently been visited, *Java* would refer to the island of Java, in Indonesia. *Java* as a type of coffee or other meanings can be determined likewise in an IR system that supports personal searching. The privacy issue related to personal searching is beyond the scope of this book.

12.3.3 Challenges to the Semantic Web as an Artificial Intelligence Application

Despite visible progress achieved in the development of the semantic web, many researchers (e.g., Legg, 2007; O'Hara, 2004; Spärck Jones, 2004) have questioned the feasibility and viability of this AI application. The semantic web is not meant to be created and maintained by human beings as what has been done in traditional IRR. Rather, AI technologies would be extensively utilized in its development and subsequent operations, which raises more questions than researchers in the area are able to answer. The notion of semantics underlying this application, on the other hand, triggers even more questions because how to perform concept searching in an automatic environment has long been a key problem that many in the field study.

There are primarily two kinds of challenges to the semantic web vision: One concerns it as an AI application, and the other relates to its anticipated capability of conveying semantics via automatic means. The former type of challenge is addressed in §12.4 when the relationship of AI and IRR is examined. The latter type of challenge can be summarized as follows.

First, who would be responsible for coding all the web resources in XML and then diagramming them with an RDF graph? Second, who would be responsible for developing and maintaining all the xmlschemas, rdfschemas, and ontologies needed to guarantee the use and interoperability of shared semantics generated in the semantic web architecture? Third, is it possible to create one ontology that could be applied in all domains, languages, and cultures in existence on this planet? These three questions are basically asked by researchers outside of W3C (e.g., Legg, 2007; O'Hara, 2004; Spärck Jones, 2004). But other questions are posed by Berners-Lee and his associates themselves (e.g., Berners-Lee, Hall, & Hendler, 2006). One question from this group, for example, is how to make all the information processed for the semantic web accessible in the public domain, because open access is one of the prerequisites the semantic web must meet.

Shadbolt, Hall, and Berners-Lee (2006) raised further questions concerning the semantic web in general when they revisited this vision. For instance, how do we effectively query huge numbers of decentralized information repositories of varying scales? How do we align and map between ontologies? How do we construct a semantic web browser that effectively visualizes and navigates the huge connected RDF graph? How do we establish trust and provenance of the content?

The views on the semantic web are changing as a result of ongoing research and technology advancement. For instance, ontology was regarded as a single entity that would include knowledge of the entire world in the semantic web architecture presented in Figure 12.1. Later, it was is found that developing ontologies focusing on smaller areas or a well-defined domain is not only realistic but could also be actually implemented, just as the knowledge base was created for expert systems in earlier days. It is always hard to predict the future. The same holds even truer regarding the future of the semantic web.

12.4 Artificial Intelligence and Information Representation and Retrieval

How far can AI go in information representation and retrieval? The answer to this question has yet to be found, chiefly because it is not a trivial task to build and program a machine that can successfully imitate the intellectual activities of human beings. This should be the most difficult nut to crack in AI research (Pescovitz, 1999).

The role of AI in information representation and retrieval today is therefore limited and should not be overstated, for two reasons. First, complex tasks in IRR depend on extensive world knowledge and on deploying it in a flexible and constructive way. Second, many information representation and retrieval operations are only shallowly done, even by people (Spärck Jones, 1991). Swanson (1988) once commented, "Although the goal of much advanced IR research is to make computers do humanlike things, the possibility that people can be human-like should not be overlooked."

Indeed, the role of people in developing AI applications for information representation and retrieval should not be overlooked. A computer does not have the subtlety, depth, range, and richness of human intelligence because it is still a million times simpler than the human brain (Hefner, 2000). Nevertheless, AI in its current state can make a contribution to situations in which either the knowledge base or inference can be limited intrinsically or the user can complement the limitations. AI is also applicable to circumstances in which AI algorithms are used in conjunction with other techniques (Spärck Jones, 1991).

Applications for information representation and retrieval based on AI alone or in combination with other techniques are growing. However, almost all such applications are either still in a research lab or already commercialized and fee based. On the other hand, various AI elements have been incorporated into many applications for information representation and retrieval. Wilks (2005) detailed some experiments with AI applications in the field of information representation and retrieval when examining the relationship between AI and information retrieval. Where is the field of information representation and retrieval heading as we enter the digital age? Research and development in AI have at least suggested some possibilities.

References

Berners-Lee, Tim. (2000). Semantic web on XML (Slide 10). [Presentation slides]. Retrieved January 18, 2009, from www.w3.org/2000/Talks/1206-xml2k-tbl/slide10-0.html

Berners-Lee, Tim, Hall, Wendy, and Hendler, James. (2006). Creating a science of the web. *Science*, 313(5788), 769–771.

Berners-Lee, Tim, Hendler, James, and Lassila, Ora. (2001). The semantic web. *Scientific American*, 284(5), 35–43.

Campbell, Philip. (2008). Community cleverness needed. [Editorial]. *Nature*, 455(7209), 1.

Carbonell, Jaime, et al. (2000). Vision statement to guide research in question answering (QA) and text summarization. Retrieved January 14, 2009, from www-nlpir.nist.gov/projects/duc/papers/Final-Vision-Paper-v1a.pdf

Cater, Arthur W. S. (2005). Question answering. In John I. Tait (Ed.), *Charting a new course: Natural language processing and information retrieval* (pp. 105–128). New York: Springer.

Cercone, Nick, and McCalla, Gordon. (1984). Artificial intelligence: Underlying assumptions and basic objectives. *Journal of the American Society for Information Science*, 35(5), 280–290.

Chen, Hsinchun. (1995). Machine learning for information retrieval: Neutral networks, symbolic learning, and genetic algorithms. *Journal of the American Society for Information Science*, 46(3), 194–216.

Chen, Hsinchun, et al. (1994). Automatic concept classification of text from electronic meetings. *Communications of the ACM*, 37(10), 56–73.

Chowdhury, Gobinda G. (1999). *Introduction to modern information retrieval*. London: Library Association Publishing.

Dent, Valeda F. (2007). Intelligent agent concepts in the modern library. *Library Hi Tech*, 25(1), 108–125.

Doszkocs, T. E. (1986). Natural language processing in information retrieval. *Journal of the American Society for Information Science*, 37(4), 191–196.

El Hadi, Widad Mustafa. (2003). Human language technology and its role in information access and management. *Cataloging & Classification Quarterly*, 37(1/2), 131–151.

Flesca, Sergio, et al. (2004). Web wrapper induction: A brief survey. *AI Communications*, 17(2), 56–61.

Godby, C. Jean, and Reighart, Ray R. (2001). The WordSmith toolkit. *Journal of Library Administration*, 34(3/4), 307–316.

Greenberg, Jane. (2003). Metadata: The fundamental component of the semantic web. *Bulletin of the American Society for Information Science and Technology*, 29(4), 16–18.

Gregg, Dawn G., and Walczak, Steven. (2006). Adaptive web information extraction. *Communications of the ACM*, 49(5), 78–84.

Hefner, Katie. (December 28, 2000). Artificial intelligence hasn't peaked (yet). *New York Times*. Retrieved October 12, 2009, from www.nytimes.com/2000/12/28/technology/28ARTI.html

Hendler, James. (March 11, 1999). Is there an intelligent agent in your future? *Nature*, 398(2763). Retrieved January 21, 2009, from www.nature.com/nature/webmatters/agents/agents.html

Jennings, Andrew, and Higuchi, Hudeyuki. (1992). A browser with a neural network user model. *Library Hi Tech*, 10(1/2), 77–93.

Kwok, Cody, Etzioni, Oren, and Weld, Daniel S. (2001). Scaling question answering to the web. *ACM Transactions on Information Systems*, 19(3), 242–262.

Lau, Annie Y. S., and Coiera, Enrico W. (2006). A Bayesian model that predicts the impact of web searching on decision making. *Journal of the American Society for Information Science and Technology*, 57(7), 873–880.

Legg, Catherine. (2007). Ontologies on the semantic web. *Annual Review of Information Science and Technology*, 41, 407–451.

Liddy, Elizabeth D. (1998). Enhanced text retrieval using natural language processing. *Bulletin of the American Society for Information Science and Technology*, 24(4), 14–16.

Lin, Jimmy, and Katz, Boris. (2006). Building a reusable test collection for question answering. *Journal of American Society for Information Science and Technology*, 57(7), 851–861.

Luhn, H. P. (1958). The automatic creation of literature abstracts. *IBM Journal of Research and Development*, 2(2), 159–165.

Mani, Inderjeet. (2001). *Automatic summarisation*. Amsterdam: John Benjamins.

Maybury, Mark T. (2002). *Toward a question answering roadmap*. Retrieved January 14, 2009, from www.mitre.org/work/tech_papers/tech_papers_02/maybury_toward/maybury_toward_qa.pdf

Maybury, Mark T. (2004). *New directions in question answering.* Cambridge, MA: MIT Press.

McDonald, Daniel M., and Chen, Hsinchun. (2006). Summary in context: Searching versus browsing. *ACM Transactions on Information Systems,* 24(1), 111–141.

Mojsillovic, Aleksandra, Gomes, Jose, and Rogowitz, Bernice. (2004). Semantic-friendly indexing and querying of images based on the extraction of the objective semantic cues. *International Journal of Computer Vision,* 56(1/2), 79–107.

Mullins, Justin. (2005). Whatever happened to machines that think? *New Scientist,* 186(2496), 32–37.

Neumann, Gunter, and Xu, Feiyu. (2004). Mining natural language answers from the web. *Web Intelligence & Agent Systems,* 2(2), 123–235.

O'Hara, Kieron. (2004). Ontologies and technologies: Knowledge representation or misrepresentation. *ACM SIGIR Forum,* 38(2), 11–17.

Over, Paul, Dang, Hoa, and Harman, Donna. (2007). DUC in context. *Information Processing & Management,* 43(6), 1506–1520.

Pescovitz, David. (March 18, 1999). Look what's talking: Software robots. *New York Times.* Retrieved October 12, 2009, from www.nytimes.com/library/tech/99/03/circuits/articles/18bots.html

Pomerantz, Jeffrey. (2005). A linguistic analysis of question taxonomies. *Journal of the American Society for Information Science and Technology,* 56(7), 715–728.

Shadbolt, Nigel, Hall, Wendy, and Berners-Lee, Tim. (2006). The semantic web revisited. *IEEE Intelligent Systems,* 21(3), 96–101.

Spärck Jones, Karen. (1991). The role of artificial intelligence in information retrieval. *Journal of the American Society for Information Science,* 42(8), 558–565.

Spärck Jones, Karen. (2004). What's new about the semantic web? Some questions. *ACM SIGIR Forum,* 38(2), 18–23.

Spärck Jones, Karen. (2007). Automatic summarising: The state of the art. *Information Processing & Management,* 43(6), 1449–1481.

Swanson, Don R. (1988). Historical note: Information retrieval and the future of an illusion. *Journal of the American Society for Information Science,* 39(2), 92–98.

Turmo, Jordi, Ageno, Alicia, and Gatala, Neus. (2006). Adaptive information extraction. *ACM Computing Surveys*, 38(2), 1–47.

Voorhees, Ellen M. (2005). Question answering in TREC. In Ellen M. Voorhees and Donna K. Harman (Eds.), *TREC: Experiment and evaluation in information retrieval* (pp. 233–257). Cambridge, MA: MIT Press.

Wilks, Yorick. (2005). Unhappy bedfellows: The relationship of AI and IR. In John I. Tait (Ed.), *Charting a new course: Natural language processing and information retrieval* (pp. 255–282). New York: Springer.

About the Author

Dr. Heting Chu is a professor in the Palmer School of Library and Information Science at Long Island University, U.S.A. She earned her BA in library science from Peking University, China, her master's degree in library and information science from McGill University, Canada, and her PhD in information studies from Drexel University, U.S.A. As she progressed in her educational pursuance, her subject orientation has moved from library science in general to information retrieval in particular. Her educational background coupled with her teaching and research experience in information representation and retrieval (IRR) enabled her in 2001 to write the first edition of this book, which was also translated into Korean in 2005 and published in India in 2009. The current second edition, on the other hand, is a product of her further work in the field of IRR. In addition, Dr. Chu has authored five books in Chinese on information retrieval and other related topics. She has also received numerous citations and requests for reprints of the many articles she published from people all over the world. Her teaching and research interests include the use of information technology in library and information science, especially in the areas of information representation and retrieval, research methods, and scientific communication.

Index

Entries are filed word-by-word. Locators followed by *t* indicate tables; locators followed by *f* indicate figures.

vector space model (*cont.*)
  space, defined, 115
  strengths, 116
  vector, defined, 115
  weighting, 115, 124
Veronica, 140
Very Large Corpus (VLC) track,
  TREC, 239, 244
video retrieval
  described, 176–178
  evaluation, 226-227
  on the internet, 178–179
video skimming, 177
Video track, TREC, 239, 240, 245
VLC (Very Large Corpus) track,
  TREC, 239, 244
vocabulary control, 5, 54, 58, 62,
  277
vocabulary switching, 66, 263
voice activation, interaction mode,
  195
vortals, 140

W

W3C (World Wide Web
  Consortium), 34
WAIS (wide area information
  servers), 11, 139–140
Web 2.0, 145, 154–155
WebCrawler, 149–150
web search engines. *See* internet
  retrieval systems
Web track, TREC, 239, 240, 245
weighted searching
  described, 75, 76
  in internet retrieval systems, 144
  precision, effect on, 81, 82
  probability model, 76, 124
  retrieval model associated, 125
  in speech retrieval, 175
  threshold, 75

vector space model, 115, 117,
  124
  weighting methods, 75–76
weighting methods, 75
wide area information servers
  (WAIS), 11, 139–140
wikis, influence on IR, 154
wildcard. *See* truncation
WIN (Westlaw Is Natural), 11, 58
WITH operator, 72, 73, 82, 97
word lists, 54, 62. *See also* go lists
word stuffing, in ranking, 147
WordNet (ontology example), 66
WordSmith, 46
World War II, influence on IRR,
  1–2, 5
World Wide Web, 29–30, 139–140
World Wide Web Consortium
  (W3C), 34
wrappers in QA, 270

X

XML (eXtensible Markup
  Language), 275–276
xmlschema, 275, 276, 280

Y

Yahoo!
  browsing, 101
  described, 63
  as directory, 63, 105, 137
  evolution, 150
  search within a browsable cate-
    gory, 106–107
  as search engine, 105–106, 151

Z

Z39.50, 79–80, 135, 140
zatocoding system, 10